Uncover Dubai: Your Go-To Guide for Exploration

Cora .O Clarkson

All rights reserved.

Copyright © 2024 Cora .O Clarkson

*Uncover Dubai: Your Go-To Guide for Exploration :
Discover the Hidden Gems of Dubai: An Insider's Travel
Companion for Adventurers*

<u>Funny helpful tips:</u>

Cultivate resilience; life will throw curveballs, but it's how you react that defines you.

Incorporate activities that challenge different muscle groups; it ensures balanced strength and growth.

Life advices:

In the ocean of time, dive deep, exploring the depths of your potential.

Building genuine relationships requires time and effort; invest in those who uplift and support you.

Introduction

This book offers a comprehensive overview of everything you need to know when visiting Dubai, one of the most popular travel destinations in the United Arab Emirates.

The guide begins by providing information on getting around in Dubai, including transportation options and tips for navigating the city. It then delves into exploring Old Dubai on foot, highlighting the historic spots and landmarks that showcase the city's rich cultural heritage.

Itineraries are suggested to help visitors plan their time in Dubai efficiently, ensuring they don't miss out on the top attractions and experiences. The guide covers a wide range of sightseeing opportunities, including tours of Dubai, historic spots, water parks, and activities that offer a typically Dubai experience.

For families traveling with children, the guide provides a dedicated section on Dubai for kids. It highlights the top attractions suitable for kids, mall play areas, and other places of interest that cater to young visitors.

Rest and relaxation options are also covered in the guide, including information on beaches, spas, and golf courses in Dubai. Readers can find recommendations for various types of restaurants in Dubai, categorized by cuisine, making it easier to explore the diverse culinary scene of the city.

The guide includes information on souks, shopping, and souvenirs, showcasing popular malls, markets, and shopping festivals. It also provides recommendations on where to stay, featuring the best hotels in Dubai for different types of travelers and budgets.

Practical information is included to assist with trip planning, such as visa requirements and the best time to travel. It also provides an overview of the modern history of Dubai and major events that have shaped the city's development. Additionally, information on the other emirates of the UAE is provided for those interested in exploring beyond Dubai, including Abu Dhabi, Sharjah, Ras Al Khaimah, and more.

The guide concludes with suggestions for other excursions outside of Dubai, including Al Ain, Musandam Peninsula in Oman, and the city of Muscat. This provides readers with options for extending their trip and exploring nearby destinations.

Overall, this book offers a comprehensive resource for travelers looking to make the most of their visit to Dubai, with information on transportation, sightseeing, dining, shopping, accommodations, and more.

Contents

GETTING AROUND IN DUBAI 1

EXPLORING OLD DUBAI ON FOOT 11

ITINERARIES 17

SIGHTSEEING 24

TOURS OF DUBAI 24

HISTORIC SPOTS 39

WATER PARKS 45

TYPICALLY DUBAI EXPERIENCES 88

DUBAI FOR KIDS 99

TOP ATTRACTIONS FOR KIDS 99

MALL PLAY AREAS 106

OTHER PLACES OF INTEREST FOR KIDS 109

REST & RELAXATION 111

BEACHES 111

SPAS 114

GOLF COURSES 124

RESTAURANTS IN DUBAI 128

JAPANESE 132

THAI 135

ITALIAN 137

INDIAN/PAKISTANI 140

CHINESE 144

ARABIC 147

IRANIAN / PERSIAN 151

EUROPEAN CUISINE..153

SEAFOOD 157

STEAK AND GRILLS 159

KID FRIENDLY RESTAURANTS...162

CAFES 165

BRUNCH 169

BARS, CLUBS & NIGHTLIFE..176

BAR RESTAURANTS...178

LOUNGE BARS / PUBS..179

COCKTAIL BARS 181

NIGHTCLUBS 184

BEACH BARS 188

STYLISH SHISHA CAFES 189

SOUKS, SHOPPING & SOUVENIRS 191

THE DUBAI MALLS (INCLUDING DUBAI MALL)..............................192

SOUKS & MARKETS..198

SHOPPING FESTIVALS & OTHER MARKETS 213

SOUVENIRS 218

WHERE TO STAY 224

BEST HOTELS IN DUBAI 225

THE GRAPESHISHA CHOICE HOTELS...226

BEST HOTELS IN DUBAI FOR FAMILIES......................................227

BEST HOTELS IN DUBAI FOR BUSINESS 228

AFFORDABLE HOTEL ALTERNATIVES 228

BUDGET HOTELS 229

HOTEL APARTMENTS 230

HOTELS ON THE PALM 230

HOTELS IN "OLD DUBAI" 231

HOTELS ON SHEIKH ZAYED ROAD 233

HOTELS NEAR THE BURJ KHALIFA – "DOWNTOWN DUBAI" 234

HOTELS IN GREATER JUMEIRAH 235

HOTELS ON DUBAI MARINA AND ON THE WALK 236

HOTELS IN THE DESERT AND OUT OF TOWN 237

HOTEL APPENDIX 238

PLANNING YOUR TRIP 263

VISAS 263

THE BEST TIME TO TRAVEL - TEMPERATURE 264

WHEN NOT TO TRAVEL 266

ARRIVING IN DUBAI 267

NEED TO KNOWS 267

MODERN HISTORY & MAJOR EVENTS 301

THE UAE FACTFILE...305

DUBAI AND THE FINANCIAL CRISIS 308

THE OTHER EMIRATES 311

ABU DHABI – THE EVOLVING CAPITAL 311

A TRYST WITH CULTURE IN SHARJAH...314

THE BASE OF FUJAIRAH 317

RAS AL KHAIMAH..318

UMM AL QUWAIN 321

AJMAN 322

OTHER   EXCURSIONS 325

GREENERY IN THE GARDEN CITY OF AL AIN 325

AL GHARBIA, THE REGION – ECLECTIC AS CAN BE.....................327

NATURE AT ITS BEST ON THE BANI YAS ISLANDS 329

THE OASIS TOWN OF BURAIMI 331

TAKING A BREAK IN DELMA ISLANDS 333

JOZOR AL SAHRA'A - THE DESERT ISLANDS OF ABU DHABI....................334

SPENDING A LIVELY DAY IN DIBBA 336

A BEACH HOLIDAY AT KHOR FAKKAN 338

EXPERIENCE THE QUAINT AND RUSTIC MASAFI 340

MUSANDAM PENINSULA – BEAUTY IN ISOLATION 341

THE CHARMING CITY OF MUSCAT 343

TRAVELLING DOWN THE HISTORICAL LANE IN OMAN..............................346

GETTING AROUND IN DUBAI

Dubai has come a long way from the days of hopping on to the back of a camel in the sweltering heat. Since then we've had Abras to take commuters and visitors across the Dubai Creek, a huge influx of taxis, air conditioned buses and more recently a modernised metro system as well having the ability to hire your own car. Dubai is now more accessible than ever before. It's not a city that you can walk across but it's now reasonably priced to travel around. Just try and avoid the rush hour.

CHOOSING YOUR TRANSPORT

Dubai is not huge or complicated once you have your bearings. If you are visiting a particular shop or restaurant though, it's best to get a landmark as many addresses may not use building numbers and on occasion don't feature on any map. Most tourists use taxis as they are reasonably priced, combined with the ever efficient 21st century metro. If you are in Dubai long enough, then it's also worth considering hiring a car.

Choosing the right mode of transport whilst on your holiday depends on many factors.

How long are you visiting for?

Is it summer or 'cool' season?

How many passengers are you travelling with?

Do you like to sightsee by foot?

How comfortable you are driving around a foreign country?

As you are no doubt aware, the weather in Dubai can get pretty uncomfortable in the warmer months (May - September). Therefore if you want to use public transport such as the metro or bus, we advise doing a bit of homework beforehand and checking out if your destination is within close reach of the station or stop. Most malls may have a station right inside the mall (Mall of the Emirates) but some places may require a walk and if it's hot, a 20 minute walk can wipe the energy from you. Taxis are always on the prowl so you can usually hop into one from outside a station stop.

It's always nice to experience the new metro system so we encourage using the metro at least once during your stay in Dubai! You may want to consider hiring a car if you feel comfortable driving in Dubai, which is renowned for wreckless drivers! The one major niggle is the parking, especially if you are planning on visiting independent shops or places that don't have their own car park - which can be many! Our advice is to travel by taxi and metro, where possible, but to hire a car if going out of Dubai.

TAXIS

There's an army of 7,000 taxi drivers roaming the city by day and night. They are plentiful and appear in hoards at key points around the city so that you rarely have to queue. Taxis did used to be a problem in the boom days, but whether it's a lack of traveller or expat or an increase to the vast number said to now swarm the streets – it certainly is not a problem anymore, especially in locations like Dubai Mall or major hotels. Taxis are fairly priced for the city – and it would be ill-advised to take an unlicensed cab, although they don't really exist. Safe, regulated and modern, most are clean, although some require a little perfume.

The other benefit of taking the taxi is getting the lowdown on what's going on. While some drivers are grumps and will just want to get you from A to B, many will be willing to strike up a conversation with you. It's a great way to understand the city from an insider perspective.

Taxis are convenient with an ample number of taxi stands and even if you want to hail one from the streets you won't be waiting too long. There are certain times of the day when getting a taxi may take longer than usual:

The work/school morning rush hour between 7-9am

The end of school rush hour between 2-4pm

The return from work rush hour between 5-7pm

Bear in mind that tourist spots such as Dubai Mall, the Atlantis waterpark etc. will incur a long wait at the queues near closing time so you might want to leave early if you have small kids in tow.

TAXI ADVICE:

Taxi drivers know most destinations, but they may not know all and if they are new to the game, they may be a little nervous.

It's better to have a close landmark ready and, of course, the phone number of the shop/restaurant etc handy.

There are six main official taxi companies in Dubai all operating on a meter basis. They have a variety of different topped roofs but are essentially the same – apart from the Ladies only pink topped roof taxi

All of the official companies charge the same rates so you can get into any.

Be wary of the private hotel taxis that you see parked outside the major hotels. While convenient, they won't necessarily operate by the meter. We have found them to sometime charge more than double and that the rate changes once you get to your destination. It is hit and miss and we don't recommend them.

If taxis are not nearby our advice is to ask your concierge to call you a cab or, if you can, walk a few minutes out of your hotel and get on the main road to hail a coloured roof taxi – or call and book one yourself.

The Ladies Taxis, driven by women and with a pastel pink roof is ideal for women uncomfortable riding with a male driver. They are not readily available to hail, so you need to keep their number handy and book in advance. Please note that the Ladies taxis only accept women and children.

TAXI PRICES

With regard to fares, the official taxi companies all have the same rate rules:

The minimum fare is 10 AED

The fare starts at 3 AED if hailed from the street and 6 if booked by phone

The fare is slightly more expensive at night or for larger cars.

The rate is 1.6 AED per kilometre

The starting airport rate is 25 AED

There are extra charges of 20 AED travelling to Sharjah or the other Emirates, but you should try and negotiate a fixed rate if going significant distances.

Taxis are exempted from the Salik Toll charge fees that regular drivers must pay.

The journey is free if the driver forgets to put the meter on or it is not working.

In practice, you'll be paying a minimum of 10 AED and an average of 25 AED per journey, depending on where you go. Taxis are generally not too badly priced especially if you are travelling in a group of 3 or 4 persons as the metro would then work out the same or more expensive. Do note that the taxi drivers are legally obliged to take you to your destination, however close it is. This may infuriate them, as they may have been queuing for a long while, but a small tip usually helps.

PRICE EXAMPLES

Examples of trip costs are below and are for the official taxis.
Private taxis will be higher:

Dubai Mall to Dubai Marina: 50 AED

Emirates Towers to Dubai Airport: 30 AED

Emirates Towers to Jumeirah Beach/Madinat Jumeirah: 40 AED

Dubai Mall to the Atlantis Hotel: 50 AED

Media City to Dubai Airport: 75 AED

Media City to Sharjah Airport: 250 AED

Dubai Airport to Dubai city: 50 AED

Dubai to Abu Dhabi: 250 - 300 AED (negotiate)

Dubai Airport to Abu Dhabi Airport: 250-300 AED (negotiate)

TAXI PHONE NUMBERS

Dubai Transport: 04 208 0808

Ladies Taxi: 04 208 0808

Metro Taxi: 04 267 3222

National Taxi: 04 339 0002

Arabia Taxi: 04 285 5111

Cars Taxi: 04 269 2900

For more information go to the Dubai Taxi website: dtc.dubai.ae

METRO

We can't imagine life before the Metro. It was only 2009 when the Dubai Metro was launched – and the roads were at breaking point! The new metro is modern, driver less, sleek and efficient. Now that most of the stations across the Red and Green lines are fully operational, it is relatively simple to travel across the city. However – your destination is unlikely to be close enough to the station and you will probably have to end up taking a taxi at the other end – especially in the heat. The coverage is pretty extensive for the major locations in Dubai. There are two interchange stations - Khalid bin Al Waleed and Union - but plans to extend the two lines to four have been shelved for the time being.

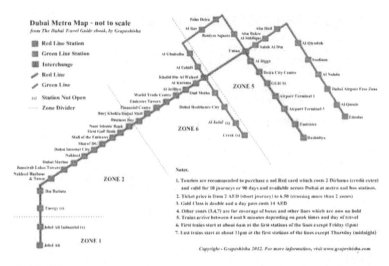

Dubai Metro

The Metro is the longest fully automated driverless metro network in the world.

There are trains running every 4 to 8 minutes with AC throughout. The lines run daily from about 6am to 1am closing at midnight on Saturday and starting at 1pm on the holy day of Friday. Having gained wide scale adoption, you're equally likely to find yourself sharing a carriage with construction workers as you are with local Emiratis. There's a ladies only carriage and a gold class carriage, if you can't stand the sweat, but you'll pay a premium. The price for journeys ranges from roughly AED 2 to AED 6 depending on the duration or distance – and double for Gold class. Kids under 5 are free. You will need to buy a Nol Card to go on the metro. For more information check out the Dubai Road & Transport Authority site. rta.ae

THE PALM MONORAIL

With all the planning that Dubai did – it seemed to have missed out linking the metro with the Monorail. This is a little bit of a pain as you'll need to get to the Gateway station (taxi drivers know it as the Palm Monorail) to get to the end of the Palm and the Atlantis hotel.

This is the only other station – and so if you are going elsewhere on the Palm, you'd have to question whether it was worth it especially at a cost of AED 15 one way per person (AED 25 return). The trains are every 23 minutes, and offer stunning views both of the Palm (if you can manage getting the front seat!) but also of the Dubai sky line. But if there's more than one of you, you may just decide to take a taxi to save time. The monorail runs from 10 am to 10 pm – and the closest Metro station to the Monorail is Nakheel which is a AED 10 ride away. There are plans to connect the monorail to the Dubai Tram system but that's not yet complete. The taxis leaving the Gateway on your return are usually expensive, so it might be worthwhile taking a taxi from the Atlantis when leaving.

DUBAI TRAM

At the time of writing, the delayed project of the Dubai Tramway or Dubai Tram was due to launch. The tram will travel between Al Sufuoh in Jumeirah past the Palm where it will interlink with the Palm Monorail Gateway going through Mina Seyahi, Dubai Marina (linking with the Metro), Dubai Marina Mall ending at Jumeirah Lake Towers (linking with the Metro again). The Tram will also loop back around the palm to Jumeirah Beach Residence.

THE NOL CARD

The NOL card is a pre pay transport card usable on public transport in Dubai, including the Metro and Bus. The tickets for the Dubai Metro are available on a tier based system dependent on how often you would use public transport. You have a choice of four different types of Nol card to choose from. For the tourist, the Red Nol card is the best option. You pre pay, can use it for 10 journeys and it's valid for 90 days. The others require photo ID and set up of an e-wallet and are not worth arranging unless you are staying for a long while. You can easily pick up your NOL card from any station, where you can pick up the maps. There are ticket machines at every station and at multiple points in Dubai, including the airport. For more information please refer to the Nol site. nol.ae

BUSES

It's completely possible to use the bus to get around Dubai, but despite our attempts, we always find it a little complicated. That's not to say that it is difficult, but you'll need to invest a little time in figuring out the routes. The buses are obviously susceptible to the Dubai traffic which is why we think the Metro is better. However, the government of Dubai have invested heavily in their new fleet to encourage local citizens as well as tourists to use them instead of cars to ease the ever growing Dubai congestion. They have even taken it as far as installing air conditioned bus stops. No matter how sleek they look and feel, not all have taken to them purely because taxis are so readily available, even though the buses run from 5am to midnight. Many who use the buses are on lower incomes but that shouldn't put you off especially if you and your destination are located near a stop. Our advice is to use them if you know exactly where you are going to and the bus route stops at your location. The other time to consider them is going between terminals at the airport. The buses take the Nol card like the metro, so make sure you are topped up. For more information about the Dubai Bus Network and finding your route, check out the RTA dedicated site: rtaprojects.me

BOATS, DHOWS AND ABRAS

The most convenient way to cross the Creek is by abra, the 1 Dirham, 3 minute, boat ride across. You should make a point of doing this short journey while in Dubai. It's one of our tourist must dos. Not only do you get from one side of the creek to the other, but you also get to see a beautiful view of the city. If it's warm, go after sunset, when all the buildings are lit up and Dubai by night is bustling. The Abra has several pick up points along the Bur Dubai and Deira side and each Abra is capable of housing about 20 passengers.

Other creek options include taking the Dubai Water Bus. For AED 4 you do a similar, but upmarket trip across. And for AED 50 you can do the creek tourist sites for an hour. You could also take the waterbus or if you're looking to see more than the creek, get a ticket on the Dubai Ferry. You can either see the Marina up to Burj AL Arab or the area close to the World islands. These are more tourist routes than transport necessities, but worth spending the money if interested. If you can stomach your food while on the river, the dhow cruise buffets are a nice evening sunset alternative.

HIRING A CAR

If you like the liberty of your own car whilst on holiday then hiring one is generally an easy affair - just make sure you can handle driving in Dubai as it is renowned for some occasionally bad driving, especially on the highway. Gulf Arabia has a reputation for young boys with their big toys drifting on and off road or Tafheet, as it is known. That aside, with parking conspicuous in most hotels, shopping malls and places of interest, it can be a useful alternative, if you are confident driving on the right. It's a bit of struggle visiting the small shops in Bur Dubai or the Gold Souk area, as on street parking is sparse. When you do find it, it's charged at around 2 AED per hour but make sure you keep topped up as the fines can be huge! Most of the large well known car hire companies are available throughout UAE and you can opt for the car to be picked up from the airport or delivered to your hotel or town. Don't get the hotel concierge to arrange your car hire as you'll more than likely pay double the going rate. Entry level cars start at AED 200 per day but can go past the AED 1000 daily mark if you're getting a top of the range 4x4 which is the expat vehicle of choice here. One point of note concerns alcohol. There is zero tolerance to having any alcohol in the bloodstream, which means a minimum jail term if you crash your car and it wasn't your fault. The other point of note is the stakes are high. If there is a death as a result of your driving, you may even be forced to pay blood money to the relatives of the victim. To hire a car you will need to be over 21 have a photocopy of your passport and entry visa, credit card, and a valid driving license from you home country (If you are in the UAE for the long term and obtain your UAE residency, you will need to obtain a UAE driving license)

For informational purposes, if you are involved in an accident in the UAE, remain in the exact place of the accident and call 999. On arrival and assessment of the accident, the police will give you some forms to complete which will then have to be given to the car hire company. You must comply with all regulations or face a fine.

On the plus side, petrol is incredibly cheap in the UAE and sometimes hiring a car can be more economical than taxi hopping, especially if you are visiting for a good few days and with family. Petrol attendants at the gas stations mean you can stay in your air conditioned luxury but make sure you also carry cash as occasionally the smaller petrol stations may not accept credit cards, especially in the outskirts.

Here are our recommended car hire firms. Don't be tempted with seemingly cheaper offers from local companies, who offer notoriously bad insurance cover, if the worst were to happen. Be safe!

Fast UAE 04 338 7171 fastuae.com

Avis 04 224 5219 avisuae.ae

Dollar 04 347 5800 dollaruae.com

Thrifty 04 347 9001 thriftyuae.com

Hertz 04 224 5222 hertz.ae

Budget 04 282 2727 budget-uae.com

SALIK - ROAD TOLLS

Dubai has installed a number of road tolls across the city. The taxi drivers are exempt so don't let them con you into paying, but if you have hired a car, you will have to pay. There are six tolling points: Al Safa, Al Barsha, Al Garhoud Bridge, Al Maktoum Bridge, AL Mamzar (Al Itthihad Road) and the Airport Tunnel (Beirut Street). Each time you pass through a Salik tolling point your vehicle is detected using Radio Frequency Identification (RFID) technology that is built into your Salik sticker tag, embedded in your windscreen. The toll of AED 4 is deducted from your prepaid toll account – or in the case of a hire car, you will be charged when you return your vehicle. For more information see salik.gov.ae

EXPLORING OLD DUBAI ON FOOT

We have three pieces of advice with regard to walking in Dubai. Firstly, make sure you don't spend the whole time in the sun. You can very quickly get heatstroke if you are not used to this type of heat. Our second piece of advice is to make sure you have water with you always to cool you down. Finally, don't even think about walking for long periods during the summer months – it's close to suicidal.

However, some areas of Dubai are perfect for walking around in the winter months and to peel back the golden façade to see what came before buildings and glamour. There are three such areas: Bastakiya, Shindhaga and Deira. These areas represent the best of Old Dubai on both sides around the creek and are the areas that you should make a point of at least visiting, even if you don't want to nosey too much around the heritage.

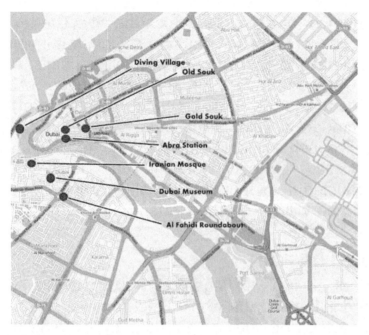

Walking tour Points of Interest in Old Dubai, Copyright OpenStreetMap contributors, CC BY-SA, Grapeshisha

BASTAKIYA

Bastakiya is the perfect bite sized chunk of rambling. For those of you who prefer to be guided, the Sheikh Mohamed Centre for Cultural Understanding offer walking tours through the area. If solo is your thing you'll probably have to get a taxi to Al Fahidi roundabout and start at Al Fahidi street. You can walk from Khalid bin al Waleed Station (Burjuman Metro Station) within the Burjuman Shopping Centre, (or the Al Fahidi Metro Station) but it will take roughly ten minutes. Even if you are not doing the tour with SMCCU, it's worth checking out their building that you will see from the roundabout.

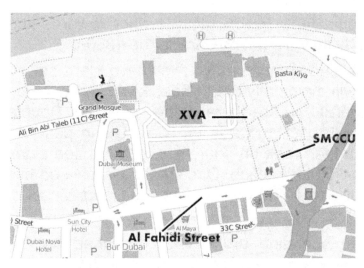

Bastakiya Walking Tour, Copyright OpenStreetMap contributors, CC BY-SA, Grapeshisha

On your right you will see Basta Art café which is a restored house where you can treat yourself to a juice or have lunch. If you angle to your left you will see the wind towers, where you can enter Bastakiya proper. On your left you will see the Majlis Gallery which is worth having at a gander at for the various exhibitions that run. There are a few more galleries and if you continue through to the right you will see the museum called Dar Ibn Al Haytham for visual arts which has some historical artefacts and also houses some Emirati art. Going further you will see the lovely flowery carving above the door of the Architectural Heritage Society which has all sorts of stuff to do with archaeology if that's your thing. The coin house is worth popping into as is Dar Al Nadwa, which is a beautifully restored structure. Use this spot as an opportunity to go upstairs and view Bastakiya from above. Further on you'll also see the eye gallery and the home of Eastern Art gallery as well.

Your next point of reference is the XVA gallery. If you veer towards you will see the XVA which is a both a hotel and a café. You'll notice it by the courtyard café. XVA is also famous for its gallery which is top class. Continue to wander around for an hour or so and check out the traditional Bedouin tent. If you move further towards the creek you will see the old city wall, dating back to the 1800s.

Continue past the doors, and sometimes you will have stalls selling arts and crafts, but you will eventually get to Bastakiya Nights, which is a great place for dinner if you are there at the right time. Double back on yourself and walk back towards the wall. Going past the Mosque on your left with the creek on your right, you will see signs for the Diwan which is the Ruler's office. Once you have passed this and made it onto the main road, you will see signs to Dubai Museum about 5 minutes walk away.

Dubai Museum is worth spending an hour to download on the history of Dubai. You'll see the large traditional dhow on exit, but once you have finished double back down the main road you originally walked down to the white domed mosque which is the Grand Mosque of Dubai. There is a very small alley next to the mosque where you will find Hindu and other objects on sale that you could take to the temple. You will very quickly come to the textile souk which is also known as the old souk. Here, under the wooden beamed coverings, it is highly likely you will get jumped on by tradesman trying to sell you pashminas, saris, Panjabi dresses and the like. At the end of the souk you will see the Iranian Mosque in the distance to your left, but go right towards the creek where you can get an Abra to the Deira. You'll also see the International Aladdin Shoes stall, where you'll be tempted to buy slippers that you will never wear.

SHINDHAGA

Shindhaga is a bolt on walk to Bastakiya. You could take on Shindhaga if you woke early and then visited Bastakiya, but if you want to cover two areas properly in one day, then plump for Bastakiya followed by Deira. Or you could cover Bastakiya and Shindhaga in one day leaving a whole day to go for the Deira souks.

That's not to say that Shindhaga is not interesting – it's just more of the same flavour as Bastakiya's history.

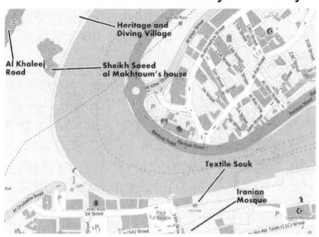

Shindhaga Walking Tour, Copyright OpenStreetMap contributors, CC BY-SA, Grapeshisha

We'd recommend starting walking from the diving village on Al Khaleej Road. You'd do well to spend some time at the Heritage Village – and then if you are that way inclined, you could visit the camel and horse museums. Let's face it – you won't do that ever again, so you might as well give it a few minutes.

Nearby, Sheikh Saeed al Makhtoum's house is where the current ruler spent his first days. It's well kept and worth visiting Shindhaga just for this as it will put the whole of Dubai into perspective. In less than one generation, the Dubai rulers have moved from relatively simple dwellings to the grandiose. Seeing this house will put things in context and give a view of what life used to be up until a few years ago.

Don't miss the traditional architecture museum next door, housed in the most traditional of renovated buildings. Continuing around the creek you will arrive at the textile souk and then the Iranian Mosques.

DEIRA

Deira's lure is the Gold Souk and will be the highlight of this walk. Once you get off the abra, you'll feel the vibe of the hawkers nearby. Follow the signs for the Old souk which is on Old Baniyas Road. Feel free to wander into the many souvenir shops – and even be tempted by some 'copy original' merchandise.

Double back on yourself and you will see the Spice souk (Sikkat Al Khalil Road). You'll actually smell it first! Don't touch the spices unless invited to, but everything is fairly priced here – which is why we like to stock up on our bits and pieces. At the end of the street, go right and then immediately left and follow the signs for the Al Ahmadiya School. Spend some time there and next door at the Heritage House.

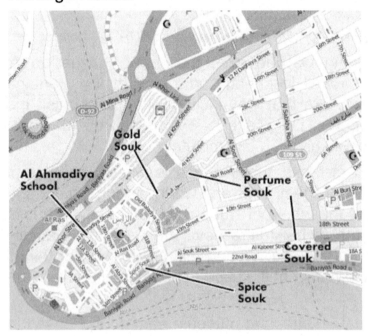

Deira Walking Tour, Copyright OpenStreetMap contributors, CC BY-SA, Grapeshisha

Walk back past the School and you will see the signs for the Gold Souk. Take a right on Old Baladiya Street which is home to local tailors and some bric a brac stores. You'll actually feel the bargaining in the air as you walk up to the souk where you'll be hit upon by the brightness of the yellow gold gleaming in the window – and the sign stating that this is "Dubai, City of Gold" - as if it wasn't. If you are there to buy, you could be there for a few hours. If not, get lost for an hour, take a perch on the bench, out of the sun and watch the flow of money and gold happen.

Come out of the exit at the other end of the Gold Souk, and you will get to the Perfume souk, where you can buy oud burners and learn the art of scent. A little further down you will arrive at the Deira Covered Souq. It's not our favourite souq, but you can finish up your souvenir shopping here if you need to. If you don't wear them, you may want to indulge in a cheap Kandura or Abaya, for your next fancy dress party back home.

ITINERARIES

Dubai offers multiple options for many travellers and with 24 hours in Dubai, what would you do you with your time? Well, Dubai has built its reputation by creating a tourist industry from scratch, to a degree that it can appear to be customised playground for everyone. Whether you want to just see what the souks are all about – or experience the concept of envisioned bling real hand, Dubai can deliver. Millions visit Dubai on a stop over every year, and many return every year to do more. What can you do in 24 hours in Dubai, when you are on a business trip? Each to their own, but we have articulated what we think are must dos if you have a short time to spend or longer. There are customised itineraries for 24 hours, two or three days or even a week.

Dubai is tourist friendly so whether you are flying through from east to west or west to east – this is where you can get your fix of future Arabia either in short bursts of a few days or for a week or more of relaxation.

24 HOURS IN DUBAI

If you are here for a brief stopover, we recommend the following to be covered during a full day.

Start your trip as early as you can in one of Dubai's oldest areas, Deira, and visit the Gold Souk. Even if buying gold is not on your agenda, you must see this place for the sheer volume of precious metal available to buy at bargain prices. The souk is half covered and uncovered so take plenty of water. If you do decide to buy – haggle and don't be shy! Shops open from 10am-10pm with a few closing between 1pm-4pm.

When you've had enough of gold, head south towards the Dubai Creek (on foot) and take a left toward a covered long alleyway which has several shops selling the most beautiful smelling spices. This is the Spice Souk and worth strolling through for about 10 minutes to see the bags of great quality Indian and Middle Eastern spices. They also sell mixed nuts and other items so this could be a good place to pick up some gifts.

Just outside the long alleyway of the souk, head to the Dubai Creek to pick up the Dhow or Abra for a ride along the Dubai Creek. These are wooden traditional boats used to transport goods back in the day. Today they are a popular method of ferrying people across the creek for 1 AED per person. The ride is only about 3-5 mins but provide awesome views. The Abra will stop near the Bur Dubai Textile souk

The Bur Dubai Textile souk located near Al Fahidi Street is very popular with the Indian, Pakistani and Middle Eastern communities. Many come here for beautiful fabric to stitch into wedding or party clothes. Tailors are also available here to make your designs sometimes in two days or even one day.   Shops again are open from 10am-10pm with a few closing between 1pm-4pm.

If you head past the Arabian Court Hotel, you should start seeing some traditional old buildings and come across Bastakiya behind the Grand Mosque. This is one of Dubai's oldest areas and building and gives an idea of what architecture was like before the oil discovery. The area is known as the Bastakiya quarter and many art galleries, cafés, shops are opening up to liven the place. It is also worth checking out the Dubai Museum for an insight into the Emirati culture and see small artefacts and short films on how Dubai became what it is today. The museum is not huge – you can cover in an hour and then break for lunch at nearby Basta Art Café, a quaint little relaxing spot in a cute garden. Lunch offered includes sandwiches and wraps but their fresh juice – especially the mint and lime - is divine!

No trip to Dubai is complete without visiting one of their glitzy malls and if we had to pick one it would have to be the huge Dubai Mall. Get a taxi from your last point and look forward to some air conditioning downtime or retail relaxation. All the brands are available here along with a cinema, huge kids play areas and the indoor Aquarium and Underwater Zoo. If you have kids, Dubai Mall will bring you some much needed sanity. Don't forget to visit the adjoining Souk Al Bahar for some lovely ornaments and pashmina, dates and gifts for loved ones.

After a few hours of strolling in Dubai Mall, take the opportunity to grab an outdoor table at one of the many al fresco restaurants dotted around the Dubai Fountain and Burj Khalifa, the world's tallest building, and wait for the music and light show to begin. If you like Lebanese food, we recommend Wafi Gourmet for juicy shawarmas, mezze and grills. Our other recommendation is Karma Kafe, with Thai fusion, Buddha Bar Style. The view is amazing from the terrace. The fountain show begins at 6pm and runs every 30 minutes, so you should book a table as soon as you arrive at Dubai Mall.

If you still have any energy left, either head back to your hotel area or stay at Dubai Mall for some shisha available at most Lebanese terraced restaurants, or check out our shisha café guide.

3 DAYS IN DUBAI

Cover everything in the 24 hr itinerary plus:

If you have kids with you, or even if you don't, you can easily spend half to a full day at one of Dubai's two famous water parks, Wild Wadi at Jumeirah Beach Hotel or the (nearly) world famous Aquaventure at the Atlantis. The rides are good for kids as well as adults and provide respite in the warm sun. If you are staying at one of these hotels, entry to the water park is free and unlimited.

After a few hours at the water park, head to Madinat Jumeirah just down the road from the Wild Wadi water park (take a taxi if you're exhausted). This is an Arabian picturesque leisure complex with two lavish hotels, Mina A'Salam and the Al Qasr. Stroll through the souk and get a feel of Arabia (although the price of their goods don't appear souk-like!) or relax for drinks/lunch/dinner at one of their many cafes and restaurants, most of which are outdoor and have awesome views of the Burj Al Arab.

If you can manage to get a convenient slot to go up the Burj Khalifa, the world's tallest building, you should probably combine this with your visit to Dubai Mall as these landmarks are all in the same area. You need to visit the ticket desk in the Dubai Mall but bear in mind you may not be offered tickets on the same day which is why we recommend booking your slot online before you arrive in Dubai.
Visiting the Burj Khalifa and taking in the awesome views will easily take an hour minimum. If you haven't done the Dubai Fountain or Aquarium, you could do these as they are all in the same area.

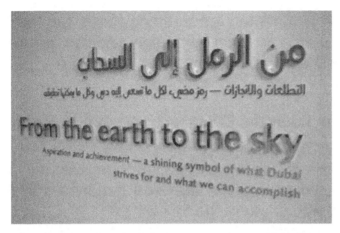

VisitDubai's crowning achievement, The Burj Khalifa

After the Dubai Mall, the next mall on your to do list should be Mall of the Emirates purely to see and perhaps even experience Ski Dubai, the indoor ski resort. Another activity to get a thumbs up from the kids, you could easily spend a couple of hours here going on the slopes, playing in the snow park or try a bob sled ride. Snow attire and equiptment is all provided and included in your entry price.

For a late afternoon/ evening excursion, don't leave Dubai without experiencing a desert safari. These are suitable for almost anyone except very young children, expectant mums and those with heart problems. Various tour companies in UAE will have packages to suit you and pick you up at your hotel. Relax and enjoy a 6 hour trip including a thrilling ride, relaxing bbq buffet, watching the sunset, belly dancers and shisha.

Don't forget to relax and soak up the sun when you're in Dubai! Shopping, eating and sightseeing can take up your holiday, but put time aside to experience Dubai's beaches. Head down to Jumeirah Road and visit Jumeirah Open Beach for free or for a small fee of 5 AED per person / 20 AED with a car Jumeirah Beach Park has facilities such as showers, play areas, bbq areas and sun loungers. If you are not staying at a beach hotel and want to experience somewhere a bit more private and exclusive than the public beaches, many hotels along Jumeirah have day passes for their beach and pool and you can also use their changing facilities, prices will start from about 200 AED per person. Enquire at your hotel.

ONE WEEK IN DUBAI

Cover everything in the 24 hours in Dubai and 3 days in Dubai itinerary and then consider the rest of what we recommend.

Don't burn out in the desert – if you have managed to cover our 3 day itinerary in Dubai, we would suggest that you combine some beach time or retail therapy with some of the following:

If you are stuck for somewhere trendy to eat, we recommend Zuma in DIFC. Brilliant Japanese cuisine and awesome atmosphere. It's the place where you can head for pre-dinner drinks/dinner and stay on for more drinking and dancing if you have the energy.

If you'd much rather view the pretty sights of Dubai whilst having your dinner, book a 4 course meal on board the Bateux Dubai, a glass dhow travelling along the creek for 2.5 hours. Under-fives are not permitted on board but enquire first.

Afternoon tea at the Burj Al Arab is one of the only ways to get access to this exclusive hotel, if you are not dining at the restaurants or staying there. For 400 AED you can enjoy a light meal at Sahn Eddar, the lobby lounge or for stunning views book a table at the Skyview Bar for afternoon tea. It's very posh, so dress smart.

Kids will love the Wonderbus tours, a bus that tours sights on land and sea! It's a 1.5 tour covering places like Heritage Village, Dubai Creek, Gold Souk, Emirates Towers and more. Alternatively, if you prefer a detailed tour of Dubai, the Big Bus Company provides detailed tours of Dubai and you can also hop on and off during the day and expore sights to your leisure. The Bug Bus Tour comes highly recommended if you want get a good overall snapshot of Dubai.

Spend a day in Abu Dhabi, UAE's capital, less than 2 hours away from Dubai. You can get your hotel to arrange a day trip by hiring your own driver and take you to some of the following landmarks: the Corniche - take a stroll along this newly renovated sea front and a welcome alternative to a crowded Jumeirah beach; visit Emirates Palace for afternoon tea; or take a drive to Yas Island and visit the F1 Grand Prix race track and if you fancy a few white knuckle rides head to Ferrari World and Yas Waterworld. On the way to or from Yas Island, consider visiting the exhibition, Manarat Al Sadiyat on Sadiyat Island, which is an impressive eye opener on Abu Dhabi's vision for 2030. The site that you must visit in Abu Dhabi is the Sheikh Zayed Mosque.

Our itineraries cover everything from 24 hours in Dubai to a full week – and although possible within the week, would require some motivation of steel with some luck with traffic! It's possible to do it all but you may want to cherry pick to what tickles your fancy versus what you consider superfluous to your holiday.

If time is on your side, there really are some great combinations of day trips to get a different balance and perspective – from time in Al Ain to splitting your holiday with some time in Oman and maybe to places like Jordan and Lebanon. Arabia is more than conflict – it's a rich area of heritage and future.

SIGHTSEEING

Dubai has created some world beating attractions in record time. If you had visited Dubai at the turn of the century, there would be Old Dubai - Bastakiya and the area around Dubai Creek. And this is where we have the divide of tourist activity – a couple of days in the historic quarter and the rest of the time in the mirage in the desert. We recommend that you see Bastakiya and old Dubai to understand the first base of Dubai but also picking through the other sexy new activities and sights. And then you will realise why Dubai is so popular. What it does, it does well. Dubai encourages you to do what you enjoy doing. Be selective on what to do, but make sure you enjoy yourself.

Apart from Bastakiya in the older part of Dubai, Dubai is not really a city to walk around and meander to new haunts. Dubai instead contains destinations of choice – a sort of a la carte tourist destination. This gives you the opportunity to pick off what you would love to do, rather than being forced to consider spots that wouldn't usually tickle your fancy.

For each sight, we have listed the following

When – what time and what day the site is open

How long – how long you should expect to spend there

Location – Where the site is located, along with landmarks and what to tell your taxi driver, if appropriate.

Cost – How much you would expect to spend in Dirhams (Dhs) for one adult.

Booking – booking details if required

More info – where you can obtain more information online, if available

TOURS OF DUBAI

Dubai can be unbearingly confusing to the uninitiated. To remind you of the key areas, here is the basic context on what you should understand when considering covering Dubai on a tour:

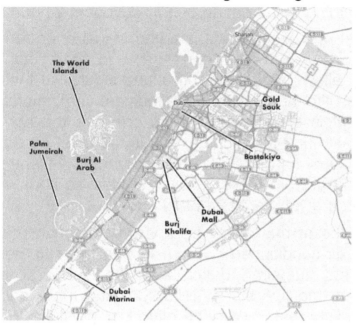

Dubai in Context, Copyright OpenStreetMap contributors, CC BY-SA, Grapeshisha

BUs TOUR OF THE DUBAI

If you're a first timer to Dubai, taking a bus tour will cover all the major landmarks and places of interest in an informative and humorous way. Apart from taxis, which can be pot luck, The Big Bus Tours offer the best way to familiarize yourself with this fascinating city of contrasts. In Dubai, there are many types of tours, but there's no point messing around with them. The Big Bus Tour is the best of the lot. In a full day you can see the whole of Dubai, with all the trimmings of intense description, humour and astonishing facts. The tour is 'hop on and hop off', so it's also flexible for you to visit some of the areas – and if you don't want to visit all the areas of Dubai, you can opt for the more manageable tour covering just the main landmarks. The main tour offered by the Big Bus Company is the day tour, but if you have time and want the easy life, you can sign up for the 48 hour tour, which gives you even more flexibility. If you have no time whatsoever, you can whizz through Dubai on the night tour and see everything – and get an overall flavour in 2 hours.

The bus picks you up at one of the malls, starting at just after 9am depending on which one – but you don't have to start then. However, starting early allows you to get off – and indulge in their additional tours of places like the souks. The guides are very helpful, and although their script is staged – it's fresh and has the right amount of balance of facts and fun. For us, this is the must do trip for the newbie to Dubai. Just turn up at Wafi, Burjuman, City Centre or Dubai Mall – and take it from there. You don't have to book in advance, but just make sure you get there early enough to pay

The open roof double decker bus gives great views, although you can opt for the cooler air-conditioned ground floor in the summer months. The tour covers Jumeirah beach and the surrounding areas such as the Palm, the five star hotels, shopping malls and Jumeirah mosque. The City tour covers the historical sites like the forts, ancient homes and architecture, Dubai Museum and the street life within Bur Dubai. Renowned tourist attractions like the Creek Park, the Spice Market and Dubai Heritage Village are also a part of the City Tour. The Beach Tour provides you with spectacular sights to feast your eyes on and capture images of the city which could never have been possible from a taxi, for example. Both the tours are covered in the price, but it all depends whether you can do it all in your 24 hour or 48 hour ticket.

Something that makes the Big Bus Tour of Dubai a huge selling point is the distance which the bus covers as a part of the itinerary. With 12 kilometres covered under the City Tour and 25 kilometres covered under the Beach Tour there is no other means of transport which would provide exposure at this scale unless you decide to shell out in hiring a car or a taxi.

POINTs OF NOTE –

The best starting point is Burjuman Mall where you can decide whether to take the city or beach tour. If you haven't been to Dubai before we recommend doing the former first. Start early!

The night tour starts at Deira City Centre at 715pm and Madinat Jumeirah at 815pm – but this is a fixed 2 hour tour with no stop offs.

Ask questions – the guides are happy to answer anything. And if they don't know, they'll call someone to find out!

Don't lose your ticket.

An alternative to the Big Bus type tour is the Wonderbus tour where an amphibious vehicle takes you through water as well as on land to various locations. It's not for everyone, but it certainly is something different

When – The Big Bus Tour of Dubai could be taken at any time as buses operate every day from nine in the morning till five in the evening. A total of 32 tours are offered every single day with departures every 30 minutes

How long – The Beach Tour lasts for 2 hours and the City Tour is one and half hours, but that is assuming you don't get off. You need the most of a full day to do the tour properly.

Location – We recommend starting at Burjuman Mall, but you could start at any of the big malls such as Wafi or Deira City Centre if you want just a city tour.

Cost – The standard price per person is around AED 240 for an adult for a one day ticket but please refer to website for different options and discounted prebooking.

More Information - bigbustours.com or call 04 340-7709

SEAWINGs PLANE TOUR OF DUBAI

The Seawings tour of Dubai is electric. One minute you are checking out the creek and the next you are circling the Burj Khalifa. The tour offers picture perfect moments and one of our most recommended trips if you can afford it. It's a unique sightseeing excursion offering a bird's eye view and likely to be the highlight of your trip.

The flights take place daily from 8 am to dusk in an amphibious Cessna caravan seaplane. The 40 minute tour of Dubai will fly by (excuse the pun) and gives you the most breath-taking view of Dubai that will supersede any of magazine paraphernalia that brought you to Dubai in the first place.

The excitement begins as you leave the Dubai Creek – as you depart and leave from water. You'll see the creek to start off with including the dhows and scenery, but Seawings comes into its own when you view the newer parts of Dubai. You get to see all the main sights and then some including the Burj Al Arab, the Burj Khalifa and the Palm and World islands. It's spectacular experiencing it from above

The plane is remarkably comfortable and has been designed so that every seat is a window seat. There are multiple packages on offer, but the most popular is the Silver package for AED 1375 per person, but there are more on offer including flying to other destinations and going to the Emirates Palace in Abu Dhabi for lunch.

If you are going to splash some cash, save some for Seawings. It may be the most expensive thing you do on your trip, but nothing quite matches it.

POINTs OF NOTE

Although this is a sea plane, it does land on the ground as well, so there's no need to worry about emergencies.

Make sure you take a spare battery for your camera (you will take loads of pictures, guaranteed)

Summer months can be hazy and thus not great for photos

We don't think it's worth paying extra for the commentary and maps, but you're welcome to spend extra!

Don't wear flip flops or high heels – as you will find it difficult to board

You need to check in at least 30 minutes before and bring your passport. You'll be provided with water on the plane – don't bring your own.

When – Daily, all year round, from 8am to dusk

How Long   – 40 minutes for the Silver trip, plus time for boarding and disembarking

Location – Flights start at Dubai Creek

Map – Dubai Creek Golf Academy, past the Park Hyatt Golf Academy

Cost – AED 1600 for the Silver trip

Booking – reservations@seawings.ae, 04 8070708 /04 8832999

More info – seawings.ae

YELLOW BOAT TOUR OF THE PALM

The gargantuan and ambitious engineering project undertaken by the Dubai Government in UAE is a world's first. The Palm Jumeirah is the largest artificial island in the world and its creation has already resulted in extending Dubai's coastline by more than 500 kilometres thus attracting some of the wealthiest investors, not to mention the leading chains of hotels and restaurants in the world. The Palm Jumeirah has evolved into one of the most fashionable, trendy and luxurious locations in the world with the uniqueness of being nestled amidst a cradle of diverse marine life with an abundance of year round sunshine.

Many people will have heard of the Palm already and it has quickly become symbolic of the ambitions of Dubai with many famous celebrities having a holiday home on the Palm. However, the view that you have of the Palm is from the sky and on the ground, the view is a little different. Firstly, the backbone of the Palm Jumeirah lies in the middle or what is known as the 'trunk' which is basically an 8 lane motorway, taking visitors and residents to the different 'fronds' or tip of the Palm.

We think one of the best ways to see the Palm is to see it from the outside. Book a tour with the Yellow Boats which will take you from Dubai Marina all around the Atlantis, past the Burj Al Arab and back. You'll get some amazing photos and be fully exhilarated by the rush of the boats

The Yellow Boats is a unique sightseeing experience. No one else offers any way to see the coast in this way. The Yellow Boats brings a fresh perspective to your Dubai trip with some of the most interesting and exciting on-water experiences. The Yellow Boats are rigid inflatable top of the line crafts and perfectly safe and great fun for families.

POINTs OF NOTE –

Yellow tours needs to be booked in advance and leaves from Dubai Marina Walk (opposite Spinneys)

As an added attraction at Palm Jumeirah for divers, two F-100 Super Sabre fighter jets were sunk after being completely stripped in a bid to create an artificial reef.

The more traditional way to experience the Palm is to visit the Atlantis the Palm either by taking a taxi there or by taking the monorail there. Time yourself though, as trying to get a taxi back at the wrong time will mean a long queue. They do come, but you're in competition with many others. Another way is to visit Aquaventure which is part of the Atlantis.

Yellow boats do a thrill seeking ride for those who love to get their adrenaline pumping.

Although it is very safe, if you get sea sick, it is best to avoid this!

When – There are fixed times depending on which tour you want, starting at 830 .

How long – Allow between 1 hour and 2 hours depending on the tour

Location – Palm Jumeirah is an identity in itself and located in the blue waters of the sea.

Cost – The all-inclusive tour of the Marina, Palm and Burj costs AED 280 and AED 210 for kids

More Info –theyellowboats.com

SMCCU TOUR OF BAsTAKIYA (SMCCU)

If you are a culture vulture, you should really consider taking the tours from the Sheikh Mohammed Centre for Cultural Understanding (SMCCU). Essentially you will be able to get a fuller picture of Emirati culture through more interaction and a meal with the Emirati as well as a guided tour through Bastakia. SMCCU is a non-profit organization set up by the Prime Minister to give a view of Emirati culture to tourists, expats and anyone who wants to listen. The main objective of this organization is to remove barriers between people belonging to different nationalities and at the same time the organization strives to raise awareness of the local religion, customs and culture of the UAE (United Arab Emirates). It's a great idea – and the Emiratis who run the tours of the mosque and of Bastakiya are really engaging and friendly.

If you want a more in depth tour of Bastakiya than our walking guides, then we suggest speaking with the SMCCU to get the bespoke treatement. The tours take place Sunday to Thursday and they go into every bit of detail you want them to. Both educational and entertaining, we recommend it wholeheartedly; especially if you have a burning question that you have never been able to get answered.

The activities organized by the organization are the main reasons as to why so many people visit SMCCU when they are vacationing in Dubai. In addition to the visit to the tour of Bastakiya there are two other ways that they can help bridge your understanding: cultural breakfasts and lunches – where you get to sample real Emirati food; and a tour of Jumeirah Mosque

Both of these are also highly recommended. You get to enjoy your breakfast in the centre which is a typical wind tower house situated in the Bastakiya quarter. The cultural breakfast is available only on Mondays and Wednesdays at ten in the morning. The cultural lunch is offered on Sundays and Tuesdays at 1 pm in SMCCU. The lunch is accompanied by a speech on the region's culture and traditions given by a local Emirati.

POINTs OF NOTE

Dress conservatively especially if you are visiting the Jumeirah Mosque. It is important to respect the Muslim culture

Visit the website cultures.ae for tour and visit schedule information as these are subject to changes.

The Sheikh Mohammed Centre for Cultural Understanding is your opportunity to understand everything about Islam and Gulf Arabia traditions. The guides are very knowledgeable and you can ask them anything. It really bridges the gap between East and West and tries to correct the stereotypes that have resurfaced since 9/11.

When – If you are planning to take the Jumeirah Mosque tour then it is at 10 am every Sunday, Saturday, Tuesday and Thursday. The Cultural breakfasts are available twice a week: Monday and Wednesday at 10 am. The Cultural Lunch is held on Sundays and Tuesdays at 1 pm.

How long – The Walking Tour is for 60 minutes

Location – Sheikh Mohammed Centre for Cultural Understanding is situated in the heart of Bastakiya Quarter in Bur Dubai. Just ask the taxi driver to take you to the traditional wind tower house in Dubai.

Cost – The walking tour costs AED 35 while the Cultural breakfast costs around 60 AED. The Jumeirah Mosque tour cost only 10 AED.

Bookings – For the Jumeirah Mosque tours booking isn't required. So it means that you can just turn up and wait at the meeting point, i.e. just outside the mosque, at the allotted time and wait for the SMCCU member to provide you with a tour of the mosque. For the walking tours, the cultural breakfast and lunch, you have to book contact the SMCCUat 043536666 or you can send them an email at smccu@cultures.ae.

More info – For more information you can visit the official site of Sheikh Mohammed Centre for Cultural Understanding at cultures.ae

HELICOPTER TOUR OF DUBAI

If you really absolutely must 'go rockstar' and pretend you are in the next James Bond movie, then the helicopter tour is for you. The view is phenomenal, the sense of nervousness is uncontrollable and so, yes, this is about as rockstar as you can get in Dubai. But taking a helicopter tour in any city is hugely expensive! It's not as expensive as Seawings, but it does eat a hole in your wallet.

Dubai by helicopter

The tour allows you to see all great spots in Dubai from the air including Burj Khalifa, Burj Al Arab – and on good days when the visibility is good you can even see Sharjah in the distance. The flight is a whirlwind, especially if you go for the 15 minute trip, so if it takes you a while to get used to flying, this is not the trip for you. However, if you love to get the adrenaline pumping, the helicopter tour of Dubai is phenomenal.

Point of Note:

You need your passport to travel so don't forget it.

You can't take any baggage with you – and kids under 3 are not allowed on.

The trip costs 800 Dhs but for 1200 (400 AED more per person) you get to see more sights including Bastakiya and the desert. You can go all out and hire the helicopter for 45 minutes or an hour, or even on an exclusive basis.

To really avoid Dubai's traffic, it's possible to be transported from the airport to the Palm, but that's just showing off.

When – Open everyday between 10am and 5pm

How long – The trip is as short as 15 minutes, but be there an hour ahead of take off

Location – The Helipad is roughly 5 minutes walk from Atlantis Dubai on the palm

Cost – Roughly 800Dhs per person for the 15 minute tour (sharing)!

Booking - You need to get your concierge to pre book this in advance. Else call 04 4262101

More information: alphatoursdubai.com

HOT AIR BALLOONING DUBAI

What better way to see the desert than by hot air balloon? Witness the unforgettable panoramic view of the dunes - it's likely that you will never experience it this way ever again. Ballooning provides a calm experience in tune with the serenity of the desert, and the feeling of the calm, clear breeze is nothing like you would experience on the ground. Be prepared to see amazing desert landscapes with rich red sand dunes, and once you've reached a good height you may be lucky enough to spot wandering camels, gazelles and date plantations.

Ballooning in Dubai

If you are planning to book a hot air balloon, be prepared for the early start. Experts say the ride at sunrise is the best in terms of air temperature and calmness. The balloon company will pick you up from your hotel (if you are staying within the urban areas of Dubai) and take you on a long drive into the heart of the desert landscape.
If this is the first time you've seen a hot air balloon in real life, you will be amazemed. It's huge! Last minute preparations of inflating the balloon will build up. No time to back out now, be brave and climb into the basket to experience the best rides of your life. Safety belts are provided, but they are only be used during exceptionally fast landings and we are told that this rarely happens.

Compared to the glitz and glamour of urban Dubai, a hot air balloon flight is a tranquil experience with the only intermittent sounds of the gas burner blasts. The entire flight lasts for approximately an hour and on touching down you'll be offered cold refreshments and a flight certificate from the pilot. Depending on where you land you may even get the opportunity to meet with some local Bedouins or farmers. It's a great experience, if you have the time and money!

POINTs OF NOTE –

Pick up time from the hotel is between usually 4- 5am. Make sure you have an early night!

The total duration of the hot air balloon adventure in Dubai is about five hours (includes pick up, and drop off), but the actual ride is about an hour.

Because it is in the desert, comfortable clothing and footwear inclusive of hats and sunglasses are strongly recommended. You may even carry a light jacket as well as protection against the early morning desert chill.

Wheelchair users and children under 5 years are not allowed on the ride. Adults with certain medical issues may also not be permitted but please check with individual tour operators.

Every ride can accommodate 2 to 24 people but it is not usually full.

There are no toilets on board!

When – The best time to book a hot air balloon flight in Dubai is early morning at sunrise and most of the tour operators also schedule it at that time. Pick up is usually between 4 and 5am

How long – While the flight lasts for one hour the entire round trip starting from pick-up point to being dropped back takes approximately 5 hours

Location –Balloon Adventures flys in the Sweihan area, but if you are staying in a hotel within the urban areas of Dubai, they will collect you and drop you back free of charge.

Cost – Roughly 1000Dhs per person

Booking - There are a handful of tour operators who are experts in hot air ballooning, however we are basing our review on an experience with Balloon Adventures Emirates 04 285 4949 ballooning.ae

TOURING DUBAI BY DUBAI METRO

Throw caution to the wind and get a bird's eye view of Dubai, from the heights of the Dubai Metro. When you arrive in Dubai you will see that it's quite possible to have the cheap tour of Dubai by Metro. You can see all the major sights – and the Metro does travel through most of Dubai, so if you are short on time and money, this is the warts and all view of the good and the bad, the new and the old.

Dubai Metro is one of the newest metro systems in the world is already proving to be one of the lifelines of a truly sprawling commercial city. You should try and use the metro itself at some point – it's the longest driverless metro in the world and one of the most modern.

The Dubai Metro sits above the city and offers great views of Sheikh Zayed Road for example. Each train is a fivecarriages long and so can fit 643 passengers both seated and standing. All trains offer three classes of accommodation namely Gold class, Women and children class and Silver Class which is economy. Try and get a seat at the front!

The Diversity of Dubai Metro

POINTs OF NOTE –

To get a first hand view of view of Dubai, get the front seat of the train if you can – but there will be competition

A ticket of Dubai Metro is flexible enough to be used in bus and taxi feeder points as well.

The four themes on which the interior of the stations are based are fire, air, earth and water and this is the deciding factor for the colour of the station.

There is a minimum charge to get to a metro station by taxi which is 10 dhs. This is the minimum charge of the taxi, so bear that in mind to your overall cost, if you are estimating cost comparisons.

If you are going to take more than one journey, but a nol card on which you can add cash. Ask the staff which one is best for you and your family.

When −The Dubai Metro is open from 6am to 11pm (midnight on Thursday and Friday)

How long − The trains travel at the speed of 90 kilometres per hour and while a red line train takes 2 hours and 23 minutes for completion of a round trip, a green line takes 1 hour 23 minutes for the same. The Dubai Metro is quick!

Location −Across 40 metro stations which are currently operating the train can be taken at any one. See the map above.

Cost −The cost of travelling in the Dubai Metro depends on class being travelled, distance etc, but even a maximum single journey is 6 Dhs.

More info −Detailed information about the Dubai Metro can be obtained at rta.ae.

HISTORIC SPOTS

AL AHMADIYA SCHOOL IN DUBAI

Al Ahmadiya school, Dubai's first school, was established in 1912 by a rich pearl merchant named Sheikh Ahmed bin Dalmouk with the intention of getting semi formal education to children in various subjects encompassing literature, sciences and religion. This school was the first of its kind when students were grouped in accordance with their age and assigned to classrooms housed in a small building behind the Sheikh's house which over a period of time underwent further expansion.

Before the establishment of Al Ahmadiya School, education in Dubai was the responsibility of religious men named 'Al-Muttawa' who used to teach children in homes with the main focus being on the Holy Koran, writing, mathematics and Arabic Calligraphy. This all-boys school reflected a pioneering effort in itself and paved the way for the introduction of formal education system in 1956 when then prohibited subjects like English, sociology and science were added to the curriculum. Since this led to a dramatic increase in the number of students, the school had to close down at its original location and move elsewhere.

This old building of Al Ahmadiya School now serves as a museum of education and that time. As a tourist site it is is interesting because the school represents an accurate reflection of Emirati life. The courtyard is especially peaceful considering how busy it is all around Deira. The historic carvings on some of the arches are probably some of the oldest in Dubai, but the teacher student mannequins are poor – and probably some of the oldest mannequins in Dubai!

POINTS OF NOTE –

Al Ahmadiya School is in close to another popular cultural landmark, Dubai Heritage House, which could also be covered at the same time.

If you are in the gold souk and debating your negotiating strategy, this museum is a few minutes walk away, and you could come here while waiting for your favourite shop to reopen during the afternoon siesta.

When – This venue is open to visitors from 0800-1930 daily except Fri, when it opens later at 1430-1930.

How Long – An hour should be enough.

Location - This school is located parallel to Dubai Creek, just off Al Khor Street.

Cost - Entry to the Al Ahmadiya School is free for all visitors.

Booking – No booking required. Just turn up.

More info - definitelydubai.com o4-2260286 dtcmaas@dubaitourism.co.ae.

THE DUBAI MUSEUM

Get your history and culture in one shot by visiting the Dubai Museum. It's the perfect place to get an accurate reflection to see where Dubai came from. Housed in the 19th century Al Fahidi fort, which, at the time, was used as the ruler's palace, a prison and then a garrison or military post, the Al Fahidi Fort is considered to be the oldest building in Dubai city and in 1970 opened its doors as the renovated Dubai Museum with a huge collection of life-size exhibits and working models of what early Dubai life was like including souks, family homes and mosques. Artefacts and collections of the pearl merchant's scales, sieves and weights all give an insight into the early trade of pearl diving, before the rich days of oil. There are also galleries depicting marine life, the desert, date gardens, general infrastructure success and more.

Bastikiya

Dubai Museum is also home to a military section where weapons of war such as curved daggers, swords, spears and shields made of sharkskin are displayed. Other than that, the museum also displays a great collection of artefacts from ancient history made out of alabaster, mud, copper, etc. All these historic finds and precious items are carefully preserved and permanently housed in the Dubai Museum for all to see. There is also a model of the wind tower room which shows photographs and diagrams of various types of wind towers.

You won't forget the slightly macabre mannequins. So bad that they are good! But don't let them be a distraction – some of the history on the old video is worth watching and with the background sounds and music – the whole museum is a real step back in time.

POINTS OF NOTE

The Dubai Museum is part of our walking tour which covers the top spots in Old Dubai

Be sure to check out pictures of the rapidly developing Dubai as well as ancient maps of the Gulf of Emirates at the entrance.

Interested in visiting an exhibit about local boats? Then go to Narish Khyma which is situated very close to the Dubai museum.

Don't even waste your time at the Dubai Museum shop. Another record for Dubai – worst museum shop in the world? Quite possibly.

When – If you are planning to visit the museum on Friday then the timing is from 2 pm to 7 pm. On Saturdays-Thursdays the museum opens at 8.30 in the morning and closes at 7.30 in the evening.

How long – This is 2 hours of your time, and a perfect place to start your view of Old Dubai.

Location – The Dubai museum, Al Fahidi Street

Cost – The cost of visiting the Dubai museum is very cheap. At only AED 3 per head this is great value.

Booking – Booking isn't required but you can contact the museum directly in case you have any queries

More info – Unfortunately the Dubai museum does not have an official website but if you have any queries you can directly contact the museum on 043531862.

VISIT JUMEIRAH MOSQUE

If you've ever wondered what a mosque looks like from the inside, take some time out of your holiday plans and visit the beautiful Jumeirah Mosque, which is one of only two mosques in Dubai open to non-Muslim visitors. The Sheikh Mohammed Centre for Cultural Understanding organise and promote these tours and its main goal is to bring awareness to the wider public on the religious practices of Islam, the culture of the UAE people and knowledge of Arabian architecture in an informal, lively and fun way. Any questions will be answered and you will go away feeling relaxed and informed.

Visitors who have been to the Sheikh Zayed Mosque in Abu Dhabi or any one of the older mosques in the Middle East may be a tad disappointed with the Jumeirah Mosque as its not on a similar size or grandeur scale. However, it does have its own charm and the SMCCU, make the visit worthwhile by answering any question you might have.

Jumeirah mosque is a dominant landmark of the area which was built as a tribute to contemporary Islamic architecture.

A mosque is visited by men only and the women perform their prayers by themselves at home. Friday is considered to be the holy day of the Islamic week and hence every Friday all the adult Muslim men are required to go to the mosque for prayer. A lot of Muslims visit the Jumeirah mosque on Fridays to offer their prayers.

The architecture within the mosque is as beautiful as the architecture on the exterior of the mosque. Inside, there is the Qibla wall, which faces towards the direction of Mecca and all Muslims are required to face the wall while praying. The holiest place in this mosque is Mihrab, which is a prayer niche located right in the centre of the Qibla wall. This indicates the exact praying direction. Minbar is a raised platform in the Jumeirah mosque which is located towards the right hand side of the Mihrab. Here the 'Imam' or the leader of the prayer delivers the Friday sermon, also known as the 'khutba' which covers various social, political and religious subjects. You will not be able to find a single picture of living beings other than plants inside the mosque because the Islamic religion forbids the practice of taking pictures of living things. The interior of this beautiful mosque is richly decorated with Arabic calligraphy and rich ornamental patterns and it is indeed a feast for the eyes.

POINTS OF NOTE

Dress conservatively. Ladies should wear either light trousers or a skirt with atleast knee length or longer. Tops should be at least short sleeved. No vest tops. Bring a shawl in case. There is traditional dress to borrow which is the abaya (long black overdress) and the shela which is used to cover the hair. Men should wear trousers/ jeans but no shorts. You will be asked to remove your shoes before you enter.

If you want to take a Jumeirah mosque tour then be sure to be present outside the mosque on Saturday, Sunday, Tuesday or

Thursday at 10 am. This is the meeting point for the tour organized by the non-profit Sheikh Mohammed Centre for Cultural Understanding.

Your guide may explain the ritual of 'wudu' which is the ritual cleansing before entering the Jumeirah mosque. You may wish to partake in this. If so, follow the instructions of your guide.

If you are planning a trip to Abu Dhabi – and the Sheikh Zayed Mosque (which is the must see tourist attraction in the UAE), then we don't recommend seeing both mosques. You only need to do one – and the mosque in Abu Dhabi is amazing.

There is a new mosque in Dubai called the Al Farooq Omar Ibn Al Khattab Mosque and Islamic Center. We call it the Blue Mosque because it is similar to the Blue Mosque in Turkey. Located in Jumeirah, it is another mosque open to Muslim's and worth a peak. Tours are daily at 1030am (no Fridays) and it's a hidden gem, not known by many tourists or expats alike. Find out more at alfarooqcentre.com

When – Tours are run every Saturday, Sunday, Tuesday and Thursday at 10am sharp. Assemble outside the mosque entrance next to The One furniture shop at 9.45am.

How long – The tours last about 75 minutes. If you are planning to have the Cultural lunch or the Cultural breakfast organized by the SMCCU then it would take longer.

Location – The Jumeirah mosque is located along the beach road or the Jumeirah Road. You should not have any problem finding it because it is a very famous mosque in Dubai and most taxi drivers will drop you off at the mosque.

Cost – It costs Dhs. 10 per person for the Jumeirah Mosque tour. Children under 12 are free. Children under 5 are permitted to accompany parents on tour as long as they are well behaved. If the child feels uncomfortable, there is a room next to the main prayer hall with toys, but a parent must accompany the child.

Booking — Booking isn't required for a Jumeirah mosque tour organized by Sheikh Mohammed Centre for Cultural Understanding. Simply show up at the meeting point at the right time and be prepared to finally understand what Islam is really all about.

More info — If you need more information or if you have any queries then you can log on to the official website of Sheikh Mohammed Centre for Cultural Understanding, i.e. cultures.ae or call them in this number: 04 3536666

WATER PARKS

WILD WADI WATERPARK

Wild Wadi, or Wild Wild Wadi, as we like to call it, is a excellent alternative to the exorbitant Aquaventure. Don't get us wrong - this is one of the most thrilling water theme parks yet and there is something for everyone. From waves to sliding straight down the slides and zipping around the curves you will be screaming for more.

The newer Atlantis is more popular, but Wild Wadi is still a long family favourite day out and is suitable for babies as well as preschoolers, teens and adults.

If you want to take the family to Wild Wadi and enjoy a leisurely time in the waves then go to Breakers Bay. If you are more of a daredevil and want to actually ride the waves the Wipe-out & Riptide is where to take your board. This is just as challenging as riding the surf on the ocean. Juha's Journey will lazily guide you down the river while you relax from the day of hard playing on the slides. For the thrill seekers there is the ultimate Jumeirah Sceirah drop at 80kms per hour. This is not for the faint hearted! For the tiny tots, there is a wave pool and themed water park where children and parents can just chill.

POINTS OF NOTE -

Wild Wadi is a water park with many water slides for going down so make sure that you wear proper swimwear

If you enjoy foot long hotdogs then make sure to stop at Ali's BBQ which is a welcome break from the slides

If you stay at the Jumeirah Beach Hotel, you have free access to Wild Wadi for your stay. It's just next door.

Ladies Day at Wild Wadi changes frequently, but is normally held on a Thursday evening where the park will also shut an hour earlier for the ladies. Please check beforehand. Ladies night is what it is - ladies only - some of whom are in their abayas going down the slides

Be sure to make use of the payment wristband, where instead of carrying cash around all day you can pay for food and drink via your wristband which you credit at the start of the day.

When - Opening times vary throughout the year so please check their website. As a rough guide, the park normally is open from 10am - 6pm during the cooler season and extends to 8pm during the warmer months. Additionally during July, every Friday the park is open till 10pm

How long - In order to experience the full park you should be prepared to spend the entire day.

Location - In Jumeriah just past the Jumeirah Beach Hotel you will find the water park.

Cost - Adult (taller then 1.1 metres) AED 225 and Sun Downer is AED 175. Entry is free of charge for children less than 2 years of age. If you pay AED 400, you can skip all the queues.

More info – wildwadi.com 04 3484444

AQUAVENTURE ATLANTIS DUBAI

Dubai Aquaventures is one of the best water parks money can buy. Honestly. The slides and rides are world class and although not a huge park, it is a full day out. Located on Palm Jumeirah as part of the Hotel Atlantis, the Aquaventure water park has been in existence since the launch of the hotel.

Legend has it that while building the Palm Jumeirah Island, excavators came across ruins which were different from the typical Arabic artefacts. The researchers concluded these might have been from the lost continent, Atlantis. It is in acknowledgement of this fact that the hotel is named as the Atlantis and a part of Aquaventure is named the Lost Chamber and dedicated to celebrating the culture, traditions and way of life of the people of Atlantis. The Lost Chamber has been built underwater in the form of a maze where you weave through the ancient streets and houses surrounded by fishes on all sides.

For the more adventurous, head to the 'Leap of Faith' which entails plunging into a shark-infested lagoon from the Ziggurat while others can wash off the heat of the desert sand dunes by undertaking a 1.5 mile long exciting river ride featuring pools, rapids, swells and 7-feet high waves.

Atlantis from afar

Dolphin Bay is a completely different experience and attraction – and probably too expensive for many. There are different packages: one to play with the dolphins – the dolphin encounter; another to swim with the dolphin – the dolphin adventure; and the Royal Swim package allows you to be pulled by the dolphins around the pool - you'll also get a hug and a kiss. The latter two require any child to be above 12, accompanied by a paying adult and be a competent swimmer. If that's too expensive, you can just get a photo taken without getting in the water. These dolphin experiences costs 600 dhs, 900 dhs and 1000dhs. At 300 dhs, just to observe, this is an expensive treat for the family. But, this is a once in a lifetime experience. And if you are a qualified diver, you can go whole hog for a scuba dive with the dolphins for a grand price of 1500 Dhs. Get in touch with Al Boom. (alboomdiving.com)

Aquaventure offers plenty of activities for even the youngest of children with an amazingly fun water playground named 'Splashers' and supervised marine adventures which are both fun as well as educational. You will definitely score brownie points with your little ones after a day out here.

There is also a dive centre associated to the waterpark, but unless you are serious about diving, we wouldn't recommend it. If you are serious about diving, this is an amazing PADI 5-star diving centre – and it could be the highlight of your trip.

The Lost Chambers is free to those staying at Atlantis – and is a half decent under water type aquarium themed park, but we think it's worth going to the Dubai Aquarium at the Dubai Mall instead.

POINTS OF NOTE –

Make sure you check the children's age requirements before committing to a day here

Don't waste your money in the lagoon, especially if time is at a premium.

For the die hards, there are 3-day passes for Aquaventure which are available but we think it is better to mix up a visit with Wild Wadi which good in its own way.

Aquaventure appears larger than it actually is, because the land covers the same area as that for the Atlantis guests and includes the pools and beach

In Summer the heat of the floor can get hot, so it's worth bringing your flip flops or water shoes – which are also useful on the floor of the river. Bring a cheap pair

Bring your own towels from your hotel if you are not staying in the Atlantis as the price to rent them is extortionate.

If the going gets tough, there is always the huge beach to chill out at.

Dolphin bay rates for Atlantis residents aren't as discounted as you might think – but as we have said this is a once in a life time experience.

When – Aquaventure, Dolphin Bay and the Lost Chambers are open all year round, however opening times will vary with the time of year so please refer to website, but invariably starting fro 10am until 7pm Take note, the weather in Dubai can get extremely uncomfortable during June to August, but on the flip side, this will probably be the quietest time in the resort.

How long – You can easily spend a full day at Aquaventure and The Lost Chambers respectively. Dolphin Bay can be done in half to a full day depending on the activities you choose.

Location – The Atlantis, The Palm is not in the centre of Dubai. It is about a 25 minute ride into Dubai city centre although if travelling during morning or evening rush hour allow more time. Alternatively, take the monorail to the Atlantis from Gateway Towers

Cost – Adult day pass for Atlantis including access to private beach 200 AED each. Child 3-13 years 165 AED. Children 2 and under are free. There are different prices for UAE residents.

Rates for different activities in Dolphin Bay vary. Ray Feeding starts from 175 AED per person and the Dolphin Encounter starts at 595 AED per person. Note that children below the age of 6 cannot participate in most Dolphin Bay activities. Day entries to The Lost Chambers start at 70 AED for children and 100 AED for adults.

Towel and locker rental is AED 50. Food and water is expensive, so consider bringing your own

Booking – online or 04 426 0000 (Aquaventure), 04 426 1030 (Dolphin Bay).

More Info - atlantisthepalm.com

DUBAI EXPERIENCES

TOURISM THINGS TO DO

AT THE TOP: BURJ KHALIFA

Six years of blood, sweat and tears and now Dubai has the tallest building in the world. By the time you read this, the record will probably have been broken. In any case, this elegant mega structure stands at 828 feet tall and has broken a multitude of world records such as the highest and fastest elevator installation, the highest outdoor observation deck, the highest place of worship, the highest restaurant and nightclub and the highest fixed lavatory in the world! Yes, that's true.

Initially named as the Burj Dubai during its development, the government of Dubai changed its name to the Burj Khalifa paying homage to the President and head of Abu Dhabi, Sheikh Khaifa bin Zayed Al Nahayan.

The tallest building in the world is made up of 900 luxury apartments, over 40 floors dedicated to office space and the first ever Armani Hotel with 160 luxury suites, studios and classic rooms. For eating and entertainment, the highest restaurant and bar in the world is At.mosphere at the 122nd floor where just a steak can set you back $100 (USD). Armani also boasts five of its own restaurants and a funky nightclub – the Armani Privé. Turning up here in your day clothes just won't do.

The world's tallest observation deck known as 'At the Top' is on the 124th floor and is a smooth 60 second ride. If you visit Dubai, the

'At the Top' viewing experience in the Burj Khalifa is one of our top things to do in Dubai - even if you are acrophobic!

You'll need to plan your visit to the top of the world in advance to achieve the viewing slot of your choice. 1700 – 1830 are probably the most popular time slots to go due to sunset views. During the popular seasonal holiday periods (Oct – May) you may have to book up to 5 days in advance to grab these popular time slots, so it's advised to make the trip to the booking office in Dubai Mall as soon as you arrive in Dubai. Our smart tip is to plan in advance and book your slot online and the likelihood of getting the day and timeslot of your choice will be a lot better. However, you don't have to visit during sunset. Visiting during the early afternoon can also be a lovely experience. So long as you have a somewhat clear day you will enjoy the At the Top experience to the fullest. Unfortunately, Dubai does have its overcast and cloudy days which could be disappointing. However, the designers behind the observation gallery have invented a clever virtual telescope in which the position you are observing through the telescope can be shown as it is on a clear day and by night/day. There are several of these telescopes available around the observation deck and cover every viewing angle.

Once you are at the top of the world, take in some of Dubai's most amazing views. Just as you can see the Burj Khalifa from every part of the city, you can see the whole city from Burj including the Palm Jumeirah, the World islands, the Emirates Towers and the rapid continuous growth of Dubai. If you are lucky enough to grab a slot after 5pm – stay and watch the Dubai musical fountain show – it's great to view it from a different angle!

There will be a photographer taking a photo of you at the top. It's not really staged, but once you get to the bottom, you will face the scourge of the best sales people in Dubai trying to sell you the memorabilia. You can pay for a photo for about 220 Dhs, which is a little steep. But they also play the game of combination products (magnets etc) or buying the rights of the photo. Don't feel forced to buy them. It is a great memento, but the photo that you really want to have is the photo from the bridge at the bottom of the Burj looking up. That one costs between 65 and 85 Dhs to get a professional one taken – or if you can take one yourself, it's free!

POINTS OF NOTE:

If you are super organised, we recommend buying your tickets online before you arrive in Dubai, so you don't have to go to the Dubai Mall immediately. If money is no object to you or you plan to spend your whole holiday at the Dubai Mall, then feel free to ignore this advice

The actual entrance to the At the Top tour is via Dubai Mall and not from Burj Khalifa.

For those who want to go even higher, you can pay AED 500 to access the even higher Sky Experience. That makes At the Top not really At the top, but you know – it's all marketing.

You can't actually go to the Armani hotel from At the Top. There is a separate entrance for this and you'll need reservations.

There's no real time limit once you get to the top, but many people don't usually stay for long as, apart from the views, there's only a memorabilia shop to purchase gifts from.

You can buy anything from Burj Khalifa Lego to Burk Khalifa branded Camel Milk chocolate, so it's a good opportunity for gifts

Make sure you arrive 15 minutes before your allocated time slot.

Be sure to gulp down as the elevator shoots up!

When – Daily, 10am to 10pm, 10am to midnight

How Long – An hour for the tour, another half an hour for the queuing and merchandise purchasing.

Location – Dubai Mall / Burj Khalifa

Cost – Adults 100 for general admission (400 for immediate entry), children (4-12 yrs) 75 for general admission (400 for immediate entry) Children under 3 are free.

Booking – To purchase tickets in advance visit tickets.atthetop.ae or visit the booking office in Dubai Mall

More info – See the official site at burjkhalifa.ae

AFTERNOON TEA AT THE BURJ AL ARAB

In Dubai there are two famous buildings called Burj – and this is the opulent one. The first self-proclaimed 7 star hotel in the world and the 5th tallest hotel in the world, the Burj Al Arab remains the icon of Dubai. It certainly lives up to its reputation and is wholly recognisable as part of brand Dubai. The Burj Al Arab in Dubai is what the Golden Gate Bridge is to San Francisco and the Eiffel Tower is to Paris. So legendary is this icon, that now the world's tallest building – the Burj Khalifa – finds it difficult to replace the Burj Al Arab as the symbol of Dubai.

Built on a man-made island about 280m from Jumeirah Beach, access is by private bridge and visitors will be declined entry if they do not have hotel or meal reservations. Inside, the décor is nothing short of Arabian luxury at its best and to some it can appear gaudy and ostentatious. But this is what rich traditional Arabia is all about. Bright hues of red and yellow illustrate the desert and warmth – and if it looks golden, it most likely is pure gold. Over 86,000 22ct gold leaf was used in covering the entire hotel – that is the definition of 'bling'. The Burj Al Arab is the opposite of minimalist so common in the modern hotel.

Moving onto the rooms, all of them are duplex suites and the deluxe suite (which, of course, if the most basic of suites available) has an area space of 169 square meters. To give you an understanding of scale, a standard five star hotel room is on average 32 square meters. The deluxe suite is decorated lavishly, just as the public areas of the hotel with a winding grand staircase, electric controls to power the curtains, doors, lights and TV and the best part – you have your own butler! Pricing for the most basic suite start at about 4000 Dhs (or $1000) per night and rise to nearly 100,000 Dhs for the most expensive Royal Suite – usually it's only royalty who can actually afford that!

If you're not willing to cough up a small fortune to stay at the Burj Al Arab, the best way to visit is to book for afternoon tea, a fancy meal or to visit the bar. Guests, whether staying the night or just visiting for a meal get treated like true VIPs. If you are keen to visit the Burj Al Arab but are on a budget, the cheapest option is either breakfast or afternoon tea at Sahn Eddar, setting you back around 250 Dhs and 400 Dhs per person respectively. Sahn Eddar is located at the lobby of the hotel and the ambience gives a true flavour of the hotel. Sitting on plush sofas, you lift your head and strain your eyes to see the end of the ceiling, but it will be hard as you curb your dizziness looking at the world's tallest atrium! A musical fountain plays soothing melodies and the vibe is totally relaxed.

If you want to absorb magnificent views of the palm islands and Dubai city, the Skyview Bar on the 27th floor offers afternoon tea packages at 450Dhs. You will be ploughed with unlimited sandwiches, cakes, treats and tea/coffee - and the views are awesome with floor to ceiling windows. The skyview bar is great at night, and if you have a spare 27,321 Dhs, you can have the most expensive cocktail in the world (that's a mere $7500). Another way to visit is to book for a proper meal - book yourself a table amongst the largest restaurant aquarium at Al Mahara, one of the best seafood restaurants in Dubai.

If marvelling at the splendour of the Burj itself is what ticks your boxes, then book at Majlis Al Bahar which is the Al fresco super romantic restaurant where you can eat in perfect view of this magic building. And if you want spend all the money you have on your bride to be, then it's possible hire the helipad and conduct your nuptuals right at the top. It'll cost you about $55k. We think the cake is thrown in. We think.

POINTS OF NOTE:

If you're not well connected, there's no way you are getting in to the Burj Al Arab – unless you have a reservation, so make sure you book in advance.

If visiting the Burj Al Arab with children, a couple of restaurants within the hotel may impose restrictions during the evenings and Skyview does not allow anyone under the age of 21 at any time of the day.

If you want afternoon tea with the family, your best bet is to book at Sahn Eddar. If you want to see amazing views with the kids from the 27th floor, the Al Muntaha restaurant is the next best priced option for lunch. Their lunch set menu is about 450 Dhs per person and children under 12 have 50% off menus, as is the case with all restaurants within the Burj Al Arab

There's an iconic photo of Andre Agassi and Roger Federer playing tennis on the helipad and another with Tiger Woods shooting a 5 iron. Don't think you'll get that opportunity! But if you have a helicopter and are a guest you can land directly at the hotel!

Other options to experience the Burj Al Arab are to try the Assawan Swa – which is probably the epitome of spa treatment opulence

The Burj Al Arab is alit with different colours at night and great to see from afar, so watch out for it after the sun drops.

The Jumeirah Beach Hotel which is built nearby is the wave to the Burj Al Arab's sail when viewed from afar.

When – Daily

How Long – Two hours for a meal and an ogle

Location – Burj Al Arab

Cost – Starts at 250Dhs for tea

Booking – Book directly with the Burj Al Arab on 04 301 7777

More info – See the official site at burjalarab.com

ATLANTIS THE PALM

2008 saw the biggest fireworks display the world has ever seen in order to launch one of the world's most glamorous (or garish to some) hotels in the world. Atlantis, The Palm Hotel in Dubai's flagship resort is located at the top of the crescent of The Palm Jumeirah. Based on a replica of its sister outlet in the Bahamas, the Atlantis, Dubai is a tad different as it sits on reclaimed land. There may not be enough superlatives in the English language to describe the magnificence of this hotel, which boasts 17 restaurants and bars, 65,000 different species of fish and a huge waterpark…not to mention a large private beach with beautiful white sand and crystal clear blue waters. Artificial and un-eco friendly as it may appear, you have to nod your head in approval as this is one mega impressive structure to talk about. Ten years ago the area that is now Palm Jumeirah was nothing but the Arabian Gulf and in a matter of years, the area was transformed into artificial land with an unimaginable amount of rock and sand to form the shape of a palm tree. And, at its furthest tip, lays Atlantis, Dubai's largest hotel.

There should be a new word to describe Atlantis. Firstly, it's huge; secondly, it's extravagant; and, finally it's placed at one of the most unique points in the world. With all that it is, we recommend visiting to have a nosey around – and if you're not staying on the Palm, this is your excuse to get on it. It brings bragging rights. The Atlantis Dubai cost approximately $1.6 billion to build and has been the main resort destination for a number of the rich and famous, but a mainstay for families, friends, and honeymooners who are all looking to experience the complete pleasure of staying at Atlantis, The Palm Hotel in Dubai. It's probably safe to say that The Atlantis Dubai is one of the most popular hotels in Dubai, and one can not imagine Dubai without it.

The Atlantis is quite a distance from Dubai city centre, so if you are choosing this hotel for your holiday to Dubai, be prepared to stay in the hotel grounds for most of your trip – the Atlantis is a resort in its own right. This isn't unfortunate unless you are on a budget and not on an all inclusive package as the restaurants aren't cheap. There are about 15 restaurants - a mixture of casual dining and award winning; Nobu to Michelin star eateries by Santi Santamaria, Giorgio Locatelli and Michel Rostang just to name a few. For entertainment there is the waterpark of the moment – Aquaventure which will thrill young and old. Beware of the Leap of Faith – it is not for the faint hearted with its 90 ft drop down a 84 degree incline - it certainly is heart popping! For the timid bunch there are many bearable slides as well as rides through the rapids not to mention a 700 metre private beach. For a real treat, you can arrange a play date with the dolphins by getting up close and personal or just enjoying an observer pass from the beach. Aquaventure has so much and you can quite easily spend a relaxing day here with the family. The park is open to hotel guests normally free of charge (check before booking with your travel agent) and the visitor rates are reasonable.

When you first reach the hotel, the first thing you will notice is that the only way to get there is via a long, semi-winding bridge to the crescent of the palm. Coming upon the Atlantis Dubai, the hotel looks as though it is rising from the gulf. All around the hotel, you are surrounded by the crystal clear waters of the Arabian Gulf. Just driving up to the hotel, you will feel a sense of fun and enjoyment heading your way. You cannot miss the mammoth hotel that rises up in front of you. It is a place of relaxation, adventure or a little bit of both!

If you don't have enough time to experience the water park, it's worth going to see Atlantis just to have a gander. It's more accessible than the Burj Al Arab, and so it feels a little like Disney World, with all the tourists looking around. As you walk through Atlantis Dubai, you cannot help but notice the magnificent array of artwork and detail throughout the hotel. As you look at the walls or even the ceilings of the Atlantis Dubai, you will see stunning displays of art everywhere. While some may say the murals and sculptures are a bit remedial, it is hard to miss the overall aquatic theme of the entire hotel, including columns, carpets, dado rails and even the doorknobs. The aquarium is not as big as the one in Dubai Mall but impressive in its own right. There are also a heap of high end stores in the hotel lobby, from Tiffany & Co to Cavallai.

If staying at the Atlantis is an option, this is a resort holiday in its own right. If planning a stay at the Atlantis, rooms are relatively expensive, but because the hotel is so large, there are many deals in association with Emirates airline. If you're in the money, you could book the famous Lost Chambers suite which is spread over 3 floors. The bottom floor is underwater offering stunning views of marine life from the bedroom, dining and bathroom areas! The Atlantis Dubai features 1,373 beautiful guest rooms and 166 luxurious suites. It is the largest hotels in Dubai. Every room is decorated with Arabic and oceanic influences. The rooms are considered quite low key and mainly decorated in natural colours of cream and beige. However, with so much to do outside of your hotel room, why would you need a room so decorated! All the rooms include balconies that let you look over into the beautiful blue waters of the Arabian Gulf or the amazing Palm Jumeirah. The bathrooms are extremely large and even have sliding screens so you can watch the plasma television while taking a luxurious bath in the spacious bathtubs.

Guest rooms and suites can provide accommodations for two adults and two children or three adults. These rooms have a number of amenities, including plasma television with a variety of channels, maid service, and bathroom amenities. However, if you want to make your stay at the Atlantis Dubai simply exquisite, rather than a room or a suite, join the Imperial Club. The rooms in the Imperial Club boast the best views and amazing dining options. Although it is more expensive than the other options at the Atlantis Dubai, you are provided with additional amenities, including access to the Imperial Club Lounge during open hours, continental breakfasts (the guest rooms and suites do not get free breakfast), afternoon tea, complimentary cocktails and canapés in the evening, complete access to the Kids Club, complimentary use of jet pool, sauna and steam facilities at the ShuiQi Spa, and special rates for the exclusive pool cabanas.

Another excuse to go to The Atlantis is for the restaurants. If you are not staying there, it is the prefect place to spend an evening. Some call the Atlantis Dubai the "Culinary Destination of Dubai." It is the perfect place to taste the unique cuisines of the world without ever having to leave the hotel. The hotel boasts 17 different restaurants, bars and lounges – everything from award winning Michelin Star restaurants to great casual dining options. No matter what your palate is, there is something to satisfy it. Award winning restaurants include Ossiano, Nobu (the first in the Middle East), Rostang, and Ronda Locatelli. Because these restaurants are extremely popular, it is very hard to get a seat without a reservation. Make sure to book your meal in one of these fabulous restaurants right upon your arrival to the hotel or even beforehand if you know your schedule. When it comes to casual dining, you can have it all, from delicious patisseries and savouries, to Mediterranean cuisine featuring the tastes of Tunisia, Algeria, Morocco, and Greece (hence the name of the restaurant – Kaleidoscope). If you have a love of Asian-inspired cuisine, try Saffron, which offers 20 stations and is a fun gastronomic journey for anyone. The hotel also offers outdoor bars and grills (some of which even offer poolside service), Arabian restaurants, and a number of kiosks offering classic healthy snacks. Make sure you eat at Atlantis, if that's the best excuse to get there.

If you can afford it, it is a fantastic holiday! The rooms are OK, but you're not here for the rooms - you're here for the whole experience. You are paying for the out of this world. Don't stay here if you are on a budget - the restaurants are expensive unless you can get a great half board deal. And staying at the Atlantis is staying at the ultimate resort - the best resort in Dubai. If you are looking to see all that Dubai offers within a week - and are more travellers or shoppers - the Atlantis is not for you, although you may want to stay here to be pampered for a few days.

It's not for everyone - things do get expensive - and being at the end of the palm means a little bit of a journey if you are exploring the city on a daily basis - but if you know Dubai, only need to venture in a couple of times - and want an experience unlike any other, the Atlantis is for you. it should be one your list of things to do this lifetime. Enjoy, whenever you do go. Because you will go - if not now, then one day.

POINTS OF NOTE:

Atlantis is a holiday in its own right. If you want to go out and see Dubai everyday, it's probably not worth staying here

If you are not staying here, it should really be experienced, either for Aquaventure or just for a nosey around.

The Palm Monorail is not connected to the main Dubai Metro yet

You don't need to book to visit, but you do need to to if you want to eat at the restaurants

Make sure you book days in advance for places like Nobu.

When – All day

How long – Anything from a couple of hours to a couple of days depending if you wanted to visit Aquaventure

Location – The Atlantis, The Palm is not in the centre of Dubai. It is about a 25 minute taxi ride into Dubai city centre although if travelling during morning or evening rush hour allow more time. Alternatively, take the monorail to the Atlantis from Gateway Towers

Cost – It's free to nosey around

Booking – online or by calling 04 426 2626 (restaurants) 04 426 0000 (Aquaventure), 04 426 1030 (Dolphin Bay).

More Info - atlantisthepalm.com

THE DUBAI MALL

Forget for a moment that this is a mall, because the Dubai Mall is so much more. It's an entertainment hub. So for all you mall haters, Dubai Mall will probably sway your opinion on shopping experiences for the better. The largest mall in the world houses over 1,200 retailers. That's heaven for some, but for those who find it hell, they may find solace in just chilling on a bench overlooking the amazing Dubai Fountain or if it's your turn to entertain the kids you'll be itching to gaze at the wonders in the Dubai Aquarium or thrill-seek at the Sega Republic Indoor Theme Park. Dubai Mall has definitely done its homework in appealing to more than just the shopaholics.

Housing well known labels from mid to top range, Dubai Mall offers an amazing variety of collections from around the world, be it the high street range or haute couture. To keep the kids amused, a replica of the famous British toy store, Hamleys has parked a spot at Dubai Mall as well as the famous American department store Bloomingdales. For all you foodies, you will be spoilt from fast food to delicacies to suit almost every palette. Pretty much any global food brand is here, so it's all about how far you are prepared to walk for you meal.

If you are in Dubai for a fleeting visit and tempted to buy some gold, Dubai Mall has its own Gold Souk, saving you a visit to the famous one in Deira. You'll find most of the famous chain stores like Marhaba and Damas and don't feel you can't bargain because you are in a mall - no piece is a fixed price! On the topic of authentic gifts, if time is short on your hands and you are in need of some ethnic gifts. Head across the Dubai Fountain, over the bridge into the Souk Al Bahar, where you'll find a modern take on a souk filled with stall like shops selling everything from shawls, authentic homeware, dates and lots more.

But as we said – **Dubai Mall is more than just for shopping**:

Dubai Fountain No trip to Dubai Mall is complete without stopping at a bench to view the amazing performance of the world's largest musical fountain, with the iconic Burj Khalifa as the backdrop – and it's free! The water jets spray up to 500 ft in the air and the light beams used in the display can be seen up to 20 miles away and is said to be visible from space. Performances are on every 30 minutes from 1800 – 2200/2300 weekday/weekend. There are also shows at 1300 and 1330 daily. There is ample space to stand and get an awesome view, but if you want to have a meal to remember, book at one of the fountain side restaurants such as Wafi Gourmet, Carluccios amongst others. The opposite side of the fountain is the Souk al Bahar where you'll find a host of outdoor restaurants with stunning views of the Burj Khalifa offering great photo opportunities.

Dubai Fountain by night

Burj Khalifa – 'At the Top' viewing experience - If your time is limited in Dubai, going on top of the Burj Khalifa has to be on your top list of things to do. The views are spectacular and the giddy may even overcome their fear of heights! You can book tickets days in advance to get the timing slot of your choice or if you are only there for a day you can buy an immediate entry ticket. All tickets can be bought in person from Dubai Mall or online.

Dubai Aquarium - If you have kids you'll give yourself at least 2 hours of sanity if you take them to the Dubai Mall Aquarium. Better still pack them off with Dad while Mum can enjoy a good gallivant round the shops. The Dubai Aquarium has one of the largest tanks in the world and has already achieved the Guinness World Record for largest viewing panel, another one to tick off the list! Dubai Aquarium has over 33,000 living animals amongst which 400 are sharks and rays combined. Alongside this there is the Underwater Zoo in which you can view an array of sea life from a suspension bridge or tree canopy. Entrance starts from 50 AED.

Sega Republic, Dubai - No UAE mall is complete without its own amusement arcade, but Sega Republic has got to be the mother of all amusement arcades with over 250 games spread over five zones. Ideal for all age groups – even adults. Entry prices start at 140 AED.

Dubai Dino - yes Dubai has it's own dinosaur housed in the mall. Granted, it was bought from US, but it's quite a sight mid shop. At 155 million years old, it'd probably as Jurassic as you will get in Dubai. It's 80 foot long and 30 ft high, so you're not going to miss it – but see how many photos are being taken in one minute. It's snap heaven for some!

Kidzania - For the younger kids, picking a career in a virtual world where you need to earn a living makes for a great couple of hours for the kids. Kids loving work? If only they knew.

Dubai Ice Rink - A great way to cool off from the summer heat is to get the blades on and head for Dubai's largest ice skating rink. Whether you are a skilled skater or a novice, the Olympic sized Ice Rink holds different themes every evening to hone your skills or just to have fun. When not in use, the Dubai Ice Rink can seat up to

2000 for functions. Prices start from 50 AED for a 2 hour session including skate hire.

Candylicious - Dubai Mall also houses the largest sweetshop in the world. Candy Time! Based opposite from the Aquarium, and 10,000 sq ft of sugar coated sweet stuff sounds like heaven and ADHD in a box. Think Charlie and the Chocolate factory for real, without Willy Wonka and the ooompa loompas!

Candylicious

And if all the above don't tickle your fancy and you like the simple things in life, the Dubai Mall has over 150 cafés, fast food outlets and fine dining restaurants and to finish off an evening choose from one of 22 screens at Dubai's largest cinema venue – Reel.

POINTS OF NOTE:

Dubai Mall is huge – if you have limited time, make sure you are focussed on what you need to do.

Don't be afraid to ask one of the concierges at every other intersection. They have amazing knowledge of the shops and how to get to each one from where you are.

Dubai Mall tends to draw you in. If you manage to stay away on your first trip to Dubai, let us know and we can sell the secret.

When – Daily, 10am to 10pm, 10am to midnight

How Long – You'll spend at least a day here

Location – Dubai Mall

Cost – Can be dangerously high, depending on temptation levels

Booking – See separate charges above.

More info – See the official site at thedubaimall.com

BASTAKIYA

Bastakiya represents the heart of historic Dubai – and is the only real Dubai that equates to the kind of exploratory tourism that you might expect from places in the Middle East. It's a small area, but it really does have a calming feel amidst the wind towers that exist at every villa. Bastakiya is a must do for Dubai, even for half a day

You can spend as long as a full day in this small area just walking through the quaint little lanes and admiring the beautifully restored architecture that was once Dubai's first commercial district dating back to the 1900s inhabited mainly by rich merchants. Many of the traditional buildings which were mainly residences have now been carefully restored and converted to cafes, museums, art galleries and shops. We don't usually recommend walking distances in Dubai, but this is one those places where it's worth breaking with the norm even though it can feel a little busy. There are great photo opportunities of Arabic architecture and lovely kept courtyards.

Traditional Windtowers in Bastakiya

In a city where modern, high rise buildings dominate, traditional old architecture sticks out beautifully and really complements the story of what Dubai used to be and what it has grown to today. The locals Emiratis are so proud of their rich cultural heritage that even though a small part of it remains today, they are keen to develop new properties in line with keeping to traditional facade themes such as the Madinat Jumeirah resort. Bastakiya or Old Dubai as it is sometimes known consisted of a series of wind towers, known as barjeels, which lined the creek on both sides and apart from lending grace to the area, they served the practical purpose of cooling the houses due to lack of any other means. These tall towers are parts of traditional courtyard houses which line the narrow streets on both sides and are amongst the few surviving symbols of distinct and unique Arabic architecture. Apart from ornate buildings there are a number of forts reflecting the defensive architecture of that generation, the most noteworthy and oldest being the Al Fahidi Fort which dates back to 1799. In a bid to maintain this ancient monument, it has now been converted into Dubai Museum while other forts like Nahar Tower which had been built in 1876, Naïf Fort and Um Royool Tower have been undergoing restoration.

To get a detailed idea as to the development of Dubai, take some time out to visit Dubai Museum It will take roughly an hour to tour around and only a short walk away you'll find the Sheikh Saeed Al Maktoum House. This building dates back to the late 1800s and now houses a unique collection of historical photos, artefacts, coins etc - great for all you historians! After this, make your way to the Heritage and Diving Village, only a couple of minutes walk more. This great re-creation of an old time village shows how settlers used to once live and make their livelihood through simple handicrafts. The late night cafeterias make it a perfect place to while away time and relax.

POINTS OF NOTE –

Visit Bastakiya as part of our walking tours of Old Dubai

Legend goes that in the era gone by the wind tower or the barjeel as it is locally known was indicative of the wealth of the family, meaning the more number of barjeels projecting towards the sky the wealthier the family residing in Bastikiya would be.

Likewise, the size of the door in a traditional house is linked to cultural behaviour in the sense that the main door permitting the men would be large so as to permit entry without having to bend while the inner doors would be smaller in size.

One of the best ways to visit Bastakiya would be to simply walk around and explore the area after an Emirati breakfast in the morning served at the Sheikh Mohammed Centre for Cultural Understanding.

Bastakiya Nights is a traditional courtyard house which has been converted into a restaurant. This is the perfect area to have a meal, particularly at dusk.

Another must-see in Bastakiya is the remnants of the Old City Wall, a gypsum-and-coral structure constructed in 1800 A.D. for the purpose of defence.

Further exploring would reveal a number of different art galleries like XVA, a contemporary art gallery which features film screenings as well, Ave Gallery and Majlis gallery which has been in operation since 1970s'.

The Basta Art Café, nestled amongst natural surroundings of trees and potted plants, is a God-send with its comprehensive menu of refreshments, sandwiches and salads. The juices here are pretty amazing.

When – Bastakiya can be visited at any time and after 10 in the morning should be ideal as most of the art galleries, museums and shops open by then.

How Long – It is possible to whizz through the entire area in an hour although art and architecture lovers can linger around for much longer.

Location – This historic district of Dubai is located along the Dubai Creek and is characterized by narrow and winding lanes and recounting the names of any of the popular landmarks like XVA Gallery or SMCCU to your taxi driver would suffice.

Cost – Obviously you are not charged for walking around Bastakiya but entry to SMCCU will cost depending on the programme you have been booked for and gaining access to the art gallery will vary from one gallery to another.

Booking – Booking may be required for the Sheikh Mohammed Centre for Cultural Understanding depending on what you want to do but otherwise most of the other venues are open to travellers and tourists without any preplanning.

More Info: See dubaiculture.ae

ABRA RIDE ACROSS DUBAI CREEK

At some point during your trip you must integrate a crossing of the Dubai Creek into your scoping out of the city. It's probably on the day that you view old Dubai and travel from Bastakiya to peek at the gleaming gold of the Gold Souk in Deira.

Forget the fact that taking an abra ride is the most cost effective to cross the Creek -it's also the most enjoyable way to witness its beauty. An abra is a small motorized water taxi, which used to be the main mode of transport many years ago. It is now a well-respected tourist icon as well as a quick getaway from Bur Dubai or Deira especially when traffic in the Al Shindagha tunnel or other bridges beggars belief. The abras are popular with tourists and commuters as they are a quick hop on hop off method of transport. They are also surprisingly therapeutic. Dn't just take our word for it!

The abra ride commences when the boat is full, at normally about 20 passengers. The fare is collected during the journey which is 1 Dirham per person. Abras are also available for private hire and whilst on a ride you'll experience one of Dubai's most authentic journeys taking in sights such as the curvy National Bank of Dubai, Creek Park, Creek Club and the dhow harbour, plus all the other beautiful landmarks and souks.

As the abra follows the snake-like channel ancient traditional Arabian houses which pass by on both sides are strongly reminiscent of the architectural style of Yemen, Saudi Arabia and even Tanzania. There is a genuine feeling of history as you step on board.

Finally, if you can stomach peeking into the murky waters, you'll be surprised that it is home to a variety of fishes, weeds and coral reef. If you do trying to take a peek, be careful not to slip in!

POINTS TO NOTE –

The best time to embark on an abra ride is at dusk on a weekday as the air is cooler, the abra not as crowded and the light would be just sufficient to enjoy the sights.

There are no life jackets so beware.

As a courtesy, it's best not to sit next to a woman you don't know or if the boat is full, leave a small gap.

Don't stand up or you will get a rollicking from the captain!

You can hire an abra exclusively for an hour for 100Dhs. Speak to the captain.

An alternative to abras are water taxis for which you can use your nol cards. They are air conditioned and perfectly fine, but you don't get the whole experience of getting on the wooden boat and feeling the history of Dubai.

When - The abras begin operating at 11 in the morning and a boat can be hailed every 20 minutes from the assigned station till 11 in the night.

How long - Each abra ride lasts for 10 minutes and the arrival and departure stations are fixed.

Location – Several Abra stations are dotted along on either banks of the Dubai Creek.

Cost – When travelling with other commuters, the cost is AED 1 (cash only) per person but for a private ride you would have to pay AED 20. Similarly, an hour long tour would cost AED 100

More Info See Dubai's official portal dubai.ae

DESERT SAFARI

The desert camps are lively and a congregation of all desert duners at the end of a thrilling ride. Colourful tents, rugs and cushions are used to create a real Bedouin feel and duners can participate in a number of activities such as camel riding, dune bashing, henna painting and so on. Indeed, what better way to remember going on a desert safari than chilling out on the Persian carpet floor within a traditional Bedouin tent, smoking a shisha, sipping Arabic coffee and munching on fresh dates?

By the early evening you get to watch the beauty and peace of a desert sunset and the barbecues kick in. Traditional belly dancers will keep you entertained and aid the digestion. We say traditional, but it really isn't a tradition in the UAE - and likely your belly dancer is probably from Eastern Europe or Turkey rather than from the region! Either way, it's fun. All good things have to come to an end and so does this trip when the vehicles head back towards the rendezvous point and leave you at your hotel. You also have the option of spending the night in the desert and if you like to be one with nature in the dark of night, without a light in site, this is for you. It's remarkable how dark darkness actually is. That's a weird comment to make, but you'll never understand how dark it can get in the desert until you experience it yourself. The stars at night are amazing

The desert safari is a balance of many things that touch on the pet loves of a tourist, from meandering through the dunes, to watching the sun set in the peace of the desert. While it doesn't quite live up to how the Bedouin used to travel, you get to see the beauty of the desert in its raw form.

While it is true that when people think of Dubai the first few images conjured up by the mind are those of shopping malls and contagious commercialization, there are certain off-beat options like going on a desert safari which take you away from the roller coaster lifestyle to sample the peace and calm of the desert.

Most of the major hotels in Dubai are pick up points for the tour operators that organise the desert safaris. The hotel you'll be staying at will certainly have all the information to organise a trip or you can use our recommended operators. The tours normally begin pick up at mid afternoon and you usually travel as a party of six - or less if you want a private group. The safaris take place in a 4 wheel drive and will make their way to the centre point of the desert, normally about a 30 min drive out of the Dubai city or towards Al Ain. The tyres are let down before you go onto the sand and the tour guide takes a peek round in case someone has a last minute panic attack.. From this point on, the real thrill and mood of being in an isolated and barren landscape sets in especially when the vehicles traverse through the sand dunes at all possible awkward angles. You really think that the car is going to topple over - and yes, they sometimes do get stuck. This phase of the desert safari is rough and exciting and lasts for around 90 minutes before finally coming to rest at a central camp.

Dunebashing in Dubai

If you're feeling queasy, then sit in the front. On the way into the desert, you sometimes stop at a camel farm to see the humped ones up close and personal. After the dune bashing you are often given the opportunity to have a go on some dune buggies for an extra charge as well as sand surfing, sand skiing or sand boarding, and riding on the camel depending on which tour operator you get. Once you get to the camp, you'll be provided with a barbeque meal and if there are enough of you a belly dancer from Eastern Europe or Russia. Of course, this is the least realistic UAE experience, but it's a lot of fun. All this while you sip on your ghawa and smoke your shisha before you get taken back to your hotel.

There is always the option to stay overnight in the desert under the stars, staying in tents. There's something to be said for being at one with the stars. You'll be woken in the morning for breakfast before your hosts drive you back to you hotel.

If you're not really into the whole shebang of dune bashing, some of the tour operators set up a very early morning drive into the desert to watch the sun come up over dates and Arabic coffee. You may even see some of the desert animals come to life at that time.

Prices start at roughly 300 Dhs per adult and you are picked up at your hotel or close by to where you are. Also, note that if there aren't enough people you might not get everything you paid for, e.g. the belly dancer – everyone has their price you know.

POINTS OF NOTE –

Because driving through the desert is not everyone's cup of tea, you should decide whether this is for you. If you get travel sick, either don't go, or sit in the front of the car. This is definitely not one for expectant mums!

Make sure that the operator you use is licensed and has insurance coverage

An up-and-down drive through the dunes would be uncomfortable on a full stomach and therefore it is advisable to have a light meal prior to the trip and avoid drinking too much water.

Light clothes and slippers/floaters are the best options to dress up in while going on a desert safari – if you are comfortable then venturing bare-foot into the sand is strongly recommended. But make sure you bring a shawl or a sweatshirt with you for when the sun goes down. It can get quite nippy in the open air.

Most people opt for the sundowner, but it's possible to opt for the dawn trip as an alternative.

Take a camera with you - but be careful not to let the sand get in!

When - A desert safari is most popular in the late afternoon although there are packages for the early morning.

How long – The time spent varies according to the package chosen and the tour operator – for example an evening safari begins at 4 in the afternoon and you would be back in your hotel by 10 at night.

Location – Going on a desert safari is best left to the experienced drivers - they'll pick you up from your hotel.

Cost – Packages start at roughly 300Dhs . You have to book in advance

More info: There are loads of operators. Our preferred ones are Arabian Adventures. arabian-adventures.com , 04 303 4888, Explorer Tours explorertours.ae04 2861991, Alpha Tours alphatoursdubai.com , 04 294 9888.

DHOW CRUISE ON DUBAI CREEK

A step up from taking an abra across the creek is to sail in style by cruising on a dhow. Taking a dhow cruise on Dubai Creek is one way to get a real feel for the old part of Dubai. Once the hub where ships would dock and all business was done, the creek is now more about tourism, though still forms an important part of business on the street. Dubai Creek is one of the places you need to experience if you visit Dubai. You don't actually have to do anything there apart from soaking up the atmosphere - but we think taking a dhow cruise on Dubai Creek gives a good feel for the history of the place – a million miles away from the skyscrapers of the modern era. The creek is a natural inlet for sea water which cuts right through the centre of the city. Also known as Khor Dubai, this is a saltwater creek which is located in the city. This creek was referred to as River Zara by the Ancient Greeks. The creek actually divides Dubai into two sections: Bur Dubai and Deira. The Dubai Creek is the only harbour or port in Dubai and its commercial importance cannot be ignored. There are some great buildings located on either sides of the creek such as Sheraton Dubai Creek, Chamber of Commerce, Deira Twin Towers, Dubai Creek Tower and the National Bank.

The standard cruise is to take the dhow to Al-Maktoum Bridge as this would enable you to see both the modern and historic landmarks of Dubai. You'll see a lot of boatmen who would be willing to take visitors on a tour from the abra stations to the mouth of the Dubai Creek and then inland to the Maktoum Bridge. This tour usually lasts for an hour or so. Seeing Dubai from the creek is different simply because so much has grown around it, yet the creek itself has remained the same.

View from the Dubai Creek

Another alternative is to take a dinner cruise on the Creek. Many tour operators offer reasonably priced tours throughout the day. There's usually some pre-recorded history blurb, but it is great to just get the breeze as you chug through the routes that many traders from Iran and all over the world have sailed. The Dhow cruise is a leisurely activity, fun for the kids but equally interesting for the adults and great for first timers in Dubai.

POINTS OF NOTE

If you have the time then you must go for a stroll around the wharf and get a glimpse of the trading heritage of Dubai. You will be able to spot a lot of dhows docking to unload their merchandise.

If you are on your honeymoon then you can make some special preparations to surprise your significant other! Even if you aren't honeymooning you can still rent the entire vessel or half the vessel in order to enjoy a private romantic cruise in the Dubai Creek.

Bateaux Dubai is the dhow cruise that stands out amongst them all on a high end huge dhow, though you may want to brave a lower end dhow to get a real experience, for which we recommend the Al Mansour Dhow

Recent dhow cruises have popped up in the Marina – but they don't compare to the real ones on the Creek.

When – You can visit the Dubai Creek at any time of the day if you are just planning to take a tour along the waterway. For a more exquisite plan, you can opt for the evening cruise under the moonlight which usually lasts for two hours. It starts from 8.30 pm and ends at 10.30 pm. Guests are picked up from their hotels between 7 pm or 8 pm.

How long – A typical Dubai Creek tour where one will be sailing through the creek in an abra would last for about an hour or less while the evening cruise lasts for two hours or more.

Location – Ask for Dubai Creek - you'll notice all the boats docked up and ready to leave. If you have booked a package then your tour operator would pick you up from your hotel.

Cost - Depending on your tour operator you can pay anything from Dhs 120 upwards. For a decent Dhow expect to pay about Dhs 300 including dinner.

Booking – ask your hotel to arrange a dhow cruise - or turn up at the creek at about 7pm. The most established dhow tours are:

Bateaux Dubai bateauxdubai.com 04 315 4777

Al Mansour Dhow radissonblu.com/hotel-dubaideiracreek 04 222 7171

Book directly and cut out the middleman

SKY DIVE IN DUBAI

Sky diving is absolutely not for the faint hearted, but if you're brave enough to jump out of a plane at almost 13,000ft, a sky dive above the magnificent city of Dubai is the best way of sightseeing all the famous landmarks at an angle and height that only a special few will ever have the experience of doing! It's no surprise that Flo Rida features skydiving in Dubai as the central activity in his video for the single Wild Ones.

You don't have to attend hours of training to undertake a free fall dive unless you want to become a qualified solo sky diver but if you're on holiday in Dubai and have a couple of thousand dirhams and, of course, are an adrenaline junkie - you must do this! First time sky divers will be chaperoned by an experienced qualified sky diver and harnessed fully and share the same parachute. Simple instructions will be given but the general advice is to be calm and enjoy the whole experience. The actual free fall time is a minute and the rest of the parachute glide is about an hour, but allow yourself three hours for the whole experience. Skydiving is strictly for over 18 years only.

For those want to experience a thrill but need a bit of indoor training first, a company called iFly Dubai offer simulated sky diving packages which they claim are so close to the real feeling of sky diving but obviously without the view! Kids as young as three as well as adults can try out the simulator. The package includes a 15 minute training session via a video demo, jumpsuits and then the actual experience in the vertical wind tunnel with a supervised expert. Kids love it and many adults use it as a stepping stone for an actual sky dive.

POINTS OF NOTE

For the genuine sky dive above Dubai city, you must be over 18 years and under 100kg or 220 lbs for safety reasons. You must not have any alcohol in your system before the dive and you must wear suitable athletic gear on the dive including trainers.

Weather plays a big part in the dive, so if it isn't a perfect day, the ride may take a little longer.

For the iFly Dubai simulator, the person going on the experience will have to sign a damage waiver form. The simulator is not for people with back, neck or shoulder injuries and women who are expecting. Additionally, you must weigh under 105kg if your height is less then 5ft 9. If you are above this height your weight should not exceed 115kg. Please call the company if you weigh more than this.

When- For the sky diving experience: Daily

For the iFly Dubai experience, fly times are normally 10am- 11pm Sun - Weds. On the weekend (Thurs and Friday) they are open till midnight.

How Long - For the sky diving experience: Allow a total of 3 hours. You may be able to go on the sky dive on the same day of booking provided there is space. For the iFly Dubai experience, allow 1 hour including the 15 minute training.

Location - For the sky diving experience, there are two locations, The Palm Jumeirah, primarily for first time jumpers and The Desert Campus off Al Ain Road for people interested in the sky diving school. For the iFly Dubai experience, they are located in Mirdif City Centre Mall, 1st Floor, South Side - Playnation.

Cost - For the sky diving experience, the first time tandem jumpers pay a package of 1750 AED which includes digital stills and video. For the iFly Dubai experience, rates for first-time flyers (child and adult) are 195 AED (although enquire for off peak rates too) there are separate rates for photo, DVD and USB souvenirs from 40 - 150 AED.

More info - For the sky diving experience please refer to the company we based our research from skydivedubai.ae. For iFly

Dubai iflyme.com

DUBAI AQUARIUM AND UNDERWATER ZOO

The Dubai Aquarium and Underwater Zoo, often called the Dubai Mall Aquarium, is a gargantuan artificial aquatic world which is home to more than 33,000 species of marine life all of which can be enjoyed through the acrylic viewing panel claimed to be the largest of its kind in the world. Although sharks and rays in population exceeding 400 are the main attractions here, other species which arouse equal amount of excitement are the gigantic grouper fish and massive hordes of pelagic fish.

Located at the ground level of the Dubai Mall, the Dubai Aquarium and Underwater Zoo is the largest suspended aquarium in the world with its aquarium tank measuring 51 metres in length, 11 metres in height and being 20 metres deep. Amongst the large variety of aquatic species, this tank boasts accommodating the largest collection of Sand Tiger sharks in the world. If you're not really into the specifics, The Dubai Aquarium is a great view - and probably a great meeting point at the mall as everyone knows where it is.

Inside the Dubai Aquarium Tunnel

A unique feature of the Dubai Aquarium is the Aquarium tunnel (you have to pay for this!) which extends for 48 metres and commencing from the ground floor, it would take you as deep as 11 metres under the surface. Walking right through the tunnel is a fascinating experience which is made educational by the presence of an Aquarium Educator who will enlighten you with amazing details of the creatures lurking around you.

At level 2 above the aquarium tank (you have to exit out into the mall to get there), there is the Underwater Zoo which features three ecosystems namely Rainforest, Rocky Shore and Living Ocean. This is like a water museum where children are thrilled to spot crocodiles, crabs, octopus, eels and even penguins not to mention a glimpse of how the fish food is prepared. The penguins are notoriously active and are a great finale to the zoo. This is the point in the Dubai Aquarium and Underwater Zoo at which it is possible to take a ride in a glass bottom boat and try to touch the fish. (for an extra cost)

One of the latest attractions at the Dubai Aquarium and Underwater Zoo is the Creepy-Crawlies section in which there are five dedicated exhibits namely an Insect Wall, a wall-mounted glass exhibit, the Iguana Enclosure, the Burmese Python Enclosure and the Tree Snake Enclosure. An attempt to cross the 'Rope Bridge' would provide a panoramic view of the Rainforest below teeming with life.

POINTS OF NOTE –

Watch out for the massive spider on the wall in the underwater zoo.

There was a leak in the mall at launch - but it's all fixed now!

The fare for a ride on the glass bottom boat can be included in the entry ticket to the aquarium.

Opposite the viewing panel is Candylicious, the largest sweet shop in the world.

On entry to the tunnel, you are offered a photo. You can decide later whether to buy it or not. Invariably you will.

There's also an option to swim with the sharks or snorkel to the delight of the watching crowds.

When – The timings are 10am-10pm between Sunday and Wednesday and 10am-midnight between Thursday and Saturday.

How long – Given the size of both the the tunnel, the Dubai Aquarium and Underwater Zoo you could spend perhaps 20 minutes in the tunnel and probably more in the the zoo, but obviously depending on how much of a water creature lover you are, you could become mesmerised by being so close to the sharks. We recommend anything from 20 minutes to 2 hours in total. Perfect if you are splitting off from the other half and her shopping.

Location – The Dubai Aquarium is located within the Dubai Mall.

Cost – free to look at the Viewing panel from outside, but behind the rope. A combo ticket for the Aquarium tunnel and underwater zoo is AED 50 while a Platinum Aquarium package inclusive of aquarium tunnel, underwater zoo and behind the scenes tunnel is AED 75. Diving and snorkelling ranges between AED 200 and 2000.

More info – thedubaiaquarium.com and contact via enquiries@thedubaiaquarium.com

THE RAS AL KHOR WILDLIFE SANCTUARY IN DUBAI

The Ras Al Khor wildlife sanctuary in Dubai is UAE's first and Dubai's only real desert wetland site. Ras Al Khor means 'head of the creek' in Arabic and occupies about 2.4 square miles on the banks of Dubai Creek comprising of mudflats, lagoons, pools, mangroves and long stretches of Sabkha, the saline flats commonly found along the coastline.

Extremely significant as the last refuge for many native species of flora and fauna, the sanctuary offers a rare glimpse of a greener Dubai which is quite different to the skyscraper focus of the Emirate. The Ras Al Khor wildlife sanctuary supports as many as 20,000 water birds belonging to many different species and according to scientists this is probably the only area in which quite a few species are present in sizeable numbers. During the winter months between October and March, this area is home to as many as 30,000 migratory birds which fly in from East African and West Asian countries. Our favourites are the flamingos seemingly out of place in this part of the world. If you like birds, you'll love the Ras Al Khow Wildlife Sanctuary. With 500 species of plants and animals, the Ras Al Khor wildlife sanctuary is an ideal spot for eco-friendly tourists.

POINTS OF NOTE –

Telescopes and binoculars are provided to tourists within the Ras Al Khor wildlife sanctuary at the three hides, camouflaged very well against the green back-drop.

This is one of few venues in Dubai where you don't have to worry about parking as all the shelters have their own car parks and are manned at all times.

While small parties can visit the area unannounced, groups consisting of more than 10 need to acquire permits from the Environment Department of Dubai Municipality.

Pink flamingos in Dubai. Yes, they're here.

Don't take the kids to Dubai Zoo – this is a lot better.

When – The Ras Al Khor wildlife sanctuary can be visited on any day from Saturday to Thursday between 9 A.M. to 4 P.M.

How Long - For bird lovers, this is a good day trip – but half a day should be enough.

Location – Any of the three shelters, one of which is at Ras Al Khor Road and the other two are located off Oud Metha Road so mentioning this to the cab driver would take you there.

Cost – Entry to this nature park is free for everyone.

More info - wildlife.ae.

CAMEL RACING

Perhaps not the most obvious thing to do on holiday but surely one of the most memorable is to view the camel races. It's a very Arabian type of sport, obviously, and predominantly male focused – and although you may compare it to horse racing or greyhounds, it has its own niche and something to experience if you have a chance.

The camel racing is at Al Lisaili Race Course and is roughly 30 minutes drive away from Dubai. Since it gets very hot during the day, the races take place early in the morning with each one lasting between 10 and 15 minutes – and they carry on back to back with no real break in between, so you can watch until you can't take any more. It's a little difficult to see which camel is which but usually the camel saddle is different in colour.

The most amusing element of the race is the view of little robot camel jockeys riding the camels. These jockeys are then controlled around the racecourse by their owners driving in their 4x4s, which all feels a bit farcical. You're most worried that the cars will crash! But it's good fun and a must do for uniqueness sake.

The Robot Camel Jockeys (resting)

POINT OF NOTE:

A few years ago, the profile of camel races were raised when it was alleged that underage jockeys from the Indian subcontinent were being used. That's all changed now with the use of the Robot

There is a pong about it all (it doesn't smell great!) – but it's all about the atmosphere!

There aren't many tourists visiting, but the locals are very friendly and happy to have you there.

Betting is illegal, so if you want to wager amongst friends, then keep it under wraps.

There used to be races at Nad Al Sheba but now Medhan has opened, that has stopped.

When – Thursdays, Fridays & Saturdays , 600am 9am with races starting from 700am onwards, from October to April

How long – 3 hours plus travelling time

Location – We recommend that you drive, and take a taxi towards Bab Al Shams. It is located near junction37 on the Al Ain Road

Cost – Free

Contact – Dubai Racing Club 04 8326951

DUBAI MIRACLE GARDEN

Weird and wonderful is what Dubai Miracle Garden is all about. An ocean of flowers in and amongst the desert certainly is miraculous. While visiting these gardens is not top of our list of things to do, Dubai Miracle Garden is evolving to include a butterfly city, an edible garden and a pick your own areas all in one. Some consider it the epitome of flowering beauty. Some horticulturists will enjoy the vast array of flowers. We think that this floral gaudiness is worth seeing once. You won't go back - there are only so many flowers you can take in one lifetime.

Point of Note:

This project has been stop start, although appears to be back open with more phases planned

They're calling it the world's largest flower garden, but it isn't actually that big. You will walk through this place in an hour.

Watch out for the massic floral clock, where a bird come to tweet every 15 minutes

Food is expensive, so we don't recommend staying.

In addition to the flower spouting cars, there is a Burj Khalifa made out of flowers and 18 metres high. That should explain to you what this place is all about.

There are supposedly 45 million flowers, but we can't verify that because they took too long to count.

When – Daily til 9pm

How long – 1 hour maximum

Location – We recommend that you drive, on the corner of Um Suqeim Roadand Sheikh Mohamed bin Zayed Road, close to Dubai Autodrome in the desert

Cost – AED 30, free under 3.

Contact –04 4228902 or vist <u>dubaimiraclegarden.com</u>

SKI DUBAI

Famous more for what it achieved than as destination in itself, Ski Dubai represented the ridiculous of the impossible – build a massive indoor ski slope in the desert. It is rather good and so if the heat is really getting to you, you can cool off at Ski Dubai at the Emirates Mall. Ski Dubai is Middle East's first indoor ski resort and the world's largest indoor ski resort. Ski Dubai not only looks like an Alpine ski resort it also provides an ultimate skiing experience with its five runs including the world's first largest indoor black run, the longest of which is 400 metres with a fall of 60 metres. Additionally there are beginner slopes and a freestyle area for the snowboarders as well as a snow park for the kids and adults.

Ski Dubai is, of course, conceptually bizarre and the space like structure viewable from the outside got the international press buzzing at the craziness of it all when it was first being built. It is unique and the mountain-themed attraction is guaranteed to provide you with complete entertainment. The snow is real – made with a year long snow making machine. This place is covered with 22,500 square meters of real snow throughout the year. Come winter or summer you can enjoy real snow whenever you like in Ski Dubai!

Points of note

Don't worry about clothing as Ski Dubai has everything you need. You will be able to find everything from winter clothing to snowboard equipment to skis here. The skis will be there to carry you downhill while there will be quad-chairlift to help reach you to the top for another round of skiing.

Not into skiing? There are other alternatives for entertainment in Ski Dubai. You can visit any of the two unique themed restaurants: the Avalanche Café which offers picturesque views of the slope and St Moritz Café which is located right at the entrance.

Meeting the penguins is one of the cutest things you can ever do

Want to ski but don't know how? In that case visit the Snow Pro, an exclusive retail shop which offers ski equipment as well as professional instructors who would provide you with guidance on how to ski or snowboard.

If you are a fitness freak you can sign up for snowrobics (theplaymania.com)

If you just want to nosey and see the slopes you can do that from the relatively warm comfort of the mall from where you can see the skiers in Kanduras and traditional gear schussing down the slopes

When – The opening times from Sundays to Wednesdays is 10 am to 11 pm. On Thursdays the park is open from 10 am till 12 midnight. On Fridays it is from 9 am till 12 midnight while on Saturdays it is open from 9 am till 11 pm.

How long – This depends on how much time you would want to spend at the ski resort. It is just like an amusement park, you can spend as much or as little time as you want.

Location – This resort is located inside the Mall of the Emirates on Sheikh Zayed Road.

Cost – For the snow park it is AED 120 for an adult and AED 110 for a child. If you want to visit the ski slope then it would cost AED 180 and AED 150 for two hours for an adult and a child respectively.. The extensions per hour cost AED 50. You can get day pass for 300 (240) Dhs. Lessons are charged separately.

Booking – If you want ski lessons or snowboard lessons then you will have to book in advance.

More info - skidxb.com and 04 4094000

THE MEYDAN DUBAI

The Meydan Race Course was inaugurated in 2010 and replaces the existing Nad Al Sheba Racecourse. The Meydan Race Course is now dubbed as one of the best race courses in the world and is has taken over as host for the Dubai World Cup – the most expensive horse race in the world.

Stretching over 7.5 million square metres the Meydan Race Course is inclusive of the Meydan Marina. The two race tracks are overlooked by the luxurious five-star hotel also called the Meydan and a huge grandstand which measures a mile in length accommodating 60,000 spectators! For horse afficionados, this is the Mecca of horse racing and November to March are the times when you can catch a race here. There are also some great restaurants at the hotel as well as the Meydan Museum and Gallery and an IMAX theatre.

We're not horse racing experts, but hear it on good authority that this is as good as it gets!

POINTS OF NOTE –

General admission to the Meydan Race Course is free but various packages can be taken up.

Starting time for the Dubai World Cup is 7pm and since it is one of the worlds's richest horse racing venues, it is a natural attraction for socialites and fashionistas the world over. It certainly is a who's who of Dubai. Don't forget your swanky hat!

A noteworthy attraction next to the Meydan Race Course is the Meydan Marina which is being designed to accommodate as many as 80 yachts.

There are other races other than the Dubai World Cup that you can attend. Get in touch with the Dubai Racing Club if you are a horse fan.

Don't forget - gambling is illegal, so you won't be able to take a punt on this one, at least while you are in the UAE.

When –The ideal time to visit would be between November and March when the races take place.

How long – A great evening of fun

Location –It is in place of the old race course Nad Al Sheba.

Cost –Admission is free of charge but there are different package rates for the Grandstand.

More Information: Email: info@dubairacingclub.com dubairacingclub.com.

TYPICALLY DUBAI EXPERIENCES

When you get to the heart of Dubai, there are a few things that help define the Emirate both from a traditional and modern standpoint.

You are probably holidaying in the Emirates for some well needed downtime and Dubai is all about the downtime. Whilst you are here, you must try and do one if not all of the experiences listed below. Some things, you may already be able to do back at home anyway, but you must try it the Emirati way – it really makes a difference and will be the 'icing' of your holiday. The one thing you won't be able to avoid is experiencing the call to prayer – or the adhan – it happens 5 times a day, including the morning, and reminds you that you are in the Muslim World. Both beautiful and eerie, this experience will remain with you long after you return, and you will be reminded of Arabia the next time you hear the chant. Enjoy!

RIDING A CAMEL

Surprisingly, there are those who actually think that there will be camels roaming the street in Dubai. This may be the desert but it sure ain't the stereotype. Finding a camel to ride can be quite difficult if you don't know where to go, but if riding one was one of the stereotypes that you have to get done, then this is where you can do it

If you are going on a desert safari, the camel ride is usually thrown in as part of the 'cultural' things to do when you are out in the desert.

Sometimes your kids may be a little too young to go on the desert safari with you, so you're pretty much stuck, but occasionally you do get lucky on some of the beaches.

If you are going to Al Marmoon Race track or Al Lisaili Race track for the Camel racing, you can ask one of the trainers at the end of the race to let you ride one. Similarly in Abu Dhabi, Al Wathba is the place for camel racing. However, if you are making a trip to Abu Dhabi as part of your trip, there is one near Marina Mall in the heritage village.

There used to be a man and his camel at Hilton Dubai Jumeirah, but it's not clear whether he still does the rides.

SMOKE A SHISHA

Shisha smoking in the UAE is a favourite national pastime. Everywhere you walk, you will come across another outdoor shisha café where locals as well as expats hang out with friends and family having drinks, coffees and snacks while puffing on a shisha. Despite the health awareness campaigns on the impact of tobacco, many cannot limit their passion for shisha and now the government want to enforce stricter guidelines on where shisha cafes can operate. For now, hotels and some outdoor dining cafes are fine to serve shisha, however the new laws mainly affect independent cafes and restaurants that operate in residential areas.

Mini shishas on sale

For those of you not 'au fait' with the shisha, it essentially is a water pipe used for smoking purposes, originating about 500 years ago. The tobacco is heated by coals and the smoke is purified and cooled through the water after which it emerges through the suction tube, from where it is smoked. The Shisha ranges from the mini (usually bought by tourists who probably won't smoke it again) to the regular metre high contraptions to the two metre monsters which grace some of the cafes. The cost to smoke one in the UAE ranges, in general, from about 35-75 Dirhams depending on whether you are in a trendy 'to be seen' place or not, though some exclusive joints can charge upward of a thousand Dirhams! Flavours vary from the popular apple (and double apple), mint, strawberry, apricot, rose through to the super cool grape. You know what we like. Grapeshisha is the choice of Sheikhs and important people.

Smoking shisha has slowly grown into western culture as alternatives have been sought for a medium between bar life and coffee life. The shisha cafes have existed for centuries from as far as India to Egypt. Shisha is prominent across the Gulf states and indeed in Dubai, where shisha can form the focal point of an evening. Some indulge during the day. Either way, if you are that way inclined, it's probably worth experiencing once to find out what it's all about. It's one of the experiences that we recommend to get a feel for the the culture, even if you just sip on your chai nana (mint tea) and watch everyone puff away, but you won't be able to avoid the sweet smell of the smoke.

You can try anywhere for shisha - they're all fine. We've listed our favourite shisha places in Dubai to suit a variety of budgets. Happy puffing!

For true Arabian opulence the One &Only Royal Mirage, Palace Courtyard is a great place for visitors, for shisha, Arabian coffee and snacks. Lovely for a chilled evening in beautiful surroundings. (04 399 9999)

At Madinat Jumeirah, head to Shimmers for shisha on the beach. Also the main courtyard at the Madinat serves great shisha with Arabian ambience. (04 3666730)

In the Mall of the Emirates, Harvey Nichols, Almaz by MOMO, brings you a more glitzy indoor experience of shisha. There is a gorgeous restaurant serving lovely Arabian food at reasonable prices aswell as a salon and juice bar. The perfect hangout for a large meal or just shisha with a relaxing cool ambience. Almaz is unlicensed. (04 409 8877)

For a night out with friends, Reem al Bawadi on Jumeirah Beach Road is a great spot. If you want a lively night – head here although may be wise to book a table if you plan to arrive after 7pm on a weekend. The variety of shisha flavours is extensive and the quality is top class. There is an excellent variety of Lebanese mezze. Thumbs up for a fun venue on a reasonable budget. (04 394 7444)

If you're near to the Dubai Creek area, head to the Dubai Creek Golf and Yacht club to QD's. Reasonably priced and great views of the creek. QD's also serves food and has a licensed bar open till 2am with a DJ. This outdoor place is also open during the hotter months but within an air conditioned tent. (04 295 6000)

Finally another favourite of ours is Shakespeare and Co in the Souk al Bahar, Dubai Mall which is a reasonably priced café style eatery. Get a table outside and you'll enjoy fantastic views of the musical fountain and the stunning Burj Khalifa while you smoke. Service is great and the snacks and breakfast menu are good. Perfect for a lazy weekend. (04 4257971)

On the Dubai Marina walk: Chandelier, a Lebanese eatery which is great for shisha but ok for food. It's normally heaving with shisha smokers so you know it must be good and the scenery is good with seating dotted next to the huge fountain.

At Jumeirah Beach Residences, go to the Al Sadaf Building, Café Tche Tche. Seating available on the terrace overlooking the Palm. Again, eating here is not as great as the shisha, so come belly full.

DUBAI STREET FOOD

If you are holidaying in the Emirates, you can't leave without sampling the nation's favourite streetfood – the shawarma. Shawarmas can be arranged open or closed ("sandwich"), the latter more popular as it is an easier way to gobble down. The open version is normally a posh sit-down way of eating it! Shawarmas consist of a soft, round flat bread filled with pieces of succulent, marinated chicken or lamb roasted on a spit and dressed with a garlic mayonnaise sauce, pickles, tomato, a few French fries all rolled up and wrapped ready to tuck into.

Strictly speaking the shawarma is of Lebanese origin, but you can get shawarmas all over the Middle East. We love them! - and although similar in nature to a greasy UK kebab, they are probably healthier - and definitely a lot tastier. We recommend you definitely try a shawarma on your trip to Dubai.

An alternative to the shawarma is the manakish, a flatbread style pizza topped with a variety of ingredients from assortments of cheese, minced meats, tomatoes, chillis and zaatar. Fresh out of the oven, the manakish are amazing, great for a snack or even a full meal. We've had manakish for breakfast, lunch, dinner, a mid day snack and post party binge.

Most of the Lebanese street food joints are open late into the night - some even 24 hours, ideal for the post club crave! Prices at the cafes and restaurants below are all very reasonable. Typical prices of shawarmas are between 5 and 8 Dhs. Bowls of hummus, moutabbal etc range from 10 – 15 Dhs each, manakish can range from 10-15 Dhs and mixed grills and other mains are between 20-35 Dhs each.

Our Dubai Favourite Shawarma Joints:

Satwa, Dune Centre, Sidra (04 345 3044). If you love mezze, you'll love the generous pot sizes of creamy hummus, moutabbal and tabouleh. The bread is baked fresh and warm and the shawarmas are good. Not a great place to sit and eat, but fab for a takeway. Open late.

Al Diyafah Road, Al Mallah (04 398 4723) Head here if you crave a quick shawarma. The chicken and lamb are tender and very reasonable on price. Again, better order this one 'to go' and eat on the pavement as you'll find more entertainment outdoors then indoors. Open late.

Sheikh Zayed Road, Saj Express. Hunger satisfying shawarmas made on their freshly baked bread give the traditional snack a strong thumbs up. The fresh juices are to die for. Open late. (04 321 1191)

Also on Sheikh Zayed Road and around Dubai, Zaatar W Zeit. Perfect to experience the manakish, try the labneh topping which closely resembles soft cheese. If you really are a dairy lover, wash it down with some labneh salty yogurt drink. Comfort food heaven! (04 343 1259)

Al Barsha, Byblos Hotel, The Deck. If you fancy eating and sitting but not blow the wallet, this open air eatery is perfect with its lounge style seating serving shisha, shawarma and most Lebanese delights. (04 448 8000)

Jumeirah, Al Wasl Road, Oasis, is a basic eatery that is popular with the beach crowd. The shawarmas hit the spot and the juices refreshing. Prices are so good that you might as well binge properly. (04 394 9353)

TEA - COFFEE

Coffee may be the Arabic drink of choice in this part of the world, but it's the Masala Chai that provides the fuel to the workers to keep the place running. It's probably worth trying both when you are out here. The coffee is slightly different to what you might experience in the West. The coffee in the UAE is called Kahva and is usually drunk at the same time as dates. Arabic coffee does not taste like your regular espresso or Americano. You may find it a little bitter and you will also notice a little spice blended in. Most of the time this is cardamom, but at some of the expensive locations, you'll find other spices are used as well. Milk is never added to this type of coffee. Some refer to Arabic coffee as Turkish coffee (or just "Turkish") interchangeably, but we have found that Turkish Coffee is the thicker darker coffee and is usually a lot stronger. Either way Arabic Coffee is an acquired taste – but one you will grow to like especially if you are a lover of different coffee blends.

Masala Tea is the drink of choice of the many Indian subcontinent workers in the UAE, from the taxi drivers to shop keepers who keep the country moving. With so many Indian expatriate workers in the country, this culture has moved with them and your masala chai here is as authentic as any. In addition to the regular tea leaves and boiling water, masala tea, contains masala or spice, usually a combination of cardamom, pepper, and ginger powder, then lashings of milk, usually evaporated plus heaps of sugar. It's a sweet concoction.

Coffee and Tea Options

You can usually get Arabic coffee at most Arabic food establishments, or you can enjoy some with your shisha at one of the many cafes. We recommend the Palace courtyard at Madinat Jumeirah. If you don't like coffee, fresh mint tea is an authentic drink to try referred to as "chai bil nana" or simply "chai nana".

Step into Karama and you will see many walking around with their white plastic cups which signifies one thing. Masala tea is close by. Any of the small stalls will offer tea at 1 AED, but you'll usually get offered it for free if you are buying clothes or spending money at one of the establishments. A place we recommend is Rangoli, but make sure you have the food as well. It's the best (and cheapest) Indian restaurant in Dubai!

HALAWA

This is an experience primarily for the ladies, however if any men are brave enough to endure a chest wax, just confirm with the relevant salon if they 'do' men!

Halawa is a completely natural form of hair removal, using sugar, lemon and water in the right proportions to make a wax. The results leave skin feeling super soft and unlike synthetic wax found in most salons in western countries, halawa or sugaring wax is ideal for those who have sensitive skin although if you haven't done any form of waxing before, you may want to try a small area first. The ancient Egyptians first discovered halawa, which is now the common way to effectively remove unwanted body hair for weeks. Many salons throughout the UAE offer halawa, as well as other standard treatments such as threading, facials, nails, massages and hair. We have listed our favourite salons that specialise in halawa below:

In all honesty, your concierge could help you with finding the best local salon or recommend one, but these are the ones we know to be good.

Zen Asia Spa, W Cluster, Jumeirah Lake Towers, opposite Damas, a short drive from Dubai Marina Metro 04 4572374

Zen Beauty Lounge, Discovery Gardens, 5 minutes from Ibn Battuta Mall, 04-4343017

The alternative is to buy your own from supermarkets like Carrefour or Lulu that you can take back home with you.

HENNA

Now becoming popular in western countries, henna tattooing has for centuries been a favourite cosmetic routine in the Middle East. Henna has taken on a new turn over the last ten years or so, and in Dubai, the city has made it easy for you to indulge in experience part of this culture. Women in the UAE get henna designs done as often as ladies paint their nails. The artists have superb talent creating the most intricate designs and the home grown and natural herbs used means the quality and colour of the final design is vivid and bold unlike the diluted cheap pastes you can get from some stores and salons in the west. Many salons have henna tattooists as standard like manicurists, and creating a design almost anywhere on the body – doesn't take much time at all. Nowadays henna tattooing has caught the eye of many males who love the tribal art. Henna appeals to many because of its temporary nature and the fact that it is 100% natural so will suit even the most sensitive of skins. Get one done on your shoulder, arm, ankle or wherever, you will be the envy of your friends and will have a short term memento of your holiday for weeks after you get back.Henna is usually for women, but it's possible to get some designs for men as well, so men, don't feel worried about trying it out.

Depending on the intricacy of the design, it can take anything between 5 minutes and an hour to get the design. Little tricks to maintain the length of time that the design stays on your hand include putting lemon on it, and putting your hand in a carrier bag and sleeping with it before washing off the dark residue. The local Emirati use henna as their nail paint of sorts and you will note that many Indians use henna during their weddings. The Indians know henna as mendhi.

The places we recommend are

Heritage for Henna. 28 stores throughout UAE based in some malls and hotels including one in Souk al Bahar. heritageforhenna.com

Sasha Beauty Salon. This salon has several stores throughout Dubai including Ibn Batutta Mall and Wafi Mall. 04 324 2070

FRIDAY BRUNCH

It's no wonder that the most modern of all traditions in Dubai was probably set up due to demand from the expats from years gone by. But it's a tradition that has stuck as part of Dubai society – gobbling as much as you of the unlimited food (and alcohol) on a Friday afternoon. It's a symbol of excess but it is certainly a lot of fun trying things you wouldn't usually try as well as indulging in your favourites. And then you have some more. And then you have even more. This is what the British do once a year at Christmas before they slouch in the sofa. There's no such hiding place in Dubai's top restaurants. Once you have had your first round and polished it off with bottles of bubbly (or non alcoholic beverage of choice), the ritual mush continue, before you write off your Friday at the beach or back in bed. In all seriousness though, many of the big name hotel restaurants cater for the Friday brunch – and the offers are fantastic value for what you get, so make sure you book in advance if you love your food.

There are many hotels to choose from but we love:

Traiteur at the Park Hyatt

Spectrum on One at the Fairmont

Al Qasr at the Al Qasr Hotel, Madinat Jumeirah

Read more in our restaurant section where we detail many more brunch options

DUBAI FOR KIDS

Dubai is a fantastic holiday destination for the family and if you have young children, you'll never fall short of things to do with them if you're visiting for a week or two. Of course they want to spend time in the hotel pool or beach splashing and running about, but sometimes this may get mundane and if it's really hot, there are a large number of great indoor spaces that put some other great cities to shame! We've short listed our favourites, but in addition to these many more parks, funlands and theme parks exist. Just enquire at your hotel concierge. Happy playing!

TOP ATTRACTIONS FOR KIDS

Dubai Aquarium and Underwater Zoo, Dubai Mall, 04 448 5200

Web:thedubaiaquarium.com

Entry Info: Combo ticket (Aquarium Tunnel and Underwater Zoo) 50 AED per person, Ultimate Aquarium Package (Combo plus glass bottomed boat ride, fish feeding and gift voucher) 100 AED person. Enquire for further packages such as snorkelling and diving. Kids under 3 are free.

Opening Hours: Sun - Weds: 10am-10pm, Thurs - Fri: 10am - Midnight

This is one attraction that will be loved by both young kids, teens and adults and probably in our opinion, one of Dubai's top three attractions. The Dubai Aquarium and Underwater Zoo resides in the Dubai Mall, so if your with the family, its a great way to let mum shop while dad takes the kids for a couple of hours. The Aquarium Tunnel is a 48 metre walk underwater walk with sharks, rays and an assortment of beautiful sea creatures swimming above and around you. The Underwater Zoo is a display of 36 aquatic creatures in a rain forest and aquarium setting where you'll see penguins, piranhas and lots more. The best view has got to be standing on top and looking down at the main Aquarium Viewing Panel - freaky! You can also experience the combined ticket separately or if you want to do more, how about a ride on the glass bottomed boat or even better, the cage snorkelling experience, will will cost additionally. Check out website for prices and info. The Dubai Aquarium and Underwater Zoo is a great attraction and should be on your must do list. If you dont want to pay to go in, enjoy the view for free from the largest viewing panel in the world, attested by the Guinness Book of Records.

Dubai offers lots for children to do

Aquaplay, Mirdif City Centre Mall

Web: aquaplayme.com

Entry Info: Rides priced individually from 5-30 AED

Opening Hours: Sat - Sun: 10am - Midnight

An indoor waterpark with fun rides like a log flume and educational water games to keep kids amused for a good couple of hours is right up our street, especially when its scorching outside and you don't fancy another top up tan. Aquaplay is a simple amusement arcade but genius as kids love it. No need to change into swim gear as aprons for kids are provided although we recommend to bring a change of clothes, incase of over excited play! Let the kids loose at

Muriel's Aquatraptions where they'll learn about the dynamics of water and enjoy spraying, squirting and messing around with different water guns, tubes and props. After having an educational water experience take them on the numerous exciting water rides like the log flume, canoes and tugboat swinging ship. Rides are priced individually, but very reasonable between AED 5-30 per ride. A great, budget alternative to the over hyped Wild Wadi and Aquaventure waterparks, but obviously not as large! Check out website for prices and info

Little Explorers, Mirdif City Centre Mall,

Web:littlexplorersme.com

Entry info: 130 AED for 1 child and 1 adult - an adult must be accompanied with child at all times, 190 AED for 1 adult and 2 children and 245 AED for 1 adult and 3 children. Additional adults are 60 AED each.

Opening Hours: Sat - Weds: 10am-10pm, Thurs - Fri: 10am - Midnight

Formerly known as Cite Des Enfants, this is another Dubai offering to keep young kids amused for hours outside the heat. Its clean and colourful concept is made up of several zones, where kids partake in many interactive games involving scientific experiments, construction, spatial awareness and group fun. The zone have cover several topics such as' I Can Do' and 'I Experiment' with interesting games within each zone, very similar to the famous science museum concepts around the world and the variety of games is generous but a parent must accompany a child at all times in order to explain the games and rules. Please note, you cant bring snacks into this venue, plus there is a no eating policy within the Little Explorers vicinity, however you will be stamped on the hand which allows you to come in and out of the area, so you pop out to the main mall for a snack/lunch and return. Little Explorers may be slightly dearer then most kid attractions in Dubai, but we highly recommend if your children are getting hot and bored with the usual beach and shopping holiday. A fun escape from the sun!

Ski Dubai, Mall of the Emirates, Al Barsha, 04 409 4000

Web: skidxb.com

Entry Info: Snow Park, Adults: 120 AED, Children under 12: 110 AED. Ski Slope (2 hours), Adult: 180 AED, Children under 12: 150 AED. Refer to website or call for info and pricing for day passes and ski lessons.

Opening Hours: Sun - Weds 10am - 11pm, Thurs 10am- midnight, Fri 9am - midnight, Saturday 9am - 11pm.

A year round indoor ski complex may sound strange, but ofcourse, anything is possible in Dubai and with temperatures climbing to just over 40 degrees in the peak of summer, going in the snow for a couple of hours is a very refreshing thought. Ski Dubai opened in November 2005 and has over 22,000 square meters, equivalent to about 3 football pitches of indoor ski area and ski lifts will take you over several slopes of varying heights and difficulty and a realistic 400 metre run. The experience is surprisingly not bad at all and will put an impressive smile on any snow enthusiasts face! After partaking in skiing, snowboarding, tobogganing, snowman building or a bobsled ride, take the family up to the Avalanche Cafe to get a bit warm and enjoy a hot chocolate. Just perfect! Your slope pass will include all the gear you need for a cold winters day including jackets, snow trousers, ski suits for kids and ofcourse skis and ski boots. Hats and gloves are not included so you should bring your own or they can be bought from the ski shop.

Aquaventure, Atlantis, The Palm Dubai, 04 426 0000

Web:atlantisthepalm.com

Entry Info: (Entry gives access to both Aqvaventure and the Atlantis beach). Adults 200 AED, Children under 1.2 M 165 AED, Children under 2 years are Free. Separate charges for locker and towel rental. Guests staying at the Atlantis have free unlimited access.

Opening Hours: Open daily 10am - Sunset, but subject to change depending on time of year - please enquire.

If you love waterparks you will have an awesome time at Aquaventure. Set in the the grounds of the Atlantis Hotel on the Palm, its not as big as its rival Wild Wadi, but still fantastic enough to while away a good half a day or even a day if you want to enjoy it thoroughly. The rides at Aquaventure cater to all ages from babies right to raring adults. If you love thrill, go on the Leap of Faith, closest feeling to free falling through water as you can possibly get - definately not for the faint hearted. Other great rides include the Plunge and Stinger. Kids will love the Rapids and the little ones will be content with the water playground and ofcourse the beach.
Foodwise, there is plenty of choice to keep everyone happy, however things that you could bring to save money and undue hassle are your own towels, as the towel rental can be a fortune. Bring flip-flops as the ground can get unbearably hot and dont forget your sunscreen and hats as Aquaventure is a mostly uncovered waterpark so it can get uncomfortable.

Wild Wadi, Jumeirah Beach Hotel, 04 348 4444

Web:jumeirah.com

Entry Info: Adults 205 AED, Children under 1.1 M 165 AED, Special Sundowner package - 2 hrs before the park closes, Adult 170 AED, Children under 1.1m 135 AED.Children under 2 years are free. Guests staying at the Jumeirah Beach Hotel have free unlimited access.

Opening Hours: Nov - Feb 10am - 6pm, March - May 10am - 7pm, June - August 10am - 8pm, Sept - Oct 10am - 7pm.

The biggest waterpark in UAE and the original is Wild Wadi. With over 30 rides and attractions you can easily spend half to a full day here and the rides will keep young children right up to the teens and adults happily amused. Wild Wadi may not have tropical and shark fish tanks that you slide into but thrills they do have and the whole place buzzes a colourful lively atmosphere. Young children and adults will love Juha's jouney, a fun lazy river ride, and the babies and toddlers will love the water play park areas. For the thrill seekers, the most talked about Jumeirah Sceirah just has to be done along with Tantrum Alley and lots more. Makesure you try the simulated wave rides Riptide and Wipeout which are only one of four in the world - surfers will be impressed! For relaxing and snacking, there are ample of loungers and cafes and restaurants dotted round the park. Pick up one of the smart wristbands and top up credit so you dont have to carry your wallet around. Check out their website for promotional offers and to avoid the rush go midweek and during school hours.

Cafe Ceramique

Branches: Town Centre, Jumeirah, 04 344 7331; Festival Centre, Dubai Festival City, 04 232 8616

Opening Hours: Daily from 9am - Midnight.

Spending a couple of hours in a painting cafe may not sound like the ideal holiday activity, but when its hot outside and the kids have had enough of beaches and malls, Cafe Ceramique can be a relaxing pleasure and is a hit with the locals and expats. Based on the cafe combined with art concept, kids choose a piece of fresh pottery such as a small plate, mug or ornament and set up painting to their heart's content. Paints and brushes are all provided, the piece then gets glazed and fired and picked up a few days later. Pretty neat experience if you haven't been before - and you dont have to have kids to go! They serve a simple lunch menu like paninis and salads and have several branches dotted round.

Children's City, Gate 1, Creek Park, Bur Dubai, 04 334 0808

Web: childrencity.ae/CHCITY

Entry Info: Adults 15 AED, Children (2-15 yrs) 10 AED, Under 2 yrs are free. Family rates are available too.

Opening Hours: Sat - Thurs 9am-8pm, Fri 3pm-9pm

Very similar concept to Little Explorers, but not as expensive and you get value for money. Children's City is an indoor interactive science museum geared toward 2- 15 yr olds with lots of hands on apparatus so the kids really get stuck in and the best thing is that it doesn't get as busy as some other places. The interior is well organised, brightly lit and very clean and features a play area for under 5 years, cafe, planetarium and a theatre. Various exhibits include looking at the human body, the world we live in, electricity and this cool simulator ride where you can pretend to ride a camel and other fun stuff. This place is pretty big so you can spend anywhere from 2 hours to half a day.

iFly Dubai, Mirdif City Centre Mall, 04 231 6292

Web: iflyme.com

Entry Info: First time flyers, Adults and Children over 3 years: 195 AED. Subsequent flyers, refer to website for pricing tiers based on minutes desired.

Opening Hours: Sun - Wed: 10am - 11pm, Thur: 10am - midnight, Fri: 9am - midnight, Sat: 9am - 11pm

Again, not an activity you would choose to take your kids to if on holiday, but if its hot, and the kids are driving you crazy , you may like to consider this. iFly Dubai simulates skydiving, it's not a simulator as such but a vertical tunnel which blasts extreme volume of air upwards so that the effect of skydiving can be achieved. All of this takes place indoors within the Playnation area of Mirdiff Mall and is suitable for kids as young as 3 years. Ofcourse there are certain groups of people whom this would be unsuitable for such as pregnant women, people suffering from back and shoulder problems. Also those who weigh above 115kg will have to confirm if they are suitable. Please refer to website for clauses. If you book the experience, you will be given a short training session which includes a video and safety positions and be given the right gear to wear such as jumpsuits, goggles, helmets and shoes. The whole flying experience is not very long about 10-15 minutes for first time flyers. If you want to go again, you dont need the training but just book by minutes you want to fly. Not the cheapest of activities!

Jumeirah Beach Park, Jumeirah Road, Jumeirah, 04 349 2555

Entry Info: 5 AED per person or 20 AED per car. Sun loungers incur separate charges. Lockers not available.

Opening Hours: Sun - Thurs: 7am - 10.30pm, Fri - Sat: 7am - 11pm, Mondays are Ladies and Children day.

If you are not staying at a hotel with its own beach, we highly recommend you take the kids to Jumeirah Beach Park. For only 5 AED entry per person, you will get access to the entire beach and its facilities such as changing rooms, toilets and showers located on either end of the beach, barbeque area, sun loungers for hire and plenty of kiosks and cafes selling decent junk food. There is also a lovely playground for young kids and huge stretches of beautiful sand. The water is refreshing and clear so makesure you take a dip! Plenty of lifeguards on duty and safety is key here so dont expect to be allowed in if the waves turn excitable. Best time to visit is during the week, avoid weekends and Fridays especially of possible, very crowded. Also take note, Mondays are normally Ladies and children day, so men not allowed. In terms of attire, Dubai is pretty laidback these days and bikinis are fine to wear, just be warned that you may get stares if there are any labourers in close viewing distances so always carry a sarong that you can cover when you want. Other than that, at most times you wouldn't even feel you are on a beach in the Middle East! The sand can get hot in the warmer months so dont forget your flip flops

MALL PLAY AREAS
KidZania, Level 2, Dubai Mall, Downtown Dubai, 04 448 5222

Web: kidzania.ae

Entry Info: Children (4 - 16 years) 130 AED, Toddlers (2-3 years) 95 AED, Babies under 2 years are free. Adults (over 17 years) 90 AED and must be accompanied with a child.

Opening Hours: Sun - Weds: 9am - 10pm, Thurs: 9am-midnight, Fri - Sat: 10am - midnight.

Very popular with the local and expat parents, KidZania really is a one of a kind kids play area. The concept is a mini city with the full works such as a school, university, companies, hospital, restaurants etc. Kids will role play their lives by going to school getting a degree or working at one of the many companies familiar in UAE - such as Emirates Airlines! In return for working they'll obtain credits or currency called KidZos which they are free to spend in the McDonalds, Waitrose or the many mini shops in Kidzania. The whole concept may sound overwhelming for a child but it works incredibly well and ideal for 6 years and over, although younger kids are able to join in, they may not get the full concept. Parents are able to stay with the younger kids or there is a supervised play room for little ones. Security is well organised here and done through an electronic bracelet in which parental info is recorded on. If you are going to visit one mall fun land, we recommend visiting KidZania, its huge and the concept is impressive and if your kids are ok being away from you for 2-3 hours, let them explore in secure surroundings while you shop in the one of the world's largest malls.

Sega Republic, Dubai Mall, 04 448 8484

Web: segarepublic.com

Entry Info: Prices are between 15 to 30 AED per attraction or go for a day pass to all rides and 200 AED credit for AED 220. This is the Platinum Power Pass and worth getting if you think you'll be spending half a day at Sega Republic.

Opening Hours: Sun - Weds: 10am-11pm, Thurs - Sat: 10am – 1AM.

Sega Republic is the Sega theme park that exists as a whole world within Dubai Mall. There's another one based in Dubai Marina Mall but this is a lot more impressive. You'll soon completely forget you were in Dubai Mall, when you step on one of the rides. Our favourite (and probably most people's) is the spinning rollercoaster. The Jungle Adventure is also good. These are the rides you'll want to revisit and so it's worth getting the power pass. Sega Republic is spread over two floors, but isn't actually that big. If you have kids aged 10 and up (or 140cm and higher), this will give them some welcome respite from you around boutique after boutique. You'll kill 3 hours here, but don't visit if your kids are young as they will be bored. Located in level 2 near the Reel Cinemas and Kidzania, this is your slice of Tokyo pop culture away from Japan. The 3D simulator rides are excellent.

Encounter Zone, Wafi City Mall, 04 324 7747

Web: wafi.com

Entry Info: For arcade games only you can purchase an e-card for 2 AED and top up when necessary. For rides in both Lunarland and Galactica you buy a wristband for 35 AED giving you 2 hours of unlimited ride usage. DN Paintball package prices start at 75 AED.

Opening Hours: Sat - Weds: 10am-10pm, Thurs - Fri: 10am - Midnight.

Another impressive mall play area is Encounter Zone. Where many malls play areas appeal to younger kids, Encounter Zone will keep the pre - teens and teens fairly amused as well as the little ones. Encounter Zone is split into two main areas Lunarland and Galactica. Lunarland is ideal for younger kids with its soft play areas, Crater Challenge; an area with slides, mazes, bridges and tunnels, and a futuristic carousel called Space Station along with the standard park arcade games. Galactica is aimed more for the over 9s and has an interactive horror show with a pg-14 parental guidance - so its scary! UAE's first indoor roller skate park called

GXpress and MaxFlight - a rollercoaster simulator ride. A recent addition to Encounter Zone is the UAE's first indoor paintball complex called DN Paintball, it proudly boasts its unique Night Fire game where you can play in the dark under UV lights. An adrenaline rushing experience but unfortunately DN Paintball is only open to boys and men - incredibly unfair!

Magic Planet, Mall of the Emirates, Al Barsha, 04 341 4000

Web: theplaymania.com/magicplanet

Further branches at: Deira City Centre Mall, 04 295 4333 and Mirdif City Centre Mall, 04 231 6311

Entry Info: 1 AED for 4 tickets. Rides are priced at individual prices.

Opening Hours: Sat - Weds: 10am-10pm, Thurs - Fri: 10am - Midnight.

This play area in the Mall of the Emirates was probably the front runner till Dubai Mall came along with KidZania, however Magic Planet still pulls in a good crowd, especially the younger kids as many malls now have thrill seeking rides to keep the older children amused. Size wise its pretty generous with about 10 large rides suitable for kids from 2 years right up to about 13 years. There is a huge bowling alley with 12 lanes and 5 pool tables plus a 4D theatre which is actually good fun. All this plus arcade games and Magic Planet's own food court with the usual kid friendly fast food joints, they can easily spend a good couple of hours here. You may like to bring some ear plugs though - it gets really noisy!

OTHER PLACES OF INTEREST FOR KIDS

These are worth checking out:

Za'abeel Park, off World Trade Centre Roundabout

A beautiful park which includes a massive adventure playground, a large lake where you can hire boats. an amphitheatre, beautiful gardens and Stargate, an indoor theme park with the usual roller coasters and soft play areas.

Safa Park, Al Wasl Road, Al Safa

A very popular and large green park, beautifully kept with a playground and a Pavilion which has fairground type attractions and a mini train taking you round the park and a gorgeous lake complete with ducks and boats to hire . Highly recommended if you are visiting in the cooler months as its probably Dubai's best traditional park.

Mushrif Park, Airport Road

Dubai's oldest and largest park at 500 hectares. Perfect for bike riding (if you happen to have brought yours!) otherwise plenty to keep kids amused with fairground type attractions like a merry go round, pirate ship, rides with camels and ponies.   There is also a mini village area with miniature buildings from around the world that the kids will adore. Plenty of picnic areas.

Wire World Adventure Park

Wild World Adventure Park, next to the Meydan Racecourse, is supposedly the largest man-made adventure park, this is for the outdoor types, when it's obviously not too hot outside. Zipliners ahoy, this park contains much more, includind massive trampolines, and ropes. About the size of four football pitches, this will make you and kids feel as if you really are Tarzan, Lord of the Arabian Jungle!

REST & RELAXATION

BEACHES

If you're staying away from the coast and want to get some beach action, you'll need to be savvy about the options. You could either pay to use the facilities of a 5 star hotel or attempt to go for one of the public beaches.

The price differential is huge. The hotels levy a charge of between AED 150 and AED 700 per person and sometimes don't allow children. That price just gets you access to the beach. You'll also have to pay for additional services such as spa facilities and water-skiing. You are recommended to call the hotel at least the night before to book a spot as some may not accept additional guests depending on the occupancy of the hotel on a specific day. Some just won't accept anyone, no matter who you are and who you know. If you are going to pay at this level, you might as well go to the Atlantis where AED 225 gets you access to Aquaventure as well. Alternatively, the Sheraton Jumeirah Beach charges an affordable AED 100 on weekdays. There are many, many options – and ultimately it comes down to which hotel you want to visit, whether you want to use the additional facilities and how much time you have. Expect to pay more for a busier beach on the weekend translates to visit the hotel beaches during the week if you can!

HOTEL BEACHES

Our favourite hotel beaches are:

Jumeirah Beach Hotel – JBH is made for families. So pay the AED 250 (AED 150 for kids) and get the view of the Burj al Arab while you get the rays.

The Quay Cluab at Mina A Salaam is quite brilliant and one of the best beach clubs. It's expensive too at AED 500 and AED 750 per person, which is why it makes sense to just stay at the hotel. It's busy, but worth the money in our view.

Habtoor Grand Beach Resort and Spa – the beach stretches pretty far down the coast. Expect to pay up to AED 150 to 200 per person

Jumeirah Zabeel Saray – our favourite hotel has our favourite beach, the hotel manages to balance exclusivity with relaxation. Make sure you book days in advance. AED 250.

Sheraton Jumeirah – pay a little and you get a lot. To get away from freeriders, this is worth spending AED 150 near the Marina

Le Meridien Mina Seyahi – AED 200-300 for one of the largest hotel beach clubs. It's more – and busier- on the weekend.

Nasimi Beach on the Palm – Where the cool cats go (without the kids), with a DJ playing in background on the weekend, this is your chance to experience Palm living for AED 300. For half the price and a little further down you can go to Riva Beach where you also get the chilled out tunes.

Fairmont the Palm offers th best of sea views but you pay top dollar for that but with limited additional perks. AED 200.

One and Only Royal Mirage – don't go here when it's peak season as you won't get in, but if you can get here, it's a great beach with lots of water sports on offer. AED 250

PUBLIC BEACHES

Your alternatives are to use the public beaches. Just be aware of the new ladies only days that have now been enforced. There are many beaches, but these are the main ones worth visiting:

Jumeirah Beach Park. Located on the Jumeirah Road, this is the most popular and best public beach in Dubai. It can get busy, so get there early and lock down your parasol and lounger. Entry is AED 5 per person. Monday and Wednesday are ladies only days.

Al Mamzar Park Beach. If you are staying closer to old Dubai, it's worth trekking a little further out for the tranquillity of Deira. In comparison to many of the other beaches in Dubai, this beach feels relatively empty, simply because of the size of the beach. It has all the amenities and is AED 5 per person. Sunday and Tuesday are ladies only days.

Jumeirah Beach Residence Open Beach. If you are staying close to the Marina, there a stretch of beach parallel to the high rises that all the residents use. It's free but doesn't have any amenities, but there are cafes nearby.

Jumeirah Open Beach. Although the Jumeirah Open Beach has white sand and perfect views of the Burj Al Arab, you do get the single men pests who stare and try and take pictures of women. The authorities clamp down on this immediately, but it can be annoying. Also knows as the Russian Beach, it is located just after the Palm Strip Mall.

Burj Beach. Although not recognised as an official beach, the area next to the Burj Al Arab is free for anyone to use. With great views of the Burj and the Palm, it's a nice spot, but there aren't any facilities.

Beach in front of Burj Al Arab

Kite Beach. Also known as Wollogong beach, due to its proximity to the university, this is a lovely spot that has become the place to be for kite surfers – surprise surprise. You can have lessons at AED 350 or go for a 3 hour intro course for AED 900. The Kite Beach is behind Sunset Mall, between the Dubai Offshore Sailing Club and Jumeirah Beach Park. See kitesurf.ae for more details.

A word of advice to the ladies: it's fine to wear a bikini on the beach as long as it's not too revealing, but it's not OK to go topless. You'll end up in jail and that's not much fun.

SPAS

If shopping is the unofficial sport of Dubai, then grooming would feature as part of the training. And if holidays were all about pampering, then Dubai would win, hands down. Both expats and local Emiratis indulge in spa treatments with as much normality as one would fill petrol in a car. It's a necessity of life. The Emirati ladies get everything from henna painting to immaculate blow dries. They certainly don't mess around with the riff raff spas – and why should you? Back in days gone by there was only one spa that the locals in the know trusted – called Spadunya – and while it used to be the spa of choice and still exists things have moved on.

Some of the spas in Dubai are astonishing to look at and once you are there they make you feel as if you have re-entered this world as an A class celebrity – that is, if you aren't one already. The spas are not discriminating and if you can pay and can get a slot, you're in for some major pampering time. And although we don't know what the benchmark is, it's quite possible the spas in Dubai rank highly with those in Asia and the best in the world. The other thing that is often overlooked is that by indulging in a spa treatment away from where you are staying in Dubai allows you to experience some of the best hotels in Dubai. So be selective when picking your spa spot. Make sure you get some glam time while you are in Dubai. After all, if you can't spend a million dollars, you might as well feel a million dollars. Our advice is to politely decline the upsell of additional products, unless you really think you are going to use them. The other thing we would say is that hammams are Turkish baths (i.e. from Turkey, not Gulf Arabia). The hotels offer modern spa treatments. There are only 2 places worth indulging in a proper hammam, the Jumeirah Zabeel Saray and the Royal Mirage. If you are offered a hammam elsewhere, it's likely not to be authentic and so not worth wasting your money on. If you want a Turkish bath, make Istanbul your next destination holiday!

HOTEL SPAS

One and Only Spa, Palm Dubai

thepalm.oneandonlyresorts.com

04 440 1010

If you are seeking a special occasion experience, then we recommend the One and Only. There are so many luxury hotels in Dubai all offering total indulgence but what sets One and Only on another level is their location and their highly rated treatments including the Rhassoul Experience for couples. Here you are given your own private couples suite equipped with private scrub area, double showers and tubs, and private relaxation area. The Rhassoul Experience is 3000 AED for two, a wage for some people, but definitely worth it for an extra special treat. Otherwise the huge selection of other treatments are not badly priced for this luxury hotel. As a guide, their 1 hr swedish massage is 500 AED and their 25 min body scrub is 215 AED. All these treatments give you access to their private spa facilities which are truly amazing. The location is so secluded you must take a private boat to get there – this is an extremely luxurious treat with privacy. It's not cheap, but both it and you are totally worth it.

Talise Spa, Madinat Jumeirah

jumeirah.com

04 366 6811

Talise is another luxurious spa with oodles of greenery and space. The spa certainly is huge with impressive indoor and outdoor features. If you want total serenity and an exit from downtown Dubai head to Madinat Jumeirah. The variety of treatments is pitched just right; their massages start from 495 AED for 60 mins and body scrubs start at 550 AED for 1 hour. Those prices in themselves are expensive, but when you consider what you also get as part of the spa facilities – it makes your money spent seem good value. You get a garden with your treatment room – and the vegetarian restaurant is top quality. The spa facilities are beautiful - an outdoor pool which is exclusive to the spa only, a refreshing indoor plunge pool and a steam/sauna room. Couples rooms are also available. Talise's signature treatments are the Hot Stone therapy with seaweed with is hugely popular with the regulars. Talise also have a Wellbeing Centre focussing on alternative therapy treatments such as hormone assessments, liver functioning etc. Be sure to keep an eye out for promotions advertised on their website before you visit as prices can be a steal, especially if you are in Dubai, off peak.

Assawan Spa & Health Club

jumeirah.com

Burj Al Arab Hotel, (04) 301 7338

If there ever was an excuse to be made to really experience the Burj Al Arab, Assawan is it. This is what all luxury spas aspire to be: there's an exclusive view of the Gulf from the 18th floor, there's an air of tranquillity surprising for such an over glamourous hotel; and ultimately the treatments are the best available. It's also on par, pricewise, with the some of its peer hotels as well as having things you can't get elsewhere, such is the exclusiveness of the Burj. The signature caviar body treatment is what Assawan is known for – but don't feel you have to do that. You can go for the caviar facial, milk bath or just for an algae wrap to tone your muscles. But apart from the bizarre and the extravagant, the regular massages and treatments are available. The icing on the cake of Assawan is the "skin jewellery" You can get real Gold or Platinum imprinted onto your skin as a tattoo. It costs 400 Dhs, but you can't get that anywhere else. Bling yourself up!

Talise Ottoman Spa

jumeirah.com

Jumeirah Zabeel Saray, (04) 453 0455

If you do want to go for a Turkish hammam, this is the only place to go. Talise is the largest spa in the UAE and probably the Middle East. It is huge, and actually feels as if you are going back to the times of the Sultans and their Ottoman Empire. The spa is quite splendid – marble and mosaics everywhere (be careful not to slip!). If palatial is what you want, this is the place to come. Talise is renowned for Ayurveda – and if that is your preference, then the Abhyanga massage is recommended.

The Spa, The Address

theaddress.com

Downtown Dubai, (04) 436 8751

The first thing to say is that you should not get confused with which Address we are recommending. The Address chain of hotels has a handful of branches in Dubai all elegantly decorated in a minimalist design. They are all pretty good in their own right but we especially love the branch at Downtown Dubai because of its central location and amazing views of the Burj Khalifa and Fountain from their relaxation rooms - truly exceptional! The Spa focusses on oriental healing techniques which can be found in all their treatments and they use ESPA products. This Spa runs a range of treatments including the unique Diamond Exfoliation which is a 30 min body polish using tiny crushed diamonds that can leave your body glittering - wonderful for weddings and not badly priced at 350 AED. Spa facilities include an Aroma Room which can also be booked in for couples and an Ice Cave. Complementary drinks and snacks available. The price is expensive for spa (it's small) but when you chilling out in the relaxation room with amazing views of the Dubai Mall and Fountain, 13 stories below – you know you're not going to get this anywhere else! Despite the size of the spa, this certainly is sheer elegance mixed with understated style.

TajSpa, Taj Palace Hotel

tajhotels.com

Al Rigga (04) 211 3114

The TajSpa at the Taj Palace Hotel may not have all the accolades that the other spas have, but it's worth seeking out. Firstly, the hotel is alcohol free, but this is the place you go to for the best chocolate massages in Dubai. There are a few offered at some of the other spas, but this is the place to come if you want to get cocoa rubbed all over your body (and who are we to judge?). If chocomania is not your thing, then the Secrets of Honey massage will make you sticky – and also turn your skin to velvet! The other chocolate massage oworth checking out if you really want to indulge is at the Sheraton Dubai which does the same thing but for a whole two hours. We think that's a little excessive - a little bit like Dubai!

SensAsia Urban Spa

sensasiaspas.com

The Village, (04) 349 8850

The Palm Jumeirah, (04) 422 7115

Mall of the Emirates, (04) 354 9228

Emirates Golf Club, (04) 417 9820

This hip and trendy chain of Spas is quite a hit with fashionistas, golfers and mummys-to-be as they have a huge variety of treatments on offer. The theme is based on the popular trendy spas in Thailand and the founder has recreated a calm yet sleek theme with the interior, treatments and services it offers. If you like pressure, don't be afraid to ask and likewise if you are a petal, be sure to mention you like it gently as standard massaging techniques involve a good amount of pressure. The surroundings are tranquil and their robes are the fluffiest around. Pricewise, it is one of the dearer spa chains in Dubai, but SensAsia regularly do special offers and recently have been doing half price promotions on some treatments on a Monday. Our favourite Sensasia is on the Palm, but the one at the Mall of the Emirates, a Sensasia Express is great for a mid shopathon pick-me-up.

Sisters Beauty Lounge, Dubai Mall

sistersbeautylounge.com

Dubai Mall, (04) 339 8500

The best beauty lounge in Dubai Mall is the Sister Beauty Mall. Although not large by Dubai standards, it certainly is popular and you can pick anything from doing your nails to a boosting head and neck massage. We quite like Sisters as they give a great massage, but also offer threading and waxing, which is perfect when you need a quick "top up" mid holiday. It's also where you can get a "cowshed" massage – which are famous in the UK and offer special toning. Retail relaxation requires, at minimum, a quick mani-padi and a neck massage before it's time to attack fashion boulevard again. Funnily enough, they also offer fake tans for those of you who can't bear then sun! But Sisters is really famous for its gold dust facial. Yes, it's 2000 Dhs of glamour. And only in Dubai!

ShuiQi Spa and Fitness

atlantisthepalm.com

Atlantis Dubai, (04) 426 2000.

The most surprising thing about ShuiQi is how serene it is in the actual spa when you enter. The least surprising thing about ShuiQi is how amazing it is. It has an amazingly long list of options depending on what you want. Even the most basic hour long face and body massage takes you to another world. And that's all you really need – ultimate relaxation away from the rigours. You may pay an arm and a leg for it, but that's why it is in the Atlantis. And if you have the budget to spend 1600 Dhs plus, we'd recommend the full 2.5 hours maxing your relaxation. It's almost a full reboot to take you back 10 years!

Spa Intercontinental

ichotelsgroup.com

(04) 7011257

Intercontinental in Festival City is a little out of the main area of Dubai but it's a day out of bliss. The spa is large, and they cater for couple treatments which make a great honeymoon treat. But what really makes this spa stand out from the others is one is it diamonds signature treatment. Yes, this is where you can get a diamond dust facial or full body treatment. At 1300 Dhs it's cheaper then the gold facial – and you will sparkle after you leave. Just don't coup yourself up in your hotel room afterwards. This is one treatment that needs to be flaunted on the town. So go and find a club that caters for superstars!

Lily Pond Spa,

lilypondspa.com

Shop 19B, Rimal 1 Building, JBR

(04)435 5780

Lily Pond Spa is a growing chain of spas that offers cheap as chips treatment and services in some of the less main stream locations. This makes it great if you are in Mirdif or are staying at the Jumeirah Beach Residence. Targeted at expats, Lily Pond is pretty busy most of the time, so you know that it's reputable. More outlets are opening all the time, so if you are in town for an extended stay and don't want to sign off your annual bonus to grooming, this is the pace to go. It's not the most high end of spots, but perfectly affordable to try out. The surroundings are nice and you can get a few treatments without breaking the bank. What's more is that there are offers all the time, so don't be afraid to ask.

Amara Spa, Park Hyatt Dubai

dubai.park.hyatt.com

(04) 602 1660

Even though Amara is set in the heart of Dubai's city centre its astonishing that you can't hear the usual Dubai chaos. Tthe interior is themed in a modern Moroccan style, with elegant marble hallways and calming fountains. The 8 private treatment rooms and residential spa rooms all have outdoor access leading to a private garden with rainshower. The majority of Amara's treatments can be booked into one of these private rooms after which you have free access to use the beautiful spa facilities which include a steam, sauna, stunning pool and more. Book a couples room if coming with a friend or other half - giving you extra privacy to enjoy tea outdoors – and make sure you stay to use the pool and gym. Prices are a bit on the steep side with a 1 hr swedish massage at 450 AED, and a 45 min body scrub at 385 AED but Amara regularly do promotions so be sure to check website or call before booking. We wish Amara was cheaper so we could go more often!

Cleopatra's Spa and Health Centre, Wafi City Mall

cleopatrasspaandwellness.com

(04)324 0000

Cleopatra's has been in operation for many years and pulls in a regular crowd of customers who just go for that much needed massage or rasul cleanse. As its name suggests the decor is Egyptian themed, just like the mall that it sits within! And the size of the spa is huge with many treatments on offer. There's everything from Elemis treatments, but if holistic is your way, go for the yoga massage - and get your chakras opened and realigned. Price wise, a 1 hr European massage is 350 AED and a 45 min body scrub start at 265 AED. All treatments give access to spa facilities which include a wet area, jacuzzi and relaxing areas. Their Pharoah's Club pool is members only but free access is may be given during promotional offers and if a spa package is booked but please enquire first. Don't be put off by the fact that this is in the mall. Cleopatra's has been successful for many years, and for good reason.

Zaitoon Wellness Spa at the Arabian Courtyard Hotel

zaitoonspa.com

(04)508 7520

The massages are rated highly here, and if you don't mind being in simple and somewhat slightly dated surroundings, Zaitoon offer some excellent choices and value for money. A swedish massage starts at 220 AED for a 50 min treatment and their signature synchronised thermal massage with "4 hands" is 400 AED for 80 mins. These days Dubai is all about five star glamour, but only a handful of places are really worth the steep prices they charge. Zaitoon Spa regularly run promotions, so be sure to ask about these before you book.

Elche Natural Beauty Salon

elche.ae

(04) 349 4942

In the depths of Jumeirah next to Jumeirah Plaza exists the Elche Beauty Salon. It's one of those places that you hear of word of mouth and through reputation. Elche is of Hungarian reputation and bases all its products on natural ingredients making this place an organic haven. The place feels a little like a hospital at times, but the products smell and feel so natural, that you are on to a good thing. Go for a facial – they will consult with you to suggest the best ones. You won't regret it.

Hello Kitty Beauty Spa

hellokittybeautyspa.com

(04) 3449598

Based in Jumeirah, Hello Kitty is near Mercato Mall in Town Centre Jumeirah. Pitched for both big girls and little girls, it is a perfect treat for both mothers and daughters, girly girls - and those that need a pampering. Hello Kitty already exists in Dubai in Dubai Mall, but this is the place for those in the know who want to get pampered Hello Kitty stylee. With Hello Kitty branding all over the place, you expect the touches of velvet hot pink and frilly fabric lamp shades. The Beauty Spa offers a separate service menu for 'Queens' and 'Princesses', offering all organic nail and beauty products for young girls. An ingenious idea and, let's be honest, this is perfect for Dubai – a place for the girls to come while the dads play a round of golf.

MALE SPAS

Signature Lounge for Men

thesignaturelounge.com

(04) 434 2110

Media City, Tower A Ground Floor, Business Central Tower (near Subway)

Let's have some equality shall we? With a huge choice of ladies only and mixed spas in Dubai, a few men only spas are beginning to open due to increasing popularity for male grooming. And while this lounge doesn't have a full on pool or sauna, the Signature Lounge is one of those places men can head off to after work or whilst the other half is pampering herself. Unlike mixed spas, Signature Spa is decorated and kitted out in masculine colours and design and equipped with mod cons and facilities men just can't do without i.e. men's magazines, wifi, apple docs and more. They offer a range of men popular treatments such as massages, facials, haircuts, shave, mani and peds and even waxing! Who says men don't care about their appearances? Pricewise, they are pretty reasonable plus run regular promotions, a 60 min European massage at 260 AED, a 60 min body scrub is 300 AED and a basic mani and ped is 130 AED, although we recommend to go for the 'Sportsman' mani ped which includes exfoliation and paraffin treatment - ooh la la!

1847, The Grooming Company

thegroomingcompany.com

Ground Level Rimal Sector

(04) 437 0252

Another one for men only, this spa pulls out all the stops for the hardcore banker types. There are 4 locations including Emirates Towers, Mirdiff Mall and at the Grosvenor House Hotel. With locations like these, you know that the service is excellent. The one that comes most recommended is on the JBR walk. You can go all in for a 4 hands massage, but if that's not what you want, then indulge in a proper shave. It will be the closest shave you ever have. And if you want to spend a little more, combine that with a gentleman's facial. Every single groggy pore will be fully cleansed.

GOLF COURSES

If you haven't heard of the Dubai Desert Classic that takes place, you're probably not interested in golf! Taking place every year in November since 1989 as part of the European Tour, it put Dubai on the golfing map. Golf doesn't strike us as a particularly Arabian sport, but there are a fair number of fantastic courses here for the golf fanatic. The grass is remarkably green for many of the courses considering its location in the desert – but the investment in irrigation systems and luxurious clubhouses demonstrates the high-end nature of golf here. And you do pay, but boy oh boy do you get some great golf.

Many of the courses have been designed by big time golfers including Colin Montgomerie, Ernie Els, Nick Faldo & Greg Norman.

And there was Tiger Woods project which has been on and off since the downturn and then cancelled as part of the fallout from his infedility scandal.

We have recommended the best golf courses that Dubai offers. Please note that the Nad Al Sheba course is now closed. Make sure you book in advance, potentially before you arrive in Dubai if you are travelling during the peak months:

Emirates Golf Course

dubaigolf.com

Sheikh Zayed Road (Interchange 5), (04)4380 2222

The Majlis, as home for the Desert Classic, is probably one of the world's best courses and by far the best course in the Middle East. There are 18 holes at Par 72. Expect to pay AED 1000 with a shared buggy. The clubhouse design is based on Bedouin tents and has the 5 star restaurant, Le Classique. The Faldo course (entitled Wadi) at the same location, also at 18 holes and par 72 is also very good, with views of the Dubai skyline. Expect to pay AED 600 during the weekdays and prove a maximum handicap of 28.

The Montgomerie

themontgomerie.com

Emirates Hills, (04)4 390 4600

The Montgomerie is a long stay spectacular 18 hole, 72 par course, catering for all abilities. It's a difficult course with multiple water hazards and sloping greens. The 17th hole has a bunker the shape of the hand and the green of the 13th hole is shaped as the UAE map – all reflective of the imagination of Colin Montgomerie. For the die hards, you can stay at the Montgomerie boutique hotel at the clubhouse.

Al Badia

albadiagolfclub.ae

Dubai Festival City, (04) 4 701 1111

Another immaculate course with lots of water features and wide fairways, Al Badia used to be called the Four Seasons, but is now run by the Intercontinental DFC, nearby. Along with the Montgomerie and the Emirates Golf Course, Al Badia is one of the top tier courses in Dubai. Pay AED 600 for a par 72.

Arabian Ranches Golf Course

arabianranchesgolfdubai.com

Arabian Ranches, (04) 4 366 3000

Built as part of the expat property boom of the early noughties and designed by Ian Baker-Finch, you will see villas enclosing the perimeter as you make way through this 72 par – 18 hole course. No water hazards but lots of sand ones! Pay AED 555 during the week.

Dubai Creek Golf & Yacht Club

dubaigolf.com

nr Al Garhoud Bridge, (04) 4 295 6000

Part of the same stable owned by the government who also run the Emirates Golf Club, this is one of the older courses in Dubai. Redesigned in 2005, you'll notice its sail inspired club house as one of the iconic buildings of Dubai. Expect to pay AED 600 at the course voted as one of the top 100 must play golf courses in the world, and where the Desert Classic has been played previous to its home at the Emirates Gold Course.

Jebel Ali Golf Resort,

jaresortshotels.com

Jebel Ali, (04) 4 814 5555

You're unlikely to play this course unless you are staying at the resort, which is a great place for families (where the father is a golf fanatic). The course is only a 9 hole, but probably one of the best 9 holers you will play

Outside of Dubai, there are 3 courses worth checking out and all in Abu Dhabi. The Abu Dhabi Golf Course (adgolfclub.com) is where the Abu Dhabi championship is held and is superb. Equally, the Gary Player designed Saadiyat Beach Golf Club (sbgolfclub.ae) provides a phenomenal backdrop to another amazing course. For something a little bit different, try out the all sand course, Al Ghazal. (alghazalgolf.ae). Yes, the whole course is made of sand, which is not as crazy as you may think, bearing in mind what part of the world you are in.

RESTAURANTS IN DUBAI

In 25 years, Dubai has gone from living off the land to providing some of the most exquisite meals that you just wouldn't believe. The Dubai food scene has been on fire for many years now, but within the last 5 years, it has really been pushing the bar sky high, in true Burj Khalifa style! Dubai's culinary scene now sits with some of the best cities in the world. It's not just about getting your juicy shawarma on the street or your freshly baked manakish. You can get those – but what has really escalated Dubai into a food capital has been the high end hotels that all need exquisite restaurants to lure in both guests and punters. The best Dubai restaurants have set themselves up as exceptionally world class - and therein lies the story as to how these restaurants have taken that step. The best Michelin star chefs are being sponsored to outclass their competitors - competition to be the best restaurant in Dubai and in a city where there is no official Michelin rating, the competition is completely open. That's good for Dubai - but not good for Dubai's waistline!

Eating out Dubai style will invariably be an impressive experience from booking until you walk out of the door. And in the 5 star outlets you could quite easily forget that you are not in London, Paris or New York. Strict health and safety regulations ensure that food is of the highest quality and you will rarely hear of restaurants being shut down due to bad hygiene.

On the flip side, even the high end restaurants which serve fantastic meals can occasionally fall short on service. This is not true for the majority of Dubai establishments but because Dubai is a global tourist destination, staff are from abroad and are all a mixed bag of roots. Therefore if you are in an Italian restaurant and want to compare your gnocchi with a potential risotto before ordering, the waiter may not always have the best answer. We call that transaction servicing - no opinion, no inside knowledge – they are just there to serve you, take your order, and get your money. That's OK sometimes but not when you're paying a developing country worker's average monthly salary for your meal.

And while there are world class, high end expensive restaurants, at the other end of the scale, there are the basic, simple outlets selling shawarmas, the vegetarian curries and the idlis. There are places like Karachi Darbar where you can eat some of the best barbecued meat, but at prices that the taxi drivers can afford. We have concentrated on providing you with a best of the best restaurants list so that you know that you have chosen wisely. If you have a week in Dubai, and your budget allows, you should try and treat yourself to some of the upscale restaurants as they quite simply are out of this world. And if you don't like the sound of our top choice, we have provided some alternatives. Give some of the more reasonably priced restaurants a chance as well. Just because a restaurant isn't as expensive doesn't mean that it isn't great.

Lamb Manakish Streetfood

If you are not satisfied, don't tip, unless it's a requirement of the restaurant. Or better still, after your meal, give the Manager some constructive feedback. You never know, you may score complementary drinks or if you are at a hotel, you may be offered a discount at a sister establishment on site, especially if you are staying there!

In terms of tipping in restaurants, 10% is the expected amount. There are no rules or common practice, however. If service is exceptional, do give more, but check with your waiter that the staff will be receiving the money and not the restaurant or worse still the restaurant owner! Occasionally a Tourist and Service charge tax is applied to all restaurants that are classified as 'Tourist' establishments. These are normally most restaurants based within hotels. If that is the case – and the tax can be up to 20%, you should only give 5 or 10% for a tip. Some other establishments will place an automatic charge of 10% on your bill. If the service is bad, it's usually tricky to argue your way out of it. And if it is not tricky, it is certainly uncomfortable. Bear in mind that service staff in the UAE are normally from the Indian Subcontinent and the Philippines and whatever money they make, a big portion of it will be sent back home. By giving a big tip, you may actually be making their whole year.

If you are going to indulge in visiting a number of fine dining establishments over a period of a week or longer, it might make sense to purchase The Entertainer which is a book of discount vouchers giving you offers like buy one get on free. There are many offers, and don't just cover restaurants, but by just using it once you can save the amount spent on buying the book. (Dhs 295). The guide is a must purchase for all expats, and are available from most supermarkets. See theentertainerme.com for more detail. You may also get some of the vouchers being sold on ebay in your own country which is a cheaper way to get hold of the vouchers. The Entertainer have also launched an app, available from their site from which you can redeem vouchers for a week without spending the price of the book. Worth checking out just before you leave as it's usually time limited.

Please note that alcohol is usually available at all restaurants based within a hotel. Independent and street restaurants will normally NOT serve alcohol by law. We have clarified those restaurants that don't serve alcohol as 'unlicensed'.

Our best restaurants are split into price bands for your convenience and we have an additional category, the Grapeshisha Choice. This is our favourite all-rounder restaurant which ticks most boxes in terms of great quality food, ambience, service, family friendly and value for money. It's not necessarily the most expensive or the best perceived – but it's our favourite and we recommend it. Our high end recommendation is the very best that money can buy. There are obviously very many restaurants all over Dubai, but we have tried to curate the best ones for you into an "uber guide" of sorts.

We get asked about whether there are any vegetarian restaurants in Dubai. Apart from Govinda's near Regent's Palace Hotel in Bur Dubai makes a play on being vegan, there aren't many that sell themselves as vegetarian restaurants. There are, however, a heap of Indian restaurants, many of which are, of course, meat free. They offer great vegetarian food at a very cheap price. Also, the restaurants in Dubai do cater for vegetarians – so even at steak houses you will get a selection of non-meat options. It's not something one must worry about in Dubai if you are vegetarian. There are more than enough choices.

What we should also mention is that there are loads of fast food joints from all over the world. Whether you want your McDonald's or Hardees, KFC or Nandos, you can find it in Dubai. You can also probably find any chain restaurant in Dubai. From Waggamammas to Ping Pong to Chili's to TGI Friday's – they are all here. And you'll find some Middle Eastern chains such as Taza Chicken, Just Falafel and Zaatar w Zeit. You'll be spoilt for choice in the malls, which while unlicensed, exist as part of the mall overall entertainment package. As we have mentioned, the malls, especially Dubai Mall, are central to the lifestyle in Dubai.

We've grouped the cuisine types into High, Mid Range and Budget and to give you an idea of pricing, we've allocated dollar signs for a 3 course meal including a glass of wine where applicable for one person. For non – alcoholic drinkers, the cost will be less.

$$$$ Dirhams 400 +

$$$ Dirhams 250-400

$$ Dirhams 150-250

$ Dirhams 150 and below

All the restaurants we've listed below have our thumbs up and should give you ample choice given your location. One final thing, Gordon Ramsay's Verre has closed down, so don't bother trying to book there. It's a shame – it was a great restaurant – but he was never there. That's no matter – as you will see, there are literally thousands of restaurants to choose from. You will be spoilt for choice. Bon appetit!

JAPANESE

High End

Nobu $$$$

The Atlantis, 04 426 2626

Nobu is world renowned. The upscale, fine dining venue which has branches worldwide including New York and London has parked itself a spot at the one of the flashiest hotels in Dubai – The Atlantis. The restaurant has been opened since launch but pulls in mixed reviews. We thoroughly enjoyed the food. Everyone will tell you about the melt in the mouth black cod in miso, which you probably won't experience anywhere else. The sashimi options are huge, and the yellow tail tuna is a big thumbs up. Be warned though, this is a boutique fare and portions are, in general, on the small side. The flip side is that everything you order will be top notch. You might want to also consider the lounge food menu which has a select few options all around the 50 AED mark but they don't, however, do the black cod. For that you must dine in the restaurant. On the negatives, children under the age of 10 cannot dine in the restaurant. Surprisingly, service is sometimes a little cold, but that said, Nobu is always full.

Also Try:

For the best sushi in Dubai: **Armani/Hashi** at the Armani Hotel, Burj Khalifa on 04 888 3444

For Glamming it up, Japanese style: **Okku** at the H-Hotel, SZR, 04 501 8888

Mid Range:

Tokyo@ The Towers $$$-$$$$

Shopping Boulevard, Jumeirah Emirates Towers, Sheikh Zayed Road, Dubai, 04 319 8088

If you are want to impress friends and family with a theatrical performance, Tokyo @ The Towers will leave you wowed with an entirely 'hands on' experience. They have a sushi bar, but the Teppanyaki tables are our favourite, where you can experience live cooking from your own personal chef. The whole show is an entertaining act, performed with such elegance. You can choose from a selection of three set menus. The interior is chic and there are several private Tatami rooms, perfect for families and business lunches.

Also Try:

For quality traditional Japanese: **Benkay** at Hotel JAL Tower, Sheikh Zayed Road, 04 3080000

For the Meydan Experience: **Shiba** at the Meydan, Nad Al Sheba, 04 381 3111

Where the Japanese eat their Japanese: **Kisaku** at Al Khaleej Palace, Deira, 04 223 1000

Trendy Location, trendy food: **Sho Cho**, at Dubai Marine Resort 04 346 1111

Authentic, chic & good for business: **Kiku**, Le Meridien Dubai, 04 286 8949

Budget:

Umi Sushi $$

Jumeirah Beach Residence, Dubai, 04 437 0208

With so many glitzy Japanese restaurants opening all over Dubai now focusing on plush interiors and on which A-List celebrity had been dining there the previous night, the real essence of sashimi and tempura has been lost. Agreed, experiencing a lavish night out amongst good food and fabulous interiors leaves you feeling content albeit short changed, but true Japanese food fanatics really do like to sample sushi for what it is and without having to preen in the salon beforehand. Umi Sushi is just that - simple sushi but good quality ingredients and good service. If you are starving and need a 'carb' kick their noodles and tempuras are scrumptious. But if you crave a good sushi platter, you can order like a king and not feel guilty about your wallet.

Also Try:

For underrated excellence: **Bonsai** at Habtoor Grand Resort & Spa, Dubai Marina 04 399 5000

Quality buffet style sushi & noodles: **Toshi** at the Grand Millennium Al Barsha 04 429 9999

Grapeshisha Choice:

Zuma $$$$

Dubai International Financial Centre (DIFC)

Cuisine: Japanese

Since opening late 2008, Zuma still maintains to create a buzz and leave potential hungry customers waiting for an evening reservation for days and even weeks at this funky large eatery. Located at the DIFC, you would think the evenings would generally be quiet - but not at Zuma. The lunch time deals are pretty good and actually work out cheaper then its sister locations in Hong Kong and London. However dinner costs are steep. But if you want fresh flavoursome sushi and their brilliant signature dishes coupled with amazing atmosphere and super interior, you may decide to throw your hands up and surrender. When booking, ask to be sat downstairs as we found the upper lounge floor to become nosier throughout the evening. It's best to head up there for drinks after dinner. Overall, a sure winner for a special occasion and if it's a thumbs up for Sheikh Mohamed bin Rashid Al Maktoum – it must be good! This is the best Japanese restaurant in Dubai, perhaps one of the best overall restaurants in Dubai, and one of the best bar venues. Make sure you book.

THAI

High End:

Pai Thai $$$

Al Qasr Hotel, Madinat Jumeirah, 04 366 6730

Set in the scenic grounds of the colossal Madinat Jumeirah Resort, Pai Thai is the perfect setting for a romantic meal for two or a cosy get together with friends. Its ideal sitting outside when the weather is just right (i.e. October – May) and you can spot all the abras making their way round the resort. If you love Thai food, you will be blown away by the food here. The meats melt in your mouth and the flavours are full of depth. We love the prawn curry and chicken satays. Portions are generous so you don't need to over order if you are a couple. Service is good but lacks a bit when the restaurant is full on the weekends. We didn't mind as this is a place to while away your time. To finish off the evening, unwind with a drink and watch the entertaining Thai dancers strut their stuff.

Also try

For funky Thai: **Mango Tree**, Souk al Bahar, Downtown 04 426 7313

The trendiest Thai in Dubai: **Buddha Bar**, Grosvenor House Dubai Marina, 04399 8888 – and then chill at **Siddhartha Lounge** afterwards 04 9176 000

(Vietnamese) You only need one Vietnamese in Dubai with this quality: **Hoi An**, Shangri-La Hotel, Sheikh Zayed Road, 04 405 2703

Mid Range:

Benjarong $$-$$$

Dusit Thani Hotel, Sheikh Zayed Road, 04 343 3333

Located in the famous branded Thai hotel, Dusit, Benjarong has an example to set and it does well. Of course, it has to be good! The interior is themed as authentic Thai, so it's all about carved dark wood furniture. Service is helpful but not overpowering and the staff are happy to recommend the popular dishes. The curries come highly recommended and we recommend the Thai Red Curry with Duck and the Maine Lobster. Portions are generous.

Also try:

For views of the Dubai Fountain: **Thiptara**, The Palace, Downtown, 04 428 7888

Amazing décor: **Blue Elephant**, Al Bustan Rotana 04 282 0000

Budget:

Lemongrass $-$$, Unlicensed

Oud Mehta (Near Lamcy Plaza) Dubai, 04 334 2325

A combination of good food, great interiors and friendly staff makes this place a favourite of Grapeshisha. When we think Thai curry craving, this is the place to come and you do not have to pay sky high prices. Lemongrass is always busy so make sure you book - especially at the weekend. The menu incorporates all of the classic Thai favourites and more with a good selection of seafood offerings too. The Penang Curry is our secret favourite! Lemongrass also has several branches in the malls known as Lemongrass Express at the Ibn Battuta Mall, Dubai Mall and Mirdif City Centre.

Also try:

For Thai/Chinese fusion in a 'rainforest' setting: **Thainese**, Ramada Continental Hotel, 04 266 2666

For Hearty homely portions: **Royal Orchid**, Marina Walk, Dubai Marina, 04 367 4040

Cheap amazing food hidden amongst Jumeirah Villas: **Smiling BKK**, near the Jumeirah Post Office, 04 349 6677

Grapeshisha choice:

Thai Kitchen $$$

Park Hyatt Dubai, 04 317 2222

Going to an older part of town, such as Deira, for dinner might now seem odd to many, but only a few years ago Deira and Bur Dubai were the downtown top areas to visit before the Palm, the Marina and DIFC came on the scene. We love the Park Hyatt, with its beautiful views of the creek and yachts, and at the same time being in the centre of Dubai's real hustle and bustle. We guarantee you that the Thai Kitchen will quell any Thai food craving – but it will also not burn a hole in your wallet. Sit indoors and admire the entertaining chefs put on a show at one of their numerous cooking stands or enjoy the peaceful creek outside. A secret tip: ask to try their mini dishes so you can sample a wider breadth of this amazing menu.

ITALIAN

High End:

Segreto $$$$

Madinat Jumeirah, Al Soufouh Road, 04 366 6125

If you want to mark a special occasion with fine dining, Segreto comes highly recommended. Firstly, the Madinat Jumeirah never ceases to please. This place oozes romantic luxury from every corner. Segreto is just the place to impress a significant other or a potential one. The restaurant is designed so that tables appear private split by lattice type dividers which look glam but are not overstated. Sit outside for pure decadence and end your night at the rooftop Centimetro Lounge for a nightcap.

Also try

Real Italian sophistication and serenity: **Armani/Ristorante**, Armani Hotel, Burk Khalifa, 04 888 3444

The most ostentatious restaurant in Dubai: **The Cavalli Club**, Fairmont Dubai, SZR, 04 3329260

Marco Pierre White at his best: **Frankie's Italian Bar and Grill**, Oasis Beach Tower, JBR, Dubai Marina, 04 399 4311

Atlantis Legend: **Ronda Locatelli**, Atlantis, Palm Jumeirah, 04 426 2626

Mid Range:

BiCE $$$

Hilton Dubai Jumeirah, 04 399 1111

Italian cuisine has to be one of the most frequented restaurant types in Dubai with a wealth of restaurants to choose from. You will find a few that score highly in great outdoor views and in food but BiCE is the place to be if you are a real Italian foodie. The interior is clean cut and sophisticated, service is super and food is fantastic. The pastas will probably be one of the best you'll ever eat and their beef and lobster carpaccios are divine. You can't go wrong with BiCE.

Also Try:

Media City Munchies: **Certo**, Radisson Blu Dubai Media City 04 366 9111

Best pizzas in Dubai: **Bussola**, Westin Dubai, Mina Seyahi, 04 399 4141

Seafood Special Italian: **Ossigeno**, Le Royal Meridien Beach Resort & Spa, Dubai Marina, 04 399 5555

Budget:

Da Vinci's $$

Millennium Airport Hotel Dubai, Al Garhoud, 04 702 8888

Da Vinci's is authentic Italian comfort food with genuinely good service. If you happen to be in the Deira area and need an Italian boost, go here. You will certainly feel comfortable here and families with kids are welcomed. The soups are lovely - try the Porcini Mushroom. For mains, a selection of favourites is on the menu including steaks and escallops. In addition to the comfort food, the best thing about Da Vinci's is their great service and value for money.

Also Try:

The happiest restaurant in Dubai: **Cucina**, JW Marriott, 04 6977977

Favourite, chilled out Pizza joint: **Marzano**, Downtown, Burj Khalifa 04 420 1136

Canal side, pizzeria: **Toscano**, Madinat Jumeirah, 04 366 6730

Grapeshisha Choice:

Jamie's Italian $$-$$$

Marina Pavilion, Festival City, 04 232 9969

With so many Italian eateries to pick as an alternative, we're opting for Jamie's as our favourite Italian. Ok, so Mr Oliver may not be a born and bred Italian, but he is one talented chef and is starting to dominate this cuisine with his modern day take on it. With numerous branches already opened in the UK, the concept is fast becoming popular as a casual yet classy dining experience. Booking is not generally required unless you go in a large group. This may not be the ideal place to 'pop the question', but there are so many of 'those' kind of eateries that we wanted to share with you something different and quirky. Foodwise, this is no nonsense hearty Italian grub. The portions are great and ingredients do taste authentic and earthy. You can opt for pastas such as the meatball or arrabiata or try the salmon steak or roast beef. The choice is varied but keeps to an Italian concept albeit straying off 'Jamie style'.

Service is great but beware of 'Jamieland' in every corner of the restaurant. If you hate him, stay away!

INDIAN/PAKISTANI

High End:

Indego by Vineet $$$$

Grosvenor House Dubai, 04 399 8888

Indego is not your typical curry house. There is nothing standard about this restaurant and we think you'll agree with us when you first step into the opulent Grosvenor House. Seating style is intimate and service impeccable. The food is based on traditional Indian flavours but with a modern twist. That doesn't mean to say the spice levels are reduced to cater for western palates, you just won't find your typical chicken madras or jalfrezi here but a host of different ingredients such as salmon and monkfish. For starters we highly recommend the crab trio. Indego is pricey, but for a spicy, romantic evening to remember, you won't regret it.

Also try

Asha Bhosle inspired food – sweet like the voice: **Asha's**, Wafi City Mall, 04 324 0000

The prettiest Indian food ever produced: **Armani / Amal**, Armani Hotel 04 888 3444

Rang Mahal is pushing to be the best: **Rang Mahal**, the Marriott Marquis 04 414 3000

Mid Range:

Amala $$$

Jumeirah Zabeel Saray, The Palm Jumeirah, Crescent Road (West), 04 453 0444

Ever been to an Indian restaurant and been totally bowled over by such a huge selection of tasty dishes that you just can't make your mind up? Well, Amala could be the answer to your ordering dilemmas. At Amala, you pay one fixed price per person and can order unlimited dishes from the a la carte menu, cooked from scratch with fresh ingredients. Dishes are perfectly portioned so as not to fill up the belly too fast. The decor is themed at Regal India but does have a subtle modern feel with its furnishings. The location is set in the luxurious Zabeel Saray Hotel on the Palm Jumeirah, an elegant and more quiet hotel to its competitor - The Atlantis. Don't let the distance of this hotel put you off, Amala is well worth the trip. Dinner only from 7pm

25 Degrees North $$

DAMAC Executive Heights Tower, TECOM, Al Barsha, 04 452 7779

It's surprising to get such a good restaurant in Al Barsha, and it is much needed. However, there's no surprise that this is one of the most popular delivery joints for the area - because the Indian food is tasty and upmarket but doesn't put you in recession mode. 25 Degrees is the new kid on the block, set up in 2013, and it's quietly setting up a reputation for itself. The restaurant is always busy - and that's a good sign. News travels fast in Dubai - so it's no wonder. There are the regular favourites on offer, but 25 Degrees North has a very nice Tangdi Wajid Ali (chicken legs marinated in spices). The fried mutton (Galawati Kebab) is something worth experiencing before you dig into your mains. Our favourite is teh Nalli Roganjosh, but for those of you with tamer taste buds will be pleased with one of the best butter chicken's in Dubai (Ask for Murg Makhani. The Shahi Tukda is originally a Pakisani dish made from bread and milk and sprinkled with nuts and is a tasty desert. Our favourite is the Awadi Kheer - comfort rice pudding. You will love it, and you will love this elegant restaurant - it is authentic and cooked with pride. The meat is fresh - and there's choices for the masses as well as dishes from back home, that bring memories of chilhood to the elder subcontinent expats. The restaurant is open planned and it's good that you can see the chefs cooking away at your meal. You may even be tempted to an extra dum biriyani. Taste buds and waist lines beware! Worth going for the business lunch is you are in the area.

Dakshin $$

Lotus Hotel, Deira Dubai, 04 227 8888

With so many curry houses occupying the Dubai scene, if all you crave is a great selection of food, good surroundings but can't pay five star prices, head to Dakshin.   It is not a dry restaurant, like many other Indian restaurants and has live entertainment on most evenings. The menu is based on mainly south Indian cuisine. Favourites are the Masala Dosa, Egg Masala Uppam and for non-vegetarian fans, their Chicken Tikka Masala is yum.

Also try

Amazing North Indian in Bur Dubai: **Aangam**, Dhow Palace Hotel, Bur Dubai, 04 4530444

Moghul style curry: **Handi**, Taj Palace Hotel, 04 2232222

For those that know Zee TVs Sanjeev Kapoor: **Khazana**, Al Nasr Leisureland, Oud Metha, 04 336 0061

Budget:

Rangoli $ (Vegetarian, Unlicensed)

Meena Bazaar, Bur Dubai, 04 351 5873

Rangolis is legendary in Meena Bazaar. It is renowned for its friendly service, fantastic 'Pani Puris' and superb value for money. If you are a tourist in Dubai, one of your stops on the itinerary has to include Mina Bazaar, the Little India of Dubai where you can get great fabrics and ready made indian suits and sarees. It's worth a wander and when you get tired and hungry, Rangoli is where you go for some very special South Asian Venegetarian. Their fresh puris, parathas, samosas and masala dosas (huge rice pancakes filled with a dry potato curry) are awesome. As a guide, four people can eat very well for 80 AED.

Delhi Darbar $ (Unlicensed)

Karama, Zabeel Road (opposite Karama post office), 04 334 7171

Deira, Sabkha Street (Nr Gold Souk), 04 235 6161

Budget quality restaurants don't get any better then this. Dubai is full of budget Indian restaurants, but it doesn't get much better than Delhi Derbar. Delhi Darbar offers good north Indian cuisine with an array of variety at the price of a shoe string. Delhi Darbar has become so popular it has now opened two more outlets in addition to the first Karama restaurant. We recommend starting off with some bihari kebabs and for mains you won't be disappointed with the classic butter chicken and palaak paneer all washed down with fluffy naans and pilau rice. The array of dhaal dishes are great too. Try whatever pleases you as you won't find prices like this back home – unless, of course you are from the Indian Subcontinent!

Also Try

World's Best Shish kebab & Biriyani : **Karachi Darbar**, Karama , 04 334 7272

Best Dubai Butter Chicken?: **Ravi Restaurant**, Satwa, 04 331 5353

The taxi driver's secret pay day restaurant: **Sind Panjab**, 04 337 5535

Best tasting buffet: **Al Ibrahimi Palace Restaurant**, 04 397 7070

South Indian Idli Specials: **Saravan Bhavan**, Karama, 04 334 5252

Double dose of Dosas, **Bombay Chowpatty**, Karama, 04 396 4937

Largest vegetarian choice in Dubai: **Kamat**, Kuwait Street Bur Dubai, 04 359 5441

Grapeshisha Choice:

Ashiana $$-$$$

Sheraton Dubai Creek Hotel and Towers, 04 207 1733

Ashiana is our favourite Indian restaurant in the UAE. This curry house has been around for years and has well established itself as Dubai's top place for fine Indian cuisine. Here, everything ticks the boxes from authentic Indian ambience, staff who are knowledgeable in the food they serve and their style of service not forgetting the delicious food. This restaurant is not one of those swanky, designer type restaurants who like to entice their clients with shimmering interiors rather then the food firsthand, but despite it's authentic and traditional feel the interior is welcoming and intriguing. The kebabs are succulent and the highly rated murg ashiana is super. A great selection of vegetarian options is an offer. Service is good and unobtrusive, unlike the live entertainment which can be fun and interesting.

CHINESE

High End:

Hukama $$$$

The Address, Downtown Dubai, 04 436 8888

Hukuma is probably the best dressed up Chinese eatery you'll find. This is not the typical black lacquered walls Chinese restaurant. Instead you'll be wowed at the sleek interiors and minimalist colours of this sophisticated restaurant which promises to give authentic Chinese flavours with a modern twist. Dishes don't taste heavily laden with soya sauce and rich tangy flavours you normally find in a Chinese takeaway. Instead you'll actually taste all the ingredients for what they truly are along with a rich layering of the key Chinese flavours. Go for the dim sum value lunch - it's the best tasting yum cha you'll ever have. The only negatives we found were the lack of knowledge by a few of the waiting staff.

Zheng He's $$$$

Mina A'Salam, Madinat Jumeirah, 04 366 6730

If you are after a quiet, romantic meal with a significant other, Zheng He's is bound to impress. Not the greatest venue for a loud bunch of friends but for couples and families, this place is picturesque. If you are visiting in the cooler months, reserve your table for outside Mina A'Salaam is a beautiful location and this restaurant boasts stunning views of the iconic Burj Al Arab. We found the interior of the restaurant to look a little dark and moody, but the food will soon lift spirits. The Jiaozi dim sum comes highly recommended, as does the juicy Peking Duck. If you love your duck in pancakes, ask them to assist in the rolling - they do such a neat job! Don't expect massive portions here – the emphasis at Zheng He's is quality and detail rather then quantity – the food is stylish, so if you are booking for a special occasion, you won't be complaining!

Also Try:

For the best in Cantonese: **Shang Palace**, Shangri-La Hotel , SZR, 04 405 2703

For high end Chinese Cuisine: **Noble House**, Raffles Dubai, 04 314 9888

Dim Sum Platter mania: **Hakkasan**, Jumeirah Emirates Towers, 04 3948 484

Mid Range:

The China Club $$-$$$

Radisson Blu Hotel, Dubai Deira Creek, 04 205 7333

The China Club is a great family friendly Chinese restaurant with delicious food, service with a smile and fairly priced by Dubai standards. The interiors are classy, but not over the top to make you feel uncomfortable in your jeans. This place is down to earth and everything here is about the food. Various dining options are available whether you want to go a la carte or set menu. By far the best value for money deal is the Yum Chai Daily Feast that runs during lunchtime and includes dim sum, noodles and a selection of rice and main course for 100 AED. The deal is half price for under 10 yrs and free for under 5s. If going for dinner we recommend the Peking duck shredded and served with pancakes and greens and their steamed black cod is divine. Yes, we love black cod!

Also Try:

For bankable high end Chinese: **Royal China**, DIFC on 04 254 5543

For duck and dim sum lovers: **Duck King** at the Beach Park Plaza, 04 342 8041

For black cod dim sum and other amazing delicacies: **The China Club**, Radisson Blu, Dubai Creek, 04 205 7333

Budget:

Noodle Bowl $-$$ (Unlicensed)

Al Diyafah Street, Satwa Dubai (Nr Dune Centre), 04 345 3381

A bright and quirky interior welcomes you as you enter Noodle Bowl. It may not be in the stylish of locations but you do get no nonsense good food at very reasonable prices. The food is a mix of Malaysian and Cantonese cuisine and the menu vast. The Tom Yum soup comes highly recommended and we liked the Ginger Chicken and Barbecued Duck dishes. Noodles are their signature trade so make sure you order some. This place is such good value for money, you can afford to try many dishes.

Also Try:

For a quick tasty meal: **Summer Palace**, Metropolitan Hotel, SZR, 04 3430000

Cheap, cheerful, great food and bad service: **Chin Chin**, Bur Dubai, 04 3983588

Dim Sum on a Discount: **Da Shi Dai**, JBR, Dubai Marina, 04 426 4636

Grapeshisha Choice:

China Sea $$ (Unlicensed)

Al Maktoum Street, Deira, 04 295 9816

Dubai is filled with many stylish restaurants which serve amazing food in stunning venues. China Sea is different. Sometimes all you want is a place that you can just turn up in your trainers, not having made a reservation and be greeted with a friendly smile and a table. China Sea is the place where you'll be satisfied with classic, authentic, comfort dishes. The decor is on the tacky side, but if you wanted plush, look at our High End recommendations! The food at China Sea is tasty, presented well, easy on the oil and always served at the right temperature. There is a huge choice of fish dishes including crab and lobster at such great value, their duck in pancakes are good and they pride themselves on their home cooked noodles. Strangely, there is a karaoke machine – which adds to our love of this odd ball place. Head here for a no frills night - you will leave smiling!

ARABIC

High End:

Al Nafoorah $$$-$$$$

Emirates Towers, Sheikh Zayed Road Dubai, 04 319 8088

Most Lebanese restaurants can be a lively affair with music, live dancing and a jolly crowd. Al Nafoorah is perfect if you like Lebanese cuisine and quiet, intimate surroundings. Located in the Emirates Towers, it can be regarded as a formal place usually frequented by lunch time and after work office workers. But its central location means it's easily accessible and the terraced alfresco seating gives it a casual but romantic vibe. The food is great with a good selection of tasty mezzes and grilled mains. For a lighter starter, try some spinach fattayers (savoury pastries).

Levantine $$$

Atlantis, The Palm Dubai, 04 426 2626

Levantine presents itself as a great opportunity to visit the Atlantis Hotel at a restaurant that, although high end, is not too extortionately priced compared to its neighbours. The menu is simple and plays on the classic mezze dishes (hot and cold) along with grilled meats and fish and fresh bread. It's the perfect place to unwind with a light dinner plus drinks and shisha overlooking the stunning views of the Atlantis so opt to sit outside if weather permits. Take note, weekends will get busy so be prepared to wave aggressively to your waiter for shisha and drinks – or shout!

Also try:

For a great lunch mezze buffet: **Café Arabesque**, Park Hyatt Dubai, Deira, Al Garhoud Road, 4 317 2222

The best Moroccan restaurant in Dubai: **Tagine**, One & Only Royal Mirage, 04 399 9999

One of Dubai's coolest Arabic restaurants and Arabic fusion at its best: **Qbara**, The Fort Complex, Wafi City, 04 7092 500

Mid Range:

Sarai $$

Dubai Marina, Jumeirah Beach Residence, 04 438 0640

You can't come to Dubai and not eat Middle Eastern food at least once. Finding a Arabic food outlet will not be hard in Dubai, as the city is littered with various options. In fact, separating the standard from the best will be the tough job. There are many good Middle Eastern restaurants situated in Dubai's finer hotels, but we found that with the majority of these, the atmosphere, interior and views normally scored higher than the food itself – not so with Sarai. The service here is homely and the waiters give honest advice based on your tastes. The interior is authentic and clean but not tacky and young families genuinely feel welcomed which is now hard to find in many five star hotel restaurants. Food is not short of delicious. Kebabs appear to be their signature trade with many variations on offer – ours arrived tender and juicy. There are many mezze dishes on offer and complementary fresh bread to keep you full for hours. Easy going, simple choices are available for kids. Just beware if you have a nut allergy as many dishes are topped with nuts.

Khan Murjan $$-$$$

Khan Murjan Souk, Wafi Mall, 04 327 9795

For buzzing atmosphere, this place will really make you feel like you're in a Middle Eastern city. Primarily, the theme of Khan Murjan is Moroccan but this ground level souk style eatery serves up a range of Middle Eastern dishes as well as different specialities during the week. The grilled meats are tender and vine leaves are the best we've tried. This place may be a bit pricier then your average Lebanese eatery, but portions are good and the atmosphere as surprisingly authentic given that this is within a faux souk within a mall. Sit back and be charmed by the musicians and after your meal, work off the belly, by taking a stroll through the souk and their many hidden stalls of secret delights.

Also try:

For Authentic Emirati Food: **Al Fanar**, Dubai Festival City Canal Walk, 04 2329233

For a set menu feast: **Al Qasr Restaurant**, Dubai Marine Hotel, Jumeirah Beach Road, 04 3461111

For tourist style ambience: **Bastakiya Nights**, Bur Dubai, Bastakiya, near the Ruler's Court, 04 353 7772

For beachside Arabic fun under a tent: **Al Khaima**, Le Royal Meridien Beach Resort and Spa, Dubai Marina, 04 399 5555

For great, fresh mezze and shisha: **Reem Al Badawi**, Jumeirah Beach Road, 04 3947444

Moroccan Berber Variety: **Almaz by Momo**, Mall of the Emirates, Barsha, Dubai, 04 409 8877

Budget:

Al Hallab $-$$

Dubai Mall, 04 330 8828

Cuisine: Lebanese

If you're visiting Dubai Mall and fancy some reasonably priced Middle Eastern food head to Al Hallab. Al Hallab offers hearty Lebanese fare which really hits the spot. If you are not overly hungry but want to sit outside and admire the glamorous views of the Musical Fountain and Burj Khalifa, then just order a mix of mezzes. Highly recommended are their fattayers and baba ganoush and for mains their minced lamb kebabs.

Also try:

For your chance to have a camel burger (yes you read that right): **Local House**, Al Fahidi Road, Bastakiya, 04 354 0705

For quality, chain equivalent Arabic food: **Automatic**, Sheikh Zayed Road (and all over Dubai), 04 321 4465

For mixed grill and shisha on the creek: **Kan Zaman**, Shindhaga Heritage Village, Port Rashid, 04 393 9913

For the best Manakish: **Zaatar W Zeit**, Sheikh Zayed (the original and best) near Shangri-La hotel 04 343 1259

For lunch on the creek: **Bait Al Wakheel**, on the creek behind the textile souk, Bur Dubai 04 353 0530

For a tasty shawarma on Sheikh Zayed Road: **Saj Express**, Sheikh Zayed Road, Oasis Tower, next to 21st Century Tower 0 4 321 1191

Gourmet Shawarma: **Wild Peeta**, World Trade Centre Plaza, 055 8957672

Grapeshisha Choice:

Wafi Gourmet $$-$$$

Dubai Mall, 04 330 8297

We love Wafi Gourmet for many reasons, but the main reason is the food. It is amazing. Every single dish is top notch. And they also have amazing sweets and baklava, nougat, dates, nuts and olives to take away – so make sure you do. These assortments make excellent gifts to take back home for your family. But in addition, if you are able to get your seat outside, you are in the prime position to watch the musical fountain – which makes for a perfect evening. You won't regret it. Pitch your arrival pre disk to get a perfect view. You will go the Dubai Mall, and you will spend longer than you think – so you might as well finish off your day trip at Wafi Gourmet.

IRANIAN / PERSIAN

High End

Shabestan $$-$$$

Radisson Blu Hotel, Dubai Deira Creek, 04 222 7171

You're unlikely to be going for a special cultural visit to Iran in the next few years, but that doesn't mean you can't go whole hog on the food. Shabestan is an Iranian restaurant serving Persian cuisine which traditionally consists of juicy kebabs, hot pots such as lamb shanks and grilled meats and fish. All the food here is superb, but beware not to fill up on the complimentary starters of hummous, bread and salad. The lamb shank (baghalah polo ba mahicheh), which has been cooked for 4 hours, is fit for a (Persian) king. Although classed as high end, Shabestan is very good value for the amount that you pay. Ask for a window seat and admire the beautiful creekside views. Shabestan is renowned as being the best Iranian restaurant in Dubai....it certainly satisfies the belly. Wonderful. If you don't want to experience the traditional band, then go on a Saturday, but they actually give some heart to the place.

Also Try:

For a romantic setting among the canals: **Anar**, Madinat Jumeirah,

Mid Range

Shahrzad $$-$$$

Hyatt Regency Deira, 04 209 6707

If many think that Shabestan is the best Iranian in Dubai, many others will plump for Sharzad. It feels a little more authentic inside, with intricate woodwork and carved ceilings. The food is tasty with lots of stews – and you get a belly dancer thrown in to turn this into a stereotypical Hollywood film scene with booming tunes. But don't let that knock the food – the lamb and chicken stews are very tasty and recommended. Have the kashk badjeman (aubergine) to start and the khoresht-e-bamieh (lamb stew) for mains. The makhloot (vermicelli with rose water, ice cream and black berries) is to die for.

Also Try:

For authentic food in a modern, setting: **Persia Persia**, Wafi City, 04 324 4100

Budget

Iranian Club $$

Oud Metha Road, 04 336 7700

The Iranian Club make you wear a headscarf (provided) if you don't have your own. So you know this is going to be a traditional restaurant when you step in. And that's exactly what you get – home cooked food – and lots of it. Definitely worth visiting if you are in the hood and you can don't have a booze problem (no booze allowed) You certainly don't come here for the atmosphere, but apparently this is as Iranian as it gets.

Also Try:

Chain style Iranian Meat Heaven: **Pars Iranian Kitchen** (multiple branches), Satwa roundabout near Rydges Plaza, 04 398 4000

Cheap Food with your (grape)shisha: **Golestan**, Airport Road, Garhoud (near Fuddrukkers), 04 2828007

(Iraqi) Massive Fish barbecued Iraqi style for your pleasure, **Al Bait Al Baghdadi**, Al Muteena Street, Deira, 04 273 7064

(Afghab) Lashings of meat and rice: **Afghan Kebab House (Al Kebab Al Afghani)**, Naif Mosque, near Deira Street, Deira, 04 222

3292.

Grapeshisha Choice

Special Ostadi, $

Bur Dubai, Al Mussalla Road, 04 3971933

The are many reasons why this is not just called Ostadi: They have hundred of different currencies laminated around the restaurant; there are some random baseball caps pinned to the wall; there are original 1985 mobile phones framed on the wall; Muhammad, the owner is like the Iranian Godfather. But what makes this place special is the meat. Meat meat meat. The lamb kebabs just keep on coming. And that's all everyone wants. Or maybe some mutton. Vegtarians stay away.

EUROPEAN CUISINE

High End:

Reflets Par Pierre Gagnaire $$$$

Intercontinental Dubai Festival City, 04 701 1111

If you have about 1000 AED per person to splash out on dinner, then this has to be 'the' place for 'that' special meal, and you won't be disappointed as this restaurant has proved itself by winning numerous awards. Service at this fine dining restaurant is impeccable and it appears as though all the staff love being there and know their job spec inside out. Food is brilliant and presented elegantly, although if you are an environmentalist you may be disappointed to learn about the extensive food miles used everyday just to get the right quality ingredients. Portions are on the generous side and they like to give complementary extras for you to taste. A more affordable option is the 3 course week day business lunch menu for 180 AED. Children under the age of 8 yrs are not allowed entry and booking in advance is required especially for weekend slots (when open).

The Ivy $$$$

The Boulevard, Emirates Towers, 04 319 8767

The Ivy comes with significant pedigree, based on its London restaurant – and the Dubai version is on a par. Well, if you are looking for the world's best shepherd's pie, it's here. Although still relatively new, this is the ticket in town for high end food. The oak panelling give the restaurant an old school feel – although it does feel a little like a men's club. That said, the food is amazing – and if you don't get to try the Ivy in London, this lifetime, Dubai is your only hope.

Also try:

For swanky French: **Margaux**, Souk Al Bahar, Downtown Dubai, Burj Khalifa, 04 439 7555

The highest restaurant in the world: **At.mosphere**, Armani Hotel, Burj Khalifa. 04 888 3828

Amazing ambience at **La Serre**, Mohamed bin Rashid Boulevard, Downtown Dubai. 04 4286888

Some say the best, we say probably one of the best meals you'll ever eat: **Rhodes Mezzanine**, Grosvenor House Hotel, Dubai Marina, 04 399 8888

Mid Range:

Bateaux Dubai $$$

Bur Dubai, 04 399 4994

Cuisine: International

This is a must for tourists and especially first timers to Dubai. The Bateux will cruise you along the enchanting old Dubai landmarks in 2 and half hours and serve you up a fantastic 4 course meal on board an air-conditioned, glass luxury dhow. Some of the landmarks you'll see are the Twin Towers, Gold Souk, Dubai Museum and lots more. Food is delicious, although a bit limited on choice, but don't let this put you off as what is on offer is all brilliantly done. Save some room for the chocolate fondant. Evening meals board at 1945 and Friday Brunches start at 1230.

The only negative is that Bateaux do not accept children under the age of five for the evening meals or the Friday Brunch. Book as soon as you can if you want to dine there during your stay.

Rive Gauche $$$

The Address, Dubai Marina, 04 436 7777

Set in the stylish The Address Hotel near Dubai Mall, Rive Gauche is The Address' signature restaurant serving elegant French cuisine. The restaurant itself is large but sectioned out to offer seating in different areas as well as outside over looking the water. The menu is not exhaustive yet has enough variety to leave you with options such as traditional French offerings like steak and frites and mussels in garlic sauce. We have to make a mention on the wonderful sides here - the mashed potatoes are heavenly. Portions are good and not over the top to let you enjoy a perfect 3 course meal, leading us on to dessert - try the yummy passion fruit mousse with buttery pastry and vanilla ice cream. A perfect evening without overly blowing your holiday wallet, you can enjoy a three course meal for two for under 650 AED.

Also try:

For hospitality and authentic German food: **Hofbrauhaus**, JW Marriott, Deira, 04 607 7977

For great value French cooking: **Le Classique**, Emirates Golf Club, Dubai Marina, 04 417 9999

Barjeel – if Creek eating is your thing, and Bateaux is out of your range, then try Blue Barjeel – you get no frills, good quality inexpensive food, 04 353 2200

Budget:

Teatro $$-$$$

Towers Rotana, 04 312 2202

It's great that among the giant five star restaurants that charge an arm and a leg for ambience and interior, there are some restaurants that still offer the same great quality and choice of food within a relaxed and charming environment but don't break the bank. Teatro is one of those friendly venues, that's perfect for a couple, family or business dinner. Choose to sit window side to enjoy Dubai skyline views. Opt for their great value set menus or choose the early bird deal which gives you 50% off your bill. Food is a mixed array of European and Asian food. Try the tempura prawns and butter chicken.

St Tropez Bistro $-$$

Century Village, Garhoud, 04 286 9029

This little cosy eatery, tucked away at the back of Century Village is the true meaning of 'no-frills'. Centrally located close to Deira and downtown Dubai, tell your taxi driver to head to Century/Irish Village. Here you'll find an assortment of restaurants from Pub style to Chinese, Italian and Persian all dotted around a pretty park. St Tropez is a small restaurant with seating inside and outdoor and is licensed. Decor is reminiscent of a French bistro with pictures of famous celebrities on the wall. St Tropez's speciality appears to be steaks, with a variety of sauces on offer. However, other yummy budget specials appear on the menu such as Chicken Cordon Bleu and the favourite Salad Nicoise.

Also try

The best deli in Dubai: **Dean & Deluca**, Souk al Bahar, 04 420 0336

Grapeshisha Choice:

Traiteur $$$

Park Hyatt Dubai, 04 317 2222

There are some really classy restaurants in Dubai, but Traiteur, for us ticks boxes on food quality, presentation and price. It's not cheap, but then again compared to similar restaurants in Dubai,

Traiteur charges fairly for what it is. Firstly the interior is bound to impress a date or equally a small group of friends with its high ceiling and spacious swanky interior. Opt to sit outside, weather permitting, with lovely views of the creek or get an indoor window seat. The open kitchen works wonderfully within the huge space and gives your tastebuds a mild tinkling as to what's in store. Food is top notch and staff will assist in your menu selection. The duck is probably the best we've ever had and the lamb is perfectly tender. Make space for desert, we are still dreaming of the crepe suzette!

SEAFOOD

High End

Ossiano $$$$$

Atlantis Dubai, Palm Jumeirah 04 426 2626

Ossiano is quite possibly the most luxurious restaurants in Dubai apart from maybe the Cavalli Club. You'll pay at least 1500 AED per person, but you'll get the best seafood of your life. You need to dress super smart, and it all feels like your working up to an amazing meal. And you are. This is gourmet fish at its best. Don't sit too close to the aquarium or you'll feel everyone is watching you although the aquarium feels huge wherever you sit!

Al Mahara $$$$$

Burj-Al Arab 04 321 1111

The Burj Al Arab's signature restaurant used to be a wonder in its own right. It is based "underwater" with a huge aquarium in the middle of the restaurant. But what you are paying for here is the whole experience – of eating at the Burj, underwater. The food is great, but not for the premiums you must pay. But it's difficult to get a reservation, so this is somewhere where demand definitely outstrips supply. Dress smart!

Also try:

For good service and amazing scallops:**Pisces**, Madinat Jumeirah 04 3668888

Medium

The Dhow $$$

Le Meridien Mina Seyahi 04 399 3333

Seafood restaurants in Dubai have a reputation for trying to stand out. And this is no different. Once you get over the fact that this is a floating restaurant, you'll realise that it has the most amazing view of the Palm, if you go for the higher seating. And that's not it – the fish is great too.

Also try,

For messy crabs and lobsters and fun: **Aprons & Hammers**, Dubai International Marine Club, Mina Seyahi Beach Resort, 04 454 7097

Budget

Bu Qtair Cafeteria $

Jumeirah

Some say this is the best fish restaurant in Dubai. It certainly is the only one of its kind. It serves only the catch of the day and is always heaving with a mixture of punters, all interested in one thing only – the amazing cheap fish curry. Located in a shack in Jumeirah, with Burj Al Arab in view, the fish here is tasty and spicy served in a coconut sauce. This Indian fish shack is popular with everyone – and it's cheap. It doesn't serve anything but the three types of fish netted that day as well as fresh paratha, but that's why it's so great. The simplicity of this shack is so anti new Dubai, that it has gained an attraction as a tourist destination in its own right, and so if you are in the area, make sure you go.

Also try

For a huge selection of fish, Lebanese style: **Fish Basket**, Oud Metha 04 336 7177

Grapeshisha Choice

Pierchic, $$$$

Al Qasr Madinat Jumeirah, 04 336 6730

This is the most romantic restaurant in town. Located at the end of a pier, you feel as if you are on a boat looking back at Dubai. This is a meal that you must do if you are on honeymoon. Get a seafood buffet and feel at peace away from the hubbub of Dubai. It's a little pricey, but you will feel a little sad walking back to main land after your meal.

STEAK AND GRILLS

High End:

Rare $$$$

Desert Palm Dubai, 04 3238888

With so many steakhouses in abundance, once you find your favourite you may never try anything different again. Situated in the idyllic Desert Palm resort, southwest of Dubai, Rare is worth the 20 minute journey from central Dubai, just for a chance to get away from it all. Rare doesn't lend itself to just a steakhouse but more a grill, it offers some variety to suit dining partners not after steak such as lamb shanks. But it is the steak that really is the front runner here, cut smooth as silk, this is the real taste and swallow test and they pass. The sides are equally elegant, with many options over and above standard fries. Try to sit outside it it's not too hot.

MJ's Steakhouse $$$$

Al Qasr Hotel, Madinat Jumeirah, 04 366 8888

MJ's is always busy and that's a sure fire sign the place serves up well. It may not be overly glitzy in its appearance, and probably more suited to business lunches than for a twentysomething birthday celebration. But if you are a meat lover and want beautiful ambience, Al Qasr has that and MJ's serves up a pretty mean selection of steaks and grills in Dubai. A varied selection of starters on hand and even vegetarians are well catered for here. Go for a very different Wagyu Beef Tartare, and opt for a side of foie gras on your steak! The open kitchen experience makes the restaurant lively and outdoor seating is perfect for couples, service is great and unobtrusive. Go if you love steak!

Also try,

Guaranteed perfection for your medium rare: **The Exchange Grill**, Fairmont Hotel, Sheikh Zayed Road, 04 311 8316

Excellent Expenses Location in DIFC and potentially the best beef in Dubai: **Centre Cut**, Ritz Carlton DIFC, 04 372 2222

High end touch to grills: **Rhodes Twenty10**, Le Royal Meridien, Dubai Marina 04 399 5555

Steak while watching tango – only in Dubai: **La Parilla**, Jumeirah Beach Hotel, 04 406 8999

Mid Range:

Rib Room $$$

Jumeirah Emirates Towers, Lobby Level, Dubai, 04 319 8088

A classic venue and a classic dining experience, Rib Room will not disappoint. From the moment you step into the chic New York style interior, you will be greeted with fantastic service explaining the generous menu. There are complementary fresh soft bagels so there's no need to order starters if you're not overly hungry and mains are generously portioned. Everyone raves about the excellent Wagyu Beef Tenderloin here with the creamy spinach and mash truffle sides. The Beef Wellington is also a "thumbs up" and made for two people. There is a good selection of non-meat options are also available. Dine at 7pm for the Early Bird Set Menu which is cheaper but also smaller quantity.

Pachanga $$$

Hilton Dubai Jumeirah Resort, 04 318 2530

This South American restaurant featuring food from Mexico, Argentina and Brazil is perfect if you're up for a lively night as oppose to a quiet romantic meal. Tuesdays are the Churrasco nights where you can select from numerous cut meats for a set price. The a la carte menu has a huge array of dishes, from which we recommend the seafood and grill platters and the lobster trio for starters. Leave space for dessert, the chocolate souffle is heaven! Arriba!

Also try:

For grill selection: **M's Beef Bistro** Le Meridien Dubai, Airport Road, 04 702 2455

The best beef carpaccio on the Palm?: **West 14th**, Oceana Beach Club, The Palm Jumeirah, 04 447 7601

To watch the Dubai Fountain: **Rivington Grill**, Souk Al Bahar, Old town Dubai, 04 423 0903

Budget:

St Tropez French Bistro $

Century Village, Garhoud, Dubai, 04 286 9029

This steakhouse clearly defines the true meaning of 'no frills' ! St Tropez offers great food at such affordable prices without compromising on quality. Located in the Century/ Irish Village and despite not being in a hotel it is still a licensed venue. You'll find St Tropez nestled at the back of the Village Park. There is not a huge amount of seating but you do have the option to sit in or outside. Inside, the decor is a little cheesy giving the place a faux bistro feel. Portions are huge so beware. For very hungry budget eaters only.

Grapeshisha Choice:

JW's Steakhouse $$$$

JW Marriott, Deira 04 6977977

The best steak house in town, JW's has been going for a number of years. Every expat who loves steak comes here and their seafood is not bad too. It's not over the top yet the service is immaculate. The only thing over the top is the old school décor and green leather seats. If you are a meat eater and on this side of town, don't miss it.

KID FRIENDLY RESTAURANTS

Restaurants that catered for children were unheard of for many years in the UAE. But as Dubai grew as a tourist destination – and a family one as well, the options for kids and families grew and grew. The options are now too difficult to count. You can pick places like Fuddruckers, or go for your regular fast food. There are even the Waggamammas or places like Pizza Express but most restaurants cater to the mini size requirements – and many offer kids meal prices at a significant discount. There are only a very few restaurants that don't allow kids at all. Below are listed a small selection of restaurants which we think are particularly sensitive when it comes to our little brats at meal times!

High End:

Beachcombers $$$

Jumeirah Beach Hotel, Dubai, 04 406 8999

Cuisine: Pan Asian

If your kids have had enough of enclosed spaces this holiday, then Beachcombers will give them some stretching space in safe grounds. As its name suggests, Beachcombers is set on Jumeirah Beach with beautiful views of the Burj Al Arab. Reserve in advance for a great dining spot outside as spaces will get booked up. The menu is all based around Malaysian Thai Indonesian favourites. Kids have their own buffet stand which serve the usual chicken nuggets, burgers and fries and kiddy favourites, but teamed with a plate of noodles - we're sure you'll find food to keep your kids and you happy. For keep them happy and occupied, the kids have their own entertainment room or can roam around on the beach whilst being in safe viewing distance from you. On brunch days there is a clown and bouncy castle ! Open daily from 7.30am - midnight, Friday Brunch 12.30 - 4pm.

Also try:

For Friday Family Brunch: **Meydan**, Nad El Sheba, 04 3811111

For a view of the golf: **Ranches Restaurant & Bar**, 04 360 7935

Mid Range:

Noodle House $$

Jumeirah Emirates Towers, 04 319 8088

Souk Madinat Jumeirah, 04 366 6730

Dubai International Financial Centre, 04 363 7093

Burjuman Centre, 04 352 6615

Cuisine: Chinese/Thai

Bright decor, huge open room with long tables and benches should get the kids thinking they're back in their school dining hall albeit with a cheery renovation. Hopefully the decor alone will assure them that this may not be such a bad dining experience. The great thing about Noodle House is the quick turnaround of your meal, but this also depends on what time you dine so with kids in tow, a midday lunch or 5pm dinner should give you decent enough service. The kids menu comprises of some really tasty colourful and healthy options such as tempura fish with broccoli, chicken/salmon with vegetable noodles or vegetable rice. For adults, the menu is vast with a selection of Chinese, Thai and Indonesian options. We're a big fan of Noodle House. Healthy, fast and tasty cuisine served in a great location – if you are a parent you will love it as well.

Cafe Ceramique $$-$$$

Jumeirah Town Centre, 04 344 7331

Dubai Festival City, 04 232 8616

Cuisine: Soups/Salads/Sandwiches/Selected Hot Snacks and Kids Menu

Cafe Ceramique provides a calm, peaceful experience - a welcome change from those loud, crowded mall play areas, plus - you don't have the messy clean up job to deal with afterward! The Cafe Ceramique chain operates in three branches across Dubai; Jumeirah Town Centre, Mall of the Emirates and Dubai Festival City. Go to Cafe Ceramique for a morning of painting and then break for lunch. Items to paint are displayed on the shelves around the restaurant and you can select however many you'd like to paint, they range from plates, cups and ornaments and all priced separately. Grab your table and paints and get creative. Food served is not bad at all. In fact, the variation on offer is significant considering the primary focus of this venue is an art cafe. Kids selections are good and healthy alternatives. A fun filled half- day out for both you and your little one(s). Collect your work of art after 1 week, so it's only worthwhile if you are staying for an extended trip. Please note, we've placed this venue in the mid range category purely because of the extra cost of ceramique painting. The price is totally dependent on how many pieces you paint and how much you eat. Open daily from 9am till Midnight.

Also try:

For ice cream with low sugar and fresh ingredients: **The Ice Factory**, JBR Walk, 04 88 71074

For the best frozen yoghurt in town: **The Frozen Yoghurt Factory**, 04 448 6401

Huge burgers, milkshakes & refills: **Fuddruckers**, 04 282 7771

Budget:

Spur Steakhouse Ranch $

Festival Centre, Dubai Festival City, 04 232 8866

Cuisine: Burgers/Steakhouse

At some point, you will have to cave in to the kids and go with the 'least healthy' option for dining, but at least Spur isn't fast food. This famous South African chain is popular with the Dubai yummy mummies, so much so that when we visited, they didn't accept reservations and we had to wait a bit to be seated. The menu has a huge variety of juicy steaks, burgers, seafood and chicken combos with fries, all with a side helping of salad. Vegetarians are catered for somewhat, but if you are after a gourmet soup and salad option, you may lack options. The real pulling point of Spur is the instant friendly and cheerful manner as you step into the restaurant. Kids are given a warm welcome and given a show round to the enclosed entertainment area which has a soft play feature and arcade games for older kids. The interior is bright and fun and the whole experience is a well oiled machine. Open Sunday - Wednesday: 10am - 10pm, Thursday - Saturday: 10am - 11pm

Also try:

Lebanese tasters: **Al Reef**, Zabeel Road, 04 396 1980

American specials: **Johnny Rockets** 04 341 2380

Grapeshisha Choice:

Cold Stone Creamery $

Mall of the Emirates, Dubai Mall and Various others

You can buy ice cream everywhere in Dubai, and get some of the best gelatos this side of Italy. But there's only one place in Dubai that puts the fun into the ice cream and that is Cold Stone. They make a real show of tossing the ice cream up from their scoopers, which the kids will love – and they continue to do it while you eat as each new customer comes in. Sometimes, they hurl the balls of ice cream across the restaurant – and not always successfully. Great Fun!

CAFES

Coffee breaks are big business in Dubai and to have coffee with company is a traditional Arabic pastime. Over the years, having a coffee has evolved to hanging out with friends, sitting alfresco and sipping on iced coffee and maybe a light snack. Unlike in most western countries where coffee shops are normally open from breakfast till late afternoon, the majority of UAE coffee shops are open for nearly 15 hours in the day - with their peak business probably more so in the evening then during the day. Emirati locals love socialising and after having their main meal at home, usually around 4-5pm, families or just the men head off after dark to kill a few hours at their favourite cafe for snacks/coffee and shisha.

Expats and visitors follow this culture and with the exceptionally beautiful weather for most of the year, take the opportunity to share some 'chill' time with your friends.

High End

Café Bateel $$ Unlicensed

Marina Walk, DIFC, Dubai Mall, 04 339 9716

Your opportunity to try dates, Arabic coffee in style is presented perfectly at the Bateel Café. As you may well know, Bateel produce the best dates, coming from Saudi and you can get a flavour of Arabian tastes at an upmarket Middle East equivalent to a traditional coffee chop. The desert variations are phenomenal.

Circle Cafe $ Unlicensed

Dubai Media City, Building #2 (CNN), 04 391 5170

Jumeirah Beach Park, 04 342 8177

Opening Hours: 7.30am-8.30pm

If you are here on work purposes and based in Media City, you'll be happy to know there is a friendly trendy cafe where you can get your daily coffee fix, fresh bagels and salads with a huge variety of fillings and toppings to suit anyone's fancy. Salad portions are huge and their toppings we must say, beat many cafes/restaurants in Dubai.

Perfect for breakfast, lunch or afternoon snack, this place is fast and efficient so you won't waste time for that all important meeting.

Also try:

Best espresso in Dubai: **Emporio Armani Café**, Dubai Mall, 04 339 8396

Venice imitation: **Café Florian**, DIFC, 04 323 1833

Mid Range:

The Lime Tree Cafe $$ Unlicensed

Jumeirah Beach Road (Villa), 04 349 8498

We have nothing bad to say about the Lime Tree Cafe. It may be famous for its yummy mummies and Jumeirah Janes and be a little pricier than a simple snack place, but you can have a hearty breakfast, lunch or even light dinner for a reasonable price and leave feeling relaxed. The atmosphere is cafe style with trendy, clean lines in decor and a perfect place to hang with kids as some of their branches have a kids' corner full of books and crayons and enough space to park a few buggies. The menu consists of an extensive breakfast choice with English and even Arabic twists – for example the breakfast platter with labneh balls, the cold and warm deli style snacks/ meals such as salads topped with grilled aubergine and halloumi. They also sell the basics such as jacket potatoes and yummy filled baguettes, pies, quiches and juicy chicken and meat kebabs. Don't leave without sampling their famous carrot cake! Since its Jumeirah branch launch in 2001, The Lime Tree Cafe has grown across Dubai, so check them out!

The ONE Deli $$

Jumeirah Beach Road nr Jumeirah Mosque, 04 345 6687

Opening Hours: 9am-9pm

What a clever way to entice you to shop after having a fulfilling lunch - plant a super trendy cafe on the top floor of a super trendy furniture store! The ONE - if you haven't heard, is one of Dubai's trendiest furniture and home wares store. But their main pulling power for punters is not their soft chanille throws, it is The ONE Deli. Yes, this place is always a hit for long lazy breakfasts or chatty lunches with friends. The decor is done ever so nicely of course using the store's own line (with price tag intact should you be interested!). The menu has a good choice and features comfort favourites for breakfast such as eggs Benedict, muesli and an array of pastries. For lunch, opt for homemade soups, salads and quiches.

Also try

For the best breakfast in Dubai (well our thoughts anyway): **Chocolate Chic**. Dubai Marina, 04 399 0433

For local organc ingredients, try **Baker and Spice**, dotted around Dubai, 04 4252240 (Souk Al Bahar)

For Giorgio's Café under the mall "stars": **Armani / Dubai Caffe**, 03 339 8396

Budget:

Basta Art Cafe $ (Does not accept Credit Cards) Unlicensed

Al Fahidi Street, Bastakiya, Bur Dubai (head to the restored Bastikya Quarter, which you'll find on the main road), 04 353 5071

Opening Hours: 8am-10pm

For true authentic atmosphere, Basta Art Cafe will whisk you away to Arabia and you'll forget about air-conditioned malls and designer handbags for a couple of hours. Seating is in their outdoor garden and there are plenty of spaces with shading, if visiting in the warmer months go in the evening. The menu consists of Arabic deli favourites as well as jacket potatoes, salads and sandwiches. We were advised to try their lime and fresh mint juice and boy is it refreshing - a perfect way to spend a peaceful couple of hours or just browsing at the many works of art in their unique art gallery. Kids will love the open space and a re-modelled majlis area with comfy cushions and low sofas - very authentic! Take note, this place may be very busy on a weekend as the surroundings are hot tourist spots. If you are not familiar with the area, Basta Art Cafe is within a stone's throw to the gold, fabric and spice souk and Deira Creek, so this is a perfect rest stop as you do your traditional tourist spots.

Also try:

For a guaranteed favourite in Dubai: **More Café**, The Dubai Mall, 04 339 8934

Grapeshisha Choice

XVA Café $

XVA Gallery, Bastakiya, Bur Dubai, 04 353 5383

Everyone's favourite tourist spot is a remarkably great little café in the middle of Bastakiya. It's small and artsy and used to be a secret spot, but you'll be lucky to get a seat. It really is a place to pop by if you are doing your Batakiya Walk, but everyone manages to pick it as their place for a vegetarian snack. Even if you don't manage to get a seat, make sure you get some mint lemonade to go. It will refresh you for the rest of the day.

BRUNCH

The concept of brunch has turned into a gastronomical Friday feast for those who live in Dubai and if you are holidaying during a Friday, you must experience the traditional 'Friday Brunch' which has now become a standard feature across Dubai. Friday is the first day of the weekend and a religious day, so you'll find most places of interest shut during the morning to allow for Friday prayers. In the past, major shopping malls would only open from 1pm, but now laws are more relaxed and the malls do open earlier. However, Thursday is the first evening of the weekend so many party hard and then relish the lie-in and slow Friday start with a trip to one of the Brunch haunts in the majority of Dubai hotels. Brunch normally starts at 12.30 and it is advised not to eat anything before you arrive, because brunch in Dubai is a eat as much you like affair. And at most licensed establishments, it's a drink as much as you like affair as well. There are booze free options, but you should know that Dubai brunches have a reputation for debauchery. In fact it was one such brunch that led to the infamous "sex on the beach" incident that lead to two British expats being imprisoned and eventually deported. But back to the food – you will be greeted with a feast of food - that will be difficult to fathom eating! If it is your first time, consider pacing yourself by walking around the various stations and plaaning your method of attack. If you really want to splash out, go for one of the high end options that offer a champagne brunch with all the trimmings (non- alcoholic packages are available and cheaper). Be sure to make a reservation in advance for any Friday Brunch venue. Enjoy, but don't overdo it. You do need to walk again!

High End:

Al Qasr $$$$

Al Qasr Hotel, Madinat Jumeirah Dubai, 04 366 6730

Cuisine: Mixed/ International.

Al Qasr has the widest choice of international food, live music, kids' activities and of course unlimited champagne. This is probably the most popular brunch location in Dubai - it's won a host of 'best brunch in Dubai' awards – so it comes with good pedigree. The moment you step into the grandeur of the Madinat Jumeirah, you will feel like royalty and no doubt be ready to feast like a King as your eyes gaze in amazement at the artwork of food displayed before you. As well as creating nearly every dish imaginable, the presentation is out of this world with mini wine glasses of condiments and puddings. The Al Qasr brunch doesn't lend itself to just one massive room but three so its important to pace yourself, starting with mini portions of sushi, lobster, tapas, mezzes, and go easy on the fresh breads and rice. Every Thai and Indian curry is available and cooked with so much depth and flavour, you can't fault the food in any way. Despite this being labelled as a 'buffet' many items are cooked from fresh according to your individual preferences. Items are replenished regularly and didn't look tired at all. Sit indoors amongst the opulent plush sofas or outside overlooking the canals and abras. Soak in the atmosphere and walk off your mains before attempting dessert – now that's a whole different experience. Brunching like a King doesn't come cheap, and the Al Qasr brunch is probably one of the most expensive brunches in Dubai, but for 550 AED you will get free flowing bubbly and alcohol. There is a non alcoholic option too and kids from 5-12 pay half price. This is one of the most expensive buffets in Dubai, but always busy - the reputation of the AL Qasr Brunch precedes it.

Traiteur $$$

Park Hyatt Dubai, 04 317 2222

Cuisine: French

Traiteur is one of our favourite restaurants in Dubai. And we also love the Park Hyatt. So what better time to spend your Friday than with a lazy brunch at one our favourite places? It's French themed with lots of different spots to go and get your various pieces of food perfection. Traiteur is classy, romantic, sophisticated and high end. If Al Qasr is all about scoffing down as much as possible, then Traiteur is all about palate. And because this isn't a rushed type affair, you will make sure you save some space for dessert. Indeed, we have known people who come to the buffet just to sample the 20 or so different desserts while sipping on champagne. Now that's just living to excess! The live jazz band ramps up your mood as well – it all makes for a perfect Friday! Expect to pay 550 fully loaded.

Also try

Eclectic Mixed International & Sumptuous: **Yalumba** at Le Meridien Dubai, Garhoud, 04 702 2328

Huge with ultimate choice: **Saffron** at The Atlantis, 04 426 2626

The best restaurant in town: **Zuma** at DIFC on 04 4255560

Mid Range:

Market Cafe $$-$$$

Grand Hyatt Dubai, 04 317 2222

Cuisine: Mixed

Market Café is kid Friendly, a great all rounder for families and those who don't require an alcoholic package - as you can pay for this separately. A huge big rainforest style layout awaits you at the Market Cafe and kids will love the space available to get away from the parents but not far enough for them to worry! Let them enjoy activities such as face painting and colouring while you get down to the nitty gritty of stuffing yourselves! The food here is all freshly laden and most of it is made to order at one of five live cooking stations. Buffet style meals are also available too and are consistently of good quality. The speciality of the Market Cafe is the juicy grill selection and rotisseries. And they also have the usual Italian, Arabic and Indian offerings. There is plenty to choose from but if you are used to the high end brunches and frills you may look down at the Market Café. We love it for its genuinely good quality food, good variety of dishes and reasonable price. Current brunch rates are 190 AED person including unlimited soft drinks. Alcohol is paid for separately. Children under 6 years are free and between 6 and 12 years will be half price. Brunch is between 12.30-4pm every Friday . Outdoor seating is available but reserve these beforehand as there aren't many tables.

Also try:

For Amazing Lobster: **The Observatory** at the Dubai Marriott Harbour Hotel & Suites, Dubai Marina 04 319 4000

For relaxed Asian treats: **Warehouse** at Le Meriden, Dubai, Garhoud on 04 282 4040

Burj Sushi Brunch at a discount: **Armani/Hashi** at the Armani Hotel on 04 8883444

Trackside Lunching: **Meydan**, Nad El Sheba on 04 3811111

Creekside brunchin': **Glasshouse**, Hilton Dubai Creek on 04 227 1111

Budget:

MORE Cafe $-$$. Unlicensed

Branches offering brunch deal:

Gold and Diamond Park: 04 323 4350

Festival City: 04 232 6299

Al Murooj: 04 343 3779

Mirdif City Centre: 04 284 3805

Cuisine: Mixed Deli Favourites

More is a healthy (and filling!) alternative to the excessive Friday brunches that are the norm in Dubai! It's so nice to try a place that offers super food that satisfies the belly and doesn't leave you demanding a 2 hour siesta. MORE Cafe is a UAE born concept created by a Dutch partnership focusing on tasty healthy eating habits in surroundings which are comfortable yet trendy and sleek. As well as serving a great menu during the week and offering a detailed takeout service, their Friday Brunch package is an amazing alternative and one that should be tried if you are fed up of the usual overpriced hotel fanfare. MORE Cafe take pride in the freshly prepared salads and offer many variations. Their eggs Benedict are yum and the variety of main courses such as hotpots and curries as well as battered fish and chips are all tasty and not heavily laden with grease. Highly recommended if you are calorie counting! Brunch package 95 AED adults and 45 AED children under 12 years. Brunch is served from 11am - 4pm Fridays.

Almaz by Momo $-$$. Unlicensed

Mall of the Emirates, 2nd Level (back of Harvey Nichols), 04 409 8877

Cuisine: North African Grills and Eggs Brunch

Almaz has a Middle Eastern vibe and style, super value and great portions. Items are made fresh to order. Momo is not your typical brunch offering mountains of international food variety, but the simple choices are great and great for vegetarians who like eggs. Surroundings are so chilled and trendy, you can easily while away a good few hours and smoke on some shisha to digest the excess! You will be offered three different brunch choices: Almaz, North African, or Berber which include a range of fried eggs, chips combo, mixed skewers of meat and potatoes and omelette with pancakes and all entrees include a tasty salad. Leave space for dessert which is a selection of moroccan pastries, brownies and cakes, ice cream, and fruit salad. Be good to yourself and do a couple of laps around the Mall of the Emirates after your feast. All this and unlimited fruit juice, soft drinks and teas for 90 AED per person. Note there is no discount offered for children and this place is unlicensed. This brunch deal at Almaz is available 11am-4pm every Friday and Saturday.

Also try:

For Pub Grub in the Pub: **Belgian Beer Café** at Crowne Plaza Dubai Festival City on 04 7011128

For Dim Sum Heaven: **Hukuma** at the Address, Downtown Dubai on 04 436 8888

Cheap Thai Sophistication: **The Thai Kitchen** at Park Hyatt Dubai, 04 317 2222

British Brunch: **Double Decker** at Al Murooj Rotana on 04 321 1111

Fry Up: **Dubliner's** at Le Meridien Dubai Hotel and Conference Centre 04 702 2455

Grapeshisha Choice:

Spectrum on One $$$-$$$$

The Fairmont Dubai, 04 311 8316

Cuisine: Mixed/International. Brunch served from 12 – 3pm

This is probably the best brunch you'll ever experience. The restaurant could be anywhere – it's a little "meh" for our liking, but with food this good and Moet on tap, who cares? As well as favourite international dishes, Spectrum focuses on seafood delights and spectacular roast carvings. Service here is fantastic and starts as soon as you walk through the door. Spectrum is one of the pioneers of the Friday brunch and has managed to maintain its spot as the place to come on a Friday afternoon. There is almost everything on order at the cooking stations: the Japanese corner will also prepare made to order dim sum and sushi; the Indian corner will flip fresh chapattis in front of your eyes and lure you with their lush curries; the carvery will serve up the juiciest roasts including turkey with all the trimmings; and that's just the beginning. Make space for the famous cheese and port room which is huge and dedicated to dairy fans. The desserts are simply to die for – our tip is to head there first and observe the amount of belly space required for after you tackle your mains. There are different brunch prices, the all out package is the Premium Bubbly Brunch at 550 AED with unlimited Moet and Chandon. Everything but alcohol is 295 AED. Kids under 5 years are free, between 6-12 years 150 AED and quite useful is the teen package at 197 AED who probably eat more than anyone.

BARS, CLUBS & NIGHTLIFE

Whether you love to party hard or chill at the bar, you won't be disappointed with the huge amount of bars and clubs Dubai has to offer. Outdoor venues are increasingly popular here, especially during October and May, but the indoor venues are also a must see, with some of the most 'blinging' and sparkling interiors you'll have ever experience. It's the outdoor bars that make the evenings especially if you are on holiday, so it's worth securing a table especially if you are not eating.

Unlike some of the bars and clubs in Europe and the States, the majority in Dubai will not charge an entry fee, however a few exclusive ones may after a certain time, so it's best to go early, grab a lovely area to sit and people watch. Alternatively, if you are able to get yourself on a guestlist, this will save you a load of hassle at the door. We have given you the information but make use of your concierge if you can. Legal entry age for bars in the UAE is 21 – and for some clubs you need to be 25. Please note that even if you are well above the legal age you may still get asked for ID especially if entering at a peak time for a highly sought after club. Girls are well respected here, and more often then not, a ladies free entry and drinks promotion will be running on at least one day of the week. Contact the relevant hotel for more details. Lastly, to really guarantee entry into a club – dress to impress. The crowd in Dubai love dressing up – even the males pay particular attention to grooming – so the more glam, the better!

The clubbing scene in Dubai is hot!

The nightlife scene in Dubai is lively with some of the world's top DJs in attendance to play the beats for you to dance the night away. Whether you are into your happy house, your soul and R&B, your Arabic beats, your hardcore, or just your regular popular fare, it is all catered for in the diverse venues that exist in Dubai. It's usually best to dress up a little as the bouncers will sometimes look for any excuse for you to not get in. It's also preferable to go as a mixed group or to turn up early. Entrance costs range from free entry to anything up to 100Dhs. Tuesday night is the traditional "Ladies night" where ladies drink for free, and Thursday is the big club night where most bars are filled to capacity. Wednesday's and Friday's also feature due to differing weekends, but Thursday is the night to hits the clubs in Dubai.

You will note that many of our recommendations are in the newer part of Dubai – and in the newer clubs. There's a whole nightclub scene in old Dubai, in the hotels there, but to say it's a little hit and miss is being kind. There are a host of cover bands which can be fun, but we find that they are always over rated. There are also venues where Mujras perform – these are young Indian sub continent girls dancing exotically to leery Indian men. We find it a little distasteful. What we also find distasteful is the number of establishments that are in place just to facilitate prostitution. None of our recommended spots are notorious for that type of activity (we think), so if that's what you want, we're sure Google can tell you where to search.

We have put together a selection of the bars and clubs that you could try out. They are usually based at the hotels due to the licensing of alcohol, and while we have only given a few to choose from, you can be sure that the Dubai nightlife is pumping. Be aware that some places are notorious for shady activities, although many have been closed down. Clubs stay open until 2 or 3 am, with some bars shutting up shop at midnight. A few of our legit, non dodgy, recommendations are listed below in various categories:

BAR RESTAURANTS

Caramel Restaurant and Lounge

Building 6, DIFCDubai

Tel: 04 425 6677

For a more relaxed bar experience with element of fun and liveliness, Caramel has lures an after work crowd for dinner and late night drinking into its airy and trendy space. The venue works well as it's not overly loud or tacky. We especially liked the outdoor leafy terrace, which does get busy so make sure you book in advance. Food here is surprisingly good – the menu is mixed with tasty international dishes, but predominantly American food such as steaks, lamb shanks, pastas and shawarmas all elegantly presented. Special promos happen during the week including a ladies night on Tuesdays and Happy Hours. You really won't want to leave! Mac and cheese is out favourite.

Left Bank

Souk Al Bahar

04 368 4501

There are two Left Banks in Dubai – one in Madinat and one in Soul Al Bahat. Theyy are both super joints, though this is the one that has been getting the more recent buzz. The place is good for dates or small groups and is an excellent start for the night. The décor is contemporary but not ultra modern which makes it very accessible.

Zuma

GateVillage6, DIFC Dubai

Tel: 04 425 5660

If you want a one stop shop and not bothered about budget, you will be thoroughly impressed with Zuma. It's probably top of the list in Dubai for a night out. Amazing sushi and funky surroundings will keep you satisfied all evening and not bother with a taxi ride to venue b. If you love sushi you will love the Tuna Tartare, but the Black Cod and Rock Shrimp tempura are equally decadent. If you don't want dinner, just snack and drink - their lounge area is ideal with low cushy sofas and the DJ really kicks ass with tunes throughout the night. Not cheap but quality is A-class. Amazing. Trust us. There's no guestlist, but if you're just drinking make a lounge reservation for weekends. Sake anyone?

Budda Bar

Grosvenor House Hotel

04 399 8888

Budda bar is well known for what it is – and it's no different in Dubai. Oriental music moving to faster beats in a glamorous setting. There's great sushi and great cocktails making for a winning combination.

LOUNGE BARS / PUBS

101

One and Only, The Palm

04 440 1030

If you are looking for a great peaceful outdoor lounge bar, 101 is one of a secret spot that offers tranquillity away from the chaos.

M Dek

Media One Hotel,MediaCityDubai

04 427 1000

Although casual in nature, M Dek has played host to many pool parties and is now pulling in an elite casual crowd. It's a great place to hangout with friends for a few pre dinner/club drinks especially when it's not overly sticky. Media One hotel is a trendy ultra modern hotel frequented by the younger working crowd. Blinging it up is not necessary here - just come to have a genuinely good time.

Irish Village

Aviation Club

04 282 4750

The Irish Village should sit in the history books of Dubai – as every expat will vouch for. This is the perfect place to watch sports or just hang out to grab a beer.

The Gramercy

DIFC

04 437 7511

The Gramercy is great sports bar for the DIFC crew, with perfect pub type food. Jazz is usually playing in the background to give that cool vibe to the place. The food is pretty good as are the drinks. This is another needed addition to DIFC.

Dhow and Anchor

Jumeirah Beach Hotel

04 366 9111

Great location and is just how you would expect a British expat type pub to be. With red leather seats and big screens for the sports, you know fish and chips is on the menu here. It's decent, although prices have slowly risen over the last years.

Blue Bar

Novotel WTC

(04) 332 0000

Part bar, part meeting point, part cover band venue, the Blue Bar has a weird feel to it that makes you love it! It's unpretentious – anyone can walk in, and it's nice little hide away that has a mish mash of clientele. If it were located anywhere else, it would be packed. Our other secret joint is The Cowboys at the President Hotel in the President Hotel. It's not cool, but has great starters and is inexpensive – great to watch the IPL with the Indian cricket lovers.

Jambase

Madinat Jumeirah

04 366 6730

This is one of our fave spots for live music. No cover band trash – just great live music and up and coming artists. Great jazz, upbeat music, turn up early for a meal and to secure your spot.

COCKTAIL BARS
DubaiMarina

04 362 7900

This is a great place to combine dinner with drinks or just arrive for drinks and snacks. Dubai Marina is famous for it's nearby glam hotels and of course boat spotting. The scenery is awesome and Aquara is the perfect place to grab a terrace spot and nosey at the beautiful yachts on show. There is an ongoing happy hour promotion during the week and come late evening the live entertainment begins with people turning the place into a dance party, definitely an evening of understated fun.

At.mosphere

122 Floor, Burj Khalifa

Tel: 04 888 3828

Instead of going for drinks at Armani Prive, get yourself across to the tallest viewpoint and enjoy champagne and strawberries amongst breathtaking views and lounge beats played by the resident DJ. At.mosphere, two floors beneath the public observation deck – At the Top has a restaurant and bar, a perfect option to hangout or perhaps spend your last night in Dubai. The bouncers might not take a liking to you in which case you won't get in. Consider booking for dinner, and trying one of the wagyu specials. This is also one of our secret spots for afternoon tea. This is the highest bar in the world – and better vies than Valut at the Marriott Marquis.

Skyview Bar

Burj Al Arab

04 301 7600

If there was ever a place to go all out, this is it – on the 27th floor of the Burj Al Ara. With great views over the beach, you can also opt to drink   the most expensive cocktail in the world. Yes, this is where you can buy the 27321 – so called because it costs 27,321 Dhs. Well, if you can afford it, then good luck to you. We would struggle at a sip. Seriously though, this is your ticket in to the Burj. You'll have to spend 275 dhs per person – so book in advance. Just know that you can order food from AL Muntaha, located next door.

360°

Roofdeck of Marina Restaurant, Jumeirah Beach Hotel

04 406 8769

The perfect place to hangout if you're on holiday or impressing some out of town guests with its picture perfect setting and the famous Burj Al Arab only an arm's length away. Rest your bum on comfy sofas and order a round, take in the breeze, smoke a grape shisha and sway to the cool tunes. Service can be a bit slow and if planning to stay all night may burn a serious hole in your wallet. This place is perfect for pre dinner/ club drinks as after 9pm it will be a mission to get into. Guests of the Jumeirah Beach Hotel are always guaranteed entry. Otherwise, sign up to the guestlist at platinumlist.ae or call the number above.

Bar 44

Grosvenor House Hotel

04 399 8888

Open:6pm – 2amdaily, Thurs open till3am.

Another bar with a view, this time on the 44th level - and it seems that 44 is the theme of the place, with 44 different champagnes on offer and even most cocktails prices at 44 dhs. When it comes to buying by the bottle, this place isn't bargain central but what do you expect – this is the Grosvenor Hotel, one of Dubai's swankiest. If a classy posh bar is what you want, without the thumping garage music, you can while away a good few hours here.

Supperclub

Jumierah Zabeel Saray

04 4530 000

This globally proven multi sensory night out is a favourite amongst the inner crowd. Combining food, art and music in one location, you can get dinner and drinks while watching a mix of performers interspersed by DJ sets.

Vu's

Emirates Towers

04 319 8088

We always find Vu's bar a little cramped, but maybe because we're no longer the cool cats we once were. And this is what this place is – a meeting place the super cool. It's unpretentious and has great "vus" from the top floor of the Emirates Tower.

The Agency

Madinat Jumeirah

04 319 8088

For the wine connoisseur this is sophisticated elegance, but as with all the best places is always busy. There are hundred of wines to pick from some of which are served by the glass.

Calabar

The Address Downtown

04 436 8888

What better spot to sip cocktails but in front of the Burj Khalifa? And so this is the place to be at dusk. There's a South American vibe here – and the terrace is where its at, so get there as soon as you can!

Neos

The Address Downtown

04 436 8888

The best spot to view the Burj Khalifa and the fountains it may be, but this place is difficult to get into. See if you can glam up to grab one drink (warning – they're expensive, even by Dubai's standards) before moving downstairs for less snooty fun at Calabar.

NIGHTCLUBS

Boudoir

Dubai Marine and Beach Resort

04 345 5995

An old favourite but still has the xfactor. The interior is sheer opulence and baroque style with rich velvet drapes and sofas. The crowd is mixed and certainly not pretentious so this is the place to come for a great night out. Saying that, people do dress up here but the dress code always appears semi/casual and no trainers. Music is normally commercial house, rnb and a healthy dose of Arabic due to the fun Lebanese crowd. It's a cool holiday experience, but beware of the bouts of smokiness which can get heavy on weekends. As with most clubs, if you want a table, there will be a min spend levied usually starting from 2500 dhs.

Entry: No entrance fee for ladies all week, however guys will be charged 100 dhs on a Thursday. Arrive as a couple and the earlier the better as Boudoir does not operate a guestlist.

400 Club

The FairmontDubai

Tel: 04 332 4900

Before the People club, 400 used to be the hot favourite and thankfully for them, it still sees huge faithful crowds which is why it can be a squeeze on the weekends. Try going on a Tuesday when the vibe is relaxed and music is a mix of Arabic, RnB and House. Interior is a mix of baroque and gothic design with funky lighting and its definitely a people watching venue so appearance is of essence. It's all about the money here and guests are presented with a huge camaraderie when ordering expensive bottles of champagne. It's a bit too pretentious for us, but that's probably because it's super exclusive.

Entry: Best to go as a couple or a mixed group and if possible get on the guestlist. For more info the400nightclub.com

Cavalli

The Fairmont Dubai

Tel: (04)55 856 6044/ 04 332 9260

For upbeat glamour, opulent surroundings and beautiful people, head toDubai's first ever designer club located at the swanky Fairmont Dubai. Come for dinner or just drinks but prepare to be dazzled by the array of swarovski crystals hanging from the ceiling and chandeliers. The interior is bold with shiny quartz floors finished in crystal dusting and the animal print upholstery actually works really well. If you love hanging out with beautiful, perfect looking people – you will love Cavalli. If you're a jeans and flat sandal type of gal, you may want to find the exit quick time. It's an experience and definitely only to embark upon for a really special occasion. If you love it here, move onto The 400 Club for afters. Seriously, the Cavalli club is another level - it looks expensive inside, and has that real high end glamour factor. But what else would expect from Roberto Cavalli?

Entry: Strictly through guestlist or prior table reservation. Go to cavalliclubdubai.com or call numbers above.

People by Crystal

Raffles Hotel

(04)55 297 2097/ (04)55 856 6557

Brace yourself for a night to remember at the Raffles. People club is rated as the new hot club of Dubai pulling in a huge VIP crowd every weekend. It is the biggest club in Dubai and replaces the previous famous bars China Moon and New Asia on the 18th and 19th Floor. Walking up a lush staircase leads to probably one of the biggest purpose built club venues you've ever seen located in a swanky glass pyramid giving nothing but stunning views of the city. Unlike in other clubs, you won't feel claustrophobic here and seating is ample. The only downer is that after midnight it starts getting really busy and crowded, but if you don't mind lots of beautiful people with stashes of cash – then you'll love it.

Entry: Strictly by guestlist. Table reservations are also advised if needed. Go to peopleofdubai.com or call the numbers above.

Armani/ Privé

Armani Hotel Dubai, Burj Khalifa

Tel: 04 888 3308

Open:10pm – 3am. Closed Sunday.

For ultimate exclusivity, a venue cannot get any more chic then at Armani/ Privé. This is where the loaded go for a regular night out and get treated with the utmost respect. Regular punters are not denied a sneak peak and surprisingly enough, guestlist is not required. Just ensure you are smartly dressed and by this they mean it, else you will be denied entry. For ladies that means full on glam but not in an overly tarty way and for men a collared shirt is a must. The décor is stunning and has the region's largest LED screen in case you get bored of VIP watching. Walk in on the weekdays and enjoy a drink at the bar or to get a table, you need to order drinks by the bottle. On the weekend a min spend is required between 2500 – 4000 dhs for either a regular table or VIP booth. At.mosphere is super cool and chic and certainly a must do for the trendy holidaymakers – if you have cash to flash!

Entry: Arrive early to avoid the queues but seriously dress to impress. Arrive as a couple or mixed group. For table bookings call number above or see dubai.armanihotels.com

Trilogy

Madinat Jumeirah

04 3668888

Trilogy is a main stay nightclub, that feels as if it has been around for ages. But the vibe inside is not tired. It's 3 floors, pretty large and plays urban music. This club is a banker if you want a good night out.

N'Dulge

Atlantis

04 426 2626

What can you say about the nightclub at the pinnacle of the palm? Well, it's for the rich couple who can afford to stay there – and those glam enough to come here as a regular. The big benefit is beng able to get your Nobu sushi at your table here – so you can eat and stay on. It's a little chaotic sometime, and a little expensive to go VIP, but being in a rave with young to middle aged rich folk letting loose to dance tracks is a lot of fun, especially when you least expect it someone shouts out "chooooon". If you are at Atlantic, make sure you pop in. N'Dulge was previously called Sanctuary.

BEACH BARS

Barasti

Le Meridien Mina Seyahi Resort

04 399 3333

If you're trying to escape the pretentious crowd and you want a no frills great night out, head for Barasti for a true holiday vibe experience overlooking the Arabian sea. Start with evening drinks and their super bar food and stay till late when the party really kicks off on the beach. Alternatively, some of the 'daytimers' come here for a relaxing breezy lunch. If you're lucky enough to be around when a top DJ or live concert is performing – buy your tickets ahead of time. Dressing here is a mix of casual and bling, but just beware it is an outdoor venue so the summers will get sticky.

Entry: No strict entry code but book a table else you will be kept waiting.

Sho Cho

Dubai Marine Resort

04 346 1111

Sho Cho is a trendy Japanese bar and restaurant that has an amazing terrace that overlooks the sea. It's a trendy location for the trendy people, that's a little too congested to be a proper club, but Sunday night is rammed for 80s night – which is the best 80s night in Dubai. But don't let that put you off or stereotype the place. It has goods selection of Japanese dishes but this is a place to be glam and watch others being glam.

Nasimi Beach

Atlantis, Palm Jumeirah

(04)55 200 4321

A more upmarket beach party pulling in the higher class punters. Book a cabana or table in advance or go early and grab a few beanbags. For the ladies, Tuesday is the night to go where there is free admission, cocktails and snack platters to share. Friday is the biggest day of the week and the pool party begins at 2pm and rocks till1am. After 4pm, expect to pay an entry fee of 100dhs or if you and a group of mates want to feel special get a VIP seating area for 4000 dhs min spend on food, shisha and drinks, in return this will buy you 12 entry tickets and of course a swanky seating area. Atmosphere is electric and the music is varied to keep everyone happy. Check out their website or facebook page for info on upcoming acts and DJs which play regularly throughout the month.

Entry: After 4pmthis is a strictly over 21 event and 100 dhs entry per person will be levied except on Tuesdays where ladies are free. For more info and reservations, call the number above or visit nasimibeach.com or search for NasimiBeach on facebook.

STYLISH SHISHA CAFES

Ewaan Lounge

The Palace,Old Town, The Address Hotel

04 428 7888

Open:4pm – 2amdaily

Beautiful place to simply relax under the stars, you won't hear loud music here, just soft Arabic beats whilst you smoke some shisha (grape of course), snack on gorgeous Arabic mezze and drinks. Alcohol is also served. Seating cannot be reserved so best to arrive by 7pm to get the best view lounge seats. A full restaurant is available inside.

The Rooftop

One and Only Royal Mirage

04 399 9999

Surely one of the best places to chill out and spend and evening , where you can smoke a shisha have great drink and listen to soothing beats. One of our favourites, this is a great place to meet up with friends.

Ikandy Bar

Shangri La Hotel

04 343 8888

Open: October – mid June 6pm (enquire first) 6pm – 2am daily.

This poolside shisha lounge is an unofficial addition to Shangri La's outlets mainly due to the fact that it is not open year round so enquire if you are planning to visit during the hotter season. The décor is very bubblegum fused with LA style glam with generously sized lounge sofas amongst drapes of white fabric. Music is mellow and just the right tempo to relax to with some grape shisha and yummy mezze lounge. All of this overlooking the pool and stunning views of the Burj make it just perfect. We couldn't really fault anything here except for the pink lighting, which actually worked nicely and we're sure Barbie would be well proud.

SOUKS, SHOPPING & SOUVENIRS

Imagine a kid in a candy shop and you can get an understanding of what a shopaholic's idea of bliss could be. It is fitting, therefore, that largest candy shop in the world, Candilicious, is located in Dubai's largest mall, the Dubai Mall. Dubai has it all when it comes to shopping: Malls, lots of them, including the Dubai Mall, one of the biggest in the world; souks, faux souks and upmarket souks; designer boutiques; tailors; street stalls; markets; and fake designer touts. It's all here in Dubai – and shopping is celebrated almost as a national sport. And for those that can't afford it, window shopping is their national sport. There's a subtle sales mechanism saying that Dubai is tax free, but that is countered by the amount spent on shipping all the goods in to Dubai. For availability, though, Dubai has everything, almost – and when there is a sale – boy is it big!

Trinkets from the Dubai Souks

People seem to congregate around shopping establishments – they are a kind of hub; somewhere to go when it's too hot, somewhere to go when there is nothing to do. That may sound a little vacuous but for a shopping fiend who wants to binge on holiday shopping, Dubai most certainly is heaven.

THE DUBAI MALLS (INCLUDING DUBAI MALL)

The only Bloomingdales outside of the US – it's in Dubai Mall. Saks 5th Avenue, it's in the Burjuman Mall here. Even Hamleys for the kids is in the Dubai Mall. Ski slope in a mall – check. And that's just a small taster. All the big global brands are here, but so are the niche and no-so-global ones. You'll find an eclectic mix of modern Arabic designers, Western brands mixed with Abaya boutiques, turning Dubai into a retail extravaganza. The draw of Dubai Mall is too great, and you will spend some time in this place, but depending on where you are staying you'll probably pop into one of the others for some well deserved escape from the sun.

Our honest view is this: whoever you are, rich or poor – you need to see the audacity of Dubai Mall, what it contains and what it represents. Dubai Mall is a must see for all tourists, whether you want to shop or not. It's not just a shopping mall, it is a core part of Dubai's landscape. Then there are the malls for the die hards, for those of you who are in Dubai for the shopping. If that's what you in Dubai to do, then get down to Burjuman, Wafi, Mall of the Emirates, Festival Centre, Deira City Centre Ibn Batuta & Mirdif, but beware of shopping mall fatigue where you don't even know which mall you are in. You'll probably go to the one that is nearest to you or most accessible. In all reality, it will all depend on where you are staying. For the Discount hunters, you might have luck in Dubai Outlet Mall and Dragonmart. And then, there are the periphery malls, which are larger plazas, expat focused, and great for the neighbourhood. They are also worth visiting, if that's what you need. And you will see all the global brands, from Department Stores to boutiques. It's also worth visiting the Arabian department store called Paris Gallery which is frequented by the local Emirati. There are no real malls that we suggest you stay away from. However, if you are broke, you should stay away from Dubai – or at least limit your credit cards!

Most malls open daily from 10am to 10pm, staying open until 11pm on Thursday and Friday, and opening at 2pm on a Friday, though

Friday is different for different malls and stores, so it's worth checking. A shopping bag from one of the Dubai malls is a memento of you shopping in Dubai. Go get it! And a final piece of advice, the air conditioning is in direct proportion to how hot it is outside. Expect a super cool breeze during the heat of summer – so make sure you have a cardigan or hoodie to keep those goose pimples at bay.

Dubai Mall

thedubaimall.com

Downtown Dubai

There is no escaping Dubai Mall. It is the hub of modern Dubai and a fine example retail gone right. While the place is one of the largest malls in the world, and would probably take a week to cover properly, it is organised by a genius – and it has to be, because the shopping with so many stores is difficult enough. There are 1200 shops within 12million square feet – which makes it the largest shopping mall in the world by area. In context that is the same area as 50 football pitches. Its size doesn't scare anyone – it brings in more and more people. In 2011 it became the world's most-visited shopping and leisure destination. It is claimed that 54 million people visited Dubai Mall, 4 million more than the number that visited New York City in the same period. It simply is monumental. Along with Bloomingdales and Gallery Lafayette, you will find every designer under the sun up and down a part of the mall called Fashion Avenue. You will also find the largest indoor gold souk in the world, Candylicious, the largest sweet store in the world, the Dubai Aquariaum, the Sega theme park, Ice rink. It's an expedition in its own right and with the range of 150 restaurants, you can power up for more retail action. There are mall concierges at every corner with maps, advice and directions but we recommend planning what you want to purchase before you enter the temptation of buying everything you see.

Mall of the Emirates

malloftheemirates.com

Sheikh Zayed Road

In any other city, the Mall of the Emirates would be the place to see or be seen but for the Dubai Mall. In its favour, there is Ski Dubai which brings a different kind of wow factor to the place, but it sometimes feels like just another big mall. There's not a full overlap with the Dubai Mall, so it's worth checking out whether you want to visit the stores here. There is, for example, a Harvey Nichols that doesn't exist at the Dubai Mall. There is an Emporio Armani Café here which is great to put your feet up – which we think better than the Armani Café in the Dubai Mall (under the birds) .

Dragonmart

dragonmart.ae

Located on the Emirates Road

There's nothing quite like Dragonmart in Dubai. It is the largest Chinese trading hub outside of China and sells a mixture of cheap tat to quality goods. It is huge, and if you are looking for a bargain, it's worth traipsing the 30 minutes by taxi to get there, but you will easily spend four hours there without thinking. It's a little bit of a maze and the place feels more like a Chinese Mall mashed up with an outlet backstreet in an industrial area of the US – a kind of globalised offshore in Dubai. You can buy anything – literally anything - here, from replica jewellery to electronic helicopters, handbag duplicates to hit and miss electronics. And this is the place to bargain as it's not as cheap as you think it should be, but haggle and you might get a good deal. It's almost the anti-Dubai which is why it's located away from the glamour – but it is certainly popular, huge and they are building an extension to double its size. The largest flea market in the world – yes, it's in Dubai. 4000 shops – that's 4 times the number at the Dubai Mall. You have been warned. Imagine all of Alibaba.com's produce being in sold in a two storey mall and you have Dragonmart.

Dubai Outlet Mall

dubaioutletmall.com

Dubai – Al Ain Road

You take the 30 minute taxi ride out into the desert for one thing and one thing only: discounted designer labels. And you think you might get them at a good discount – but it's pot luck. There are 250 shops with a few food outlets. The place feels a little clinical, but it can be worthwhile. Start at the first floor at the sport brand name stores such as Nike, Puma and Adidas before going down to try out The Outlet and The Deal before venturing forth. The deals are usually not bad, but it's also a matter of luck with regard to when the stores receive new goods. If you are a less popular size, you will get a bargain here!

Deira City Centre Mall

deiracitycentre.com

Al Ithihad Road

City Centre Mall is an everyman's mall – it's always busy and caters for the every day. Before the new wave of malls appeared, this was the main mall the people used to shop at. And it remains popular. The mall doesn't have as many high end brands as Dubai Mall, Burjuman and the like but there is a good selection of stores catering for 'normal' salaries. It can get a little congested and claustrophobic in comparison to the airier new malls.

Festival Centre

festivalcentre.com

Dubai Festival City

As Dubai grows further out, so the malls follow. Part of the newish Dubai Festival City, this mall is located with great views of the creek. It can a little far to come if you are staying in Jumeirah, for example. It's a great mall, but not worth the trek across from the main holiday spots unless you have a reason to be in Festival City.

Burjuman

burjuman.com

Khalifa bin Zayed Street, Bur Dubai

Apart from Saks Fifth Avenue, there's not much you can't get from any other store in Dubai. That said, there are high end brands here, such as D&G and DKNY, as this is how this mall was pitched prior to the arrival of Dubai Mall, so you might bag yourself a deal. Burjuman feels like a high end mall and is the best mall in the area.

Ibn Battuta Mall

ibnbattutamall.com

Jebel Ali

In our eyes, IBM, as it is referred to, is over themed. Is that even possible? In Dubai it is. Based upon places visited by the 14th Century Berber explorer - namely China, India, Persia, Egypt, Tunisia and Andalucia - it is large and spacious, but due to its location, it may be a little far out for some. But as a mall on the outskirts of Dubai it makes it more of an escape than some of the other malls. The themed areas make shopping in Dubai in this location something of a museum type experience which kids will love. There's even a hot air balloon that rises to a height to give you a view of the Marina

Wafi City Mall

wafi.com

Dubai Healthcare City

Wafi is in an area themed as Egyptian and you won't miss the pyramid at the front entrance and is also connected to the Raffles hotel. It's a label focused place, you will find many local Emirati shopping here, but you will find it smaller than some of the other malls. However, the souk extension of Khan Murjan is the big drawing point of the mall — as well as some of the restaurants including Asha's.

Mirdiff City Centre Mall

mirdifcitycentre.com

Mirdiff

We love Mirdiff City Centre Mall because it is great for the kids with iFly and playnation, which makes the trip across town worthwhile. Play, shop, play, shop, eat – everyone's happy. As it's a little further out, this one is only worth going to if you have kids to keep entertained.

Emirates Towers Boulevard Plaza

boulevarddubai.com

Exclusive high end, small plaza containing the highest concentration of designer names in Dubai. Worth popping in if you are on the way to Agency. Despite its size – it's only on 2 floors of the business tower - some fashionistas just shop here and nowhere else. It's high end – and probably one of the cleanest plazas you will ever find – perhaps because Sheikh Mohamed is often in the area.

Other Malls worth a mention include:

Mercato Mall - small Italian themed mall in Jumeirah mercatoshoppingmall.com

Lamcy Plaza – lower brand, ie normal priced clothes, for the masses

lamcyplaza.com

Marina Mall- Quiet, Expat focused Mall serving Marina residents

dubaimarinamall.com

Al Ghurair City – oldest mall in Dubai, favoured by Emiratis

alghuraircentre.com

The Village Mall - get down here on Jumeirah Beach road for the exclusives and up and coming brands. This is where you will find Ayesha Depala, which the ladies will love and another boutique called S*auce. You can also find other one offs at Candella.

thevillagedubai.com

In addition try out The Sahara Centre on the way to Sharjah as well as Mega Mall in Sharjah. In Abu Dhabi, Marina Mall and Abu Dhabi Mall are the ones worth visiting,

SOUKS & MARKETS

A souk is a market area of an Arab city where you can get anything from fresh food to artefacts such as a shisha and tourist type objects. In Dubai, these have taken on different forms with only a few traditional ones that you might associate with the Arab world. But that's not bad thing, the choice of souks and markets in Dubai gives a different experience to those in depths of deeper Marrakesh. Here's how we have split them up:

Nouveaux Souks – these are souks that have been created with a traditional feel, but with the luxury of air conditioning and all the mod cons.

Gold and the Gold Souk – Dubai is renowned for its gold and this gold souk has to be seen to be believed.

Traditional Souks in Old Dubai – The souks that give Dubai its reputation and that continue to operate to this day

Tailored Clothes markets & Mina Bazaar – get bespoke items made during your trip.

New markets – Markets and shopping areas that have popped up as New Dubai has established itself

NOUVEAUX SOUKS

We have put together the best souks worth checking out all for different reasons. Whether you want an Arabian coffee pot or a handwoven carpet, some prayer beads or other intricacies of Arab culture, these are the places to go to:

Khan Murjan, Wafi Mall.

Khan Murjan is a new area in the basement of Wafi City Mall, which has more than 150 shops with traders selling a variety of handicrafts. Of all the nouveaux souks, this is the one that we recommend. You're transported back to the olden days in the dark feel of Arabia – a complete contrast from the bright lights of Wafi. The ambience is authentic with dark wood features and small shops selling shawls, belly dancing gear and more. If you can catch it during the day you will see the light coming through the amazing stained glass window. And once you have finished your shopping, have some coffee or shisha near the waterwheel in the courtyard.

Souk, Madinat Jumeirah

The Souk at Madinat Jumeirah precedes Khan Murjan by a few years and in its airy wooden interior, you feel somewhat taken back in time. The stores are more expensive, but some of them are exclusive. This is worth a stroll if you are spending an evening at Madinat Jumeirah.

Souk Al Bahar, Downtown Burj Dubai

Souk Al Bahar (soukalbahar.ae) is located in at Downtown Burj Dubai just the short walk across the bridge from Dubai Mall. Even though the walk is a short one, you will take a while to get there because the first thing you see is the marvel of the Burj Khalifa – and as you cross the bridge you will be tempted to take that perfect shot with the Burj in the background. But you'll eventually make it - and it will be worth it. The Souk Al Bahar has a modern day feel and attitude to a souk, with restaurants and some retail shopping outlets including several pashmina shawl shops, souvenir and Moroccan lighting. For a meal to remember, get an outdoor table at one of the bordering restaurants. We like Urbano (Italian), or try Sammach (Seafood), or one of our favourites, Zahr El Laymoun (healthy Lebanese) and enjoy fantastic views of the Burj Khalifa and Dubai Fountain while you eat. You may want to reserve a table as you walk up to the Souk – as this is a perfect evening and tables are limited.

Al Jaber Gallery, Mall of the Emirates, Dubai Mall, Souk Al Bahar

Sometime you want to just get the gifts without the buzz of the market. This is exactly what Al Jaber does. There are many locations but we like the one in Souk Al Bahar. You can pick up your bits and pieces, gifts and souvenirs so it seems as if you have done the trawl for your friends and family. This is market shopping cheating at its best. No haggling, no buzz, just good quality souvenirs in one place.

GOLD & THE GOLD SOUK

The most famous of all the souks in Dubai is the Gold Souk. Dubai has the reputation of being the City of Gold, so much so that Raffles Spa offers a 24 carat gold facial. We don't recommend it if you are on a budget, but we do recommend a trip to the Gold Souk. If you have not been, it truly is a marvel to see hundreds of gold shops all together, selling this age old investment. And while, historically, gold has been an investment, the temptation for adornment remains. With the numerous styles on offer, it is very difficult to walk away from the UAE without getting your own piece of bling.

The Gold Souk

Many regular holidaymakers to Dubai cannot leave without making at least one stop to the famous Deira Gold souk. If you are looking to buy gold jewellery for a wedding, for yourself or looking to sell off your old unwanted gold, the gold souk is the place to come. Gold souks in the UAE are the biggest re-importer of gold so the selection on offer at the various outlets are huge, especially the one in Deira. Quality is brilliant as careful monitoring regularly takes place in order to avoid fake pieces being sold. The price of gold items are very competitive because workmanship charges are more reasonable compared to western countries. With the hustle and bustle of over 300 stores gleaming at you in all their splendour, the gold souk is on our top list of things to do in Dubai.

Inside the Gold Souk

The first sounds that you will hear when you enter the souk are the calls to purchase "copy handbag", or "copy watch good price". If you are interested you can follow them to their backroom to see the merchandise. If you are not interested then be careful not to give them any eye contact or they wont leave you alone!

If you want to combine Meena Bazaar with the Deira Gold Souk, why not take a 5 minute abra ride across Dubai creek. The small shops within Deira gold souk normally operate on a split shift basis, so you'll find the independent stores will shut between 2-5pm. The larger chains such as Damas and Marhaba may work through the day, but do enquire first. If you are holidaying when it is extremely warm it's best to visit the gold souk from 5pm.. If you can handle the heat – go earlier! If visiting on a Friday, most shops will be shut till 4pm.

Gold Shops

With all the shops just selling gold, it can be overwhelming. Ultimately, if you are there to purchase gold, then you will need to find something you like. If you are not planning to buy gold, it's worth checking out for the atmosphere alone as you will never experience this anywhere else in the world!

In terms of specific gold shops, there are so many stores available, but we have checked out a few that stand out and would be a good place to start with. Damas is the big player offering the most up to date designs. Their collection is mainly Arabian, but they stock a large variety of Italian, European and Indian pieces. Damas is reputed as being one of the expensive stores, so heavy haggling may not work here! Marhaba have a variety of branches throughout Dubai selling a lot of western style jewellery. This is a great store and can indulge in some serious bargaining. JoyAlukkas is a big seller of Indian designs and has a number of stores in the UAE. Other stores worth checking out are Barakat and Yasin jewellery. Remember, everyone has a different taste – be sure to check out a number of stores and then buy from where you feel comfortable. Marhaba, Damas and Barakat are our favourites.

If you feel special enough to leave around a chunk of gold on your desk – why not get a paperweight to make you feel like a king. The famous jewellers Damas hold a few designs in the form of an oryx, flowers and shoes to suit anyone's hobbies.

Another brilliant gift idea is to have your name written in Arabic and then carved in gold as a pendant, bracelet or ring. The beautiful Arabic calligraphy is a timeless form of design and sure to be a hit for any gift.

Selling Gold Jewelley

Selling gold jewellery in Dubai to help the cause of another jewellery set is the smart way to go if you have gold sitting in your archive jewellery box. Use it up and upgrade in Dubai! In the Gold Souk in Deira, about 30% of shops will offer an exchange on old gold. You will know as there are signs on the front door saying 'We exchange old gold for new gold'. A few good shops we know of are Kanz, G.B and Barakat. All have several branches within the Deira Gold souk. Obviously, exchanging gold means you have to like the gold pieces that these particular shops have. If you like several items of jewellery in different shops or are just after selling your old gold for some cash, then there are two shops we know of in Deira Gold Souk which will offer you a quote in cash in exchange for your old gold. Al Taj, which is located in the alley of gold shops surrounding the covered part of the gold souk and Al Khatib, also not far from Al Taj. It's best to get directions from any shop keeper. These two shops will give you a valuation of your gold by separating your pieces into 18k, 22K and 24k groups and weighing each of the groups. They are experts in assessing gold so don't try and sell off your gold plated items – they will know! Remember to bring your passport as no other form of ID will be accepted.

The process is quick and normally you can sell your gold and get your cash within 30 minutes depending on how much you have. The quote you receive if selling for cash rather then exchanging for new gold doesn't vary immensely but you may lose about 5% if you prefer the cash to new gold. Bear in mind though that some are particularly picky about certain factors such whether the gold has a hallmark or not. Although it is not usual, they may be concerned whether there is a certificate or a receipt. But this is only likely to happen if they believe something illegal is taking place.(There are a number of measures taking place to prevent illegal trading of gold) so before travelling, if you have any of these documents, it might be worth taking it with you along with your gold. However from most people we have spoken to – trading in old gold is not a complicated process. To prevent any issues, the two cash only trade in stores will request the CID to turn up to take a photo of the gold and to sign off on the sale. You won't get ripped off, but equally, if you are dealing in illegal goods, don't expect to get away with it. As well as gold, souks sell a vast amount of diamonds, however trading-in your unwanted diamonds is probably not a good idea. If you are keen to do this at the gold souk it is best to get a valuation from an independent expert first. Trading-in diamonds in the souk is generally not advised as most stores are not experts in valuing diamonds therefore a genuine deal may not be given.

Gold in Dubai Airport dubaidutyfree.com

Buying gold at Dubai Aiport could be a last minute thing. Also, if you are visiting Dubai on a stopover and have no opportunity to get out of the airport area, you may be tempted to shop for gold and other items at the Dubai Duty Free. Speaking with many people, we have come across mixed reviews for buying gold here. Generally, over the years, the level of customer service at the gold shops in the Dubai Duty Free has declined, however if you know exactly what you want then shopping at Dubai Duty Free is not a bad option. Most people have commented that sometimes good deals can be had here. However, we have spot checked the value of what you can get versus the gold souk and Dubai Airport doesn't come close.

The Gold and Diamond Park goldanddiamondpark.com

The Gold and Diamond Park can be found on Sheikh Zayed Road, between interchange 3 and 4. Not as busy as the Deira Gold Souk, which can be good and bad, they stock a larger variety of gemstones and, of course, diamonds. So, if diamonds are your thing, go to the gold and diamond park. If it's predominantly a gold item you are after, then go to the gold souk. There are about 90 retailers and some of the popular well known chains such as Damas and Marhaba. The prices are a lot cheaper than the west, so, once you have proposed, this is the place to come and get your perfect diamond, although haggling down the price when with your loved one – may feel a little weird. Some of the diamonds here are massive! Be careful you don't knock yourself out – but as a negotiation point aim for 50% of the starting point and work back to between 30-40%. If you are creating your own piece you will have less room to manoeuvre, but do make sure you push down and shop around. Only a fool pays the first price.

Gold Souk in Dubai Mall

If you are only visiting Dubai for a day and time is of a constraint, the Dubai Mall, the world's largest mall, has its own indoor gold souk with familiar brands such as GB, Marhaba and Damas. This area is a separate section within the mall with about 40 shops all together round a centre point. The shops will be open all day in accordance with mall opening hours. You won't get the same noisy souk vibe, but if you need to gold shop – you can do it in a peaceful air-conditioned environment. It's also quiet, so you won't have to wait long to see anyone.

Tips on purchasing gold

Choice - The UAE is a large importer of gold offering a variety of designs from Indian style, to Arabic and modern Italian and European pieces.

Tax free - There is no VAT on the gold in the UAE, which makes prices particularly cheap. You might find that prices are up to 40% cheaper than those in the west.

Shop around - There are an endless number of stores offering similar products. Once you have found the item you like, make sure you haggle down to get the best price, before comparing that same item with another shop. Feel free to walk away and come back for the best price you have haggled to – it is all part of the game.

Weight and Workmanship - The price is based on the type of gold (24K, 22K etc.) and how much it weighs. The price per gram is usually displayed at each store. If not, make sure you ask specifically for what is the price of gold on the day as the price of gold is variable depending on the day. There will then be a charge for workmanship depending on length of time taken, how intricate the design is and whether a craftsman or machine was used. With a little bit of mental arithmetic therefore, you can quite easily work out what percentage charge is being charged for the workmanship. And usually, this will revolve around a fixed amount for the workmanship around the gold that doesn't change. But in your negotiations you will never know how much that is! But if maths makes you uncomfortable, ask for the calculator – and let the negotiations begin.

Safe and secure - There is significant monitoring of the stores so that customers can be sure that the shops are providing a good product that is real gold.

Colours - Designs are constantly changing and white gold is becoming more and more prevalent in the souks these days, with chromium designs also being offered.

Trade in - Many tourists have their old gold on the shelf and come to trade in for cash or as payment towards a new design. It is certainly possible to sell gold in Dubai. Not all stores buy gold, but many do, and some will accept an exchange. Bear in mind, though that some are particularly picky about certain factors: whether the gold has a hallmark; whether there is a certificate; or whether you have a receipt. (There are a number of measures taking place to prevent illegal trading of gold)

New designs - if you want to get the newest pieces, then base your trip around the shopping festivals. Many bring out their new ranges to coincide with DSF and DSS when much business takes place.

Custom made - if you want your own piece designed, that can also be done, depending on the time frame. It is best to get in touch beforehand or as soon as you get into town so that your piece is perfect. Having pictures of what you want is also a big help.

Copies - Duplicate designs exist all over and you could get your Bulgari gold set for a snip in comparison the legitimate price, not that we condone this flagrant infringement of copyright! Talking of copies you will hear the calls of "copy watch, copy handbag" being pitched at you, to lure you to rooms filled with fake Louis Vitton, Gucci and other big names.

What is available - everything is available from chains to sets, diamond rings to bangles, watches to cufflinks to money holders. If you want it, it will be here.

Shop times - The shops at the souks operate on a split shift basis, so there is basically a break for the afternoon between 2 and 5. Either get there early or aim for the evening until about 1030pm. You can buy gold at Dubai Airport but we think you get a better choice, better price and better experience at the Gold Souk in Dubai

Cash is king - You can bargain down to the last Dirham if you pay in cash. While credit cards are accepted, your Dollar or Dirham can make a big difference if you are planning a big purchase.

TRADITIONAL SOUKS

Deira, is renowned for the famous gold souk. However, once you begin your adventure, you may want to explore the surrounding backstreets.

Perfume Souk Dubai

If you want to concoct your own Arabic scent, and you have sampled the scents of the Arabian Oud and similar smells in the malls, then the Pefume Souk is for you. The smell of Arabian perfume is completely different to western scents and is oil based, so consider this before you commit your money. The Perfume is located near the Deira Gold souk. if the creek is behind you (in the distance) walk towards your right.

Spice souk Dubai

The spice souk is the one souk that actually feels like a souk. The smell of spice is great as you walk through the tight alleyways and streets. Worth the walk through to see all the spices piled high, and to buy your discount saffron. The spice souk is worth experiencing for atmosphere alone and is located the other side of the Gold Souk.

In addition to the Perfume Souk and Spice Souk there are the fish market and the fruit and vegetable market. We don't recommend going to visit these at all as they are essentially for trade. If you haven't seen a fish market before, then it's worth getting up early to see the fish market, but for no other reason other than you like to watch people buying fish and like the pong.

We also do not recommend the electronics souk, where it is impossible to judge the quality of product and the Deira covered souk, which consists of odd clothing plus cheap tat for your house.

Textile Souk

The textile souk is by far the most traditional of all the souks that exist in Dubai. Close to the creek, this was once an amalgamation of different Emirati stores that now have seemed to focus on Indian and Pakistani clothing. You can get all your material for a Salwar Kameez and get it tailored. But ultimately you'll just want to walk through, get a feel for the atmosphere and sample some pashminas – and if you haven't – then this may be a place to pick up some souvenirs.   Also known to some locals as the Old Souk, this is a walk through that you must do.

Karama Market Dubai

Also known as both Karama Souk and Karama Complex, Karama Market has a reputation for selling the best in fake goods that Dubai has to offer. If that's your thing you can find almost anything you want in varying degrees of quality from sunglasses and watches to t-shirts handbags and shoes – as well as some odd and unusual tat. Be ready for the ear invasion as you are offered different goods at different prices, but these shop keepers revel in the haggling to the point that they actually enjoy it. Although the authorities are aware of what really goes on here, karama has become part of the landscape of Dubai. Occasionally there are swoops of some specific stores, but you're unlikely to get stopped both here or on your way out of the country. Don't expect rock bottom prices, but do expect to negotiate – and pay in cash to guarantee your final "last last price" discount. , this is fake central. If that is what you want, this the place to get your knocked off goods. Make sure you check the spelling of brand names – many people have walked off with a Cucci instead of Gucci or equivalent – until it was pointed out to them back home.

TAILORED CLOTHES & MEENA BAZAAR

Some people come to Dubai for the prime reason of tailoring their clothes. Some even make a business out of it. If you want tailored clothes, Dubai can make to measure, from colourful Indian outfits, to tailored suits. Many tailors exist all over Dubai, but the big concentration of them is at Mina Bazaar. For the average Joe getting a tailored suit is a luxury in the West, so getting one made while on holiday is a luxury and an experience. We give you the knowledge of what you need to know before you part with your hard earned cash.

Meena Bazaar, open on a split shift basis, is also known as Souk al Kabeer or the Textile souk. It is noisy and has the brightest most colourful store fronts. It is also falling apart and a little tacky but is worth a trip to see the heart of India in the heart of Dubai. You could combine Meena Bazaar with the Deira Gold Souk by taking the 5 minute abra ride across Dubai creek.

First off, you need to get to Mina Bazaar, which is also known as Cosmos Lane, and is located close to Bank Street which is also known as Computer Street, sometimes. It all sounds confusing but it's easiest to take a taxi there, since they will all know where to go and parking usually is a tad traumatic. Worst case, you can try and get to the Sheraton 4 points or Astoria Hotel, ask someone the direction and walk there in less than five minutes.

For suits, some tailors will copy your items, while some prefer to measure you up from scratch. Copying of items usually takes more time, but in the main, you can expect to get a suit tailored between 3 days to one week – you may need to have up to 3 fittings, so if you are visiting the UAE rather than residing here, make sure that the tailor is aware of your urgency.

Prices will be split between material and labour, though many shops will provide you with an all in service. For a regular tailor in Mina

Bazaar, the price for tailoring an business suit should between 400 and 1000Dhs, and then the material cost by yard will depend on your taste. Material to make a suit will cost anything between 50 to 500Dhs per yard, and for the average size man, 3 and a half yards is what you need for a jacket and trousers up to about 4 and half if you are a little bigger. And then, for a fixed tailoring charge over and above this, you will have your suit. So, for about 1500Dhs you can have a top quality tailored suit that fits you perfectly, which is less than an average off the peg in the West. The standards are very good, and you can make your alterations until you have your perfect fit. You can also get an extra pair of trousers. Shirts cost about 150 Dhs each but could be a lot more depending on the material and options. You'll get all the options from whether you want cut away collars to types of buttons, so make sure you are very specific, or the cheap option will be assumed.

We recommend Mina Bazaar in Bur Dubai, although others would recommend going to the Afghani market in Deira. We don't find the quality is as good there. If you have time, then check them both out. Which store should you go to for your tailoring? Well, it really is best to look around and see who you feel comfortable with, and who can fit you in. An option would be to go to Al Nahda Tailors or Kucheen for men, and Dream Girl Tailors or Grace Tailors for women, all located at Mina Bazaar. Once you are there, ask around and you'll be pointed in the right direction.

We have no qualms in recommending Parmar tailors on Al Nahda Street. They are well established, have regular clientele, and if you want to spend the extra buck on some top end tailoring, then we Parmar Tailors are the ones for you (parmartailors.com), While the other tailors produce good value for money, Parmar have established a reputation for themselves as the best. You will be paying a lot more; typically 300Dhs for a shirt and 2000Dhs for a suit on average, but the quality can not be questioned. They also have a separate women's shop located a few doors away. They are based a

3 minutes walk down from Al Fahidi Street on Al Nahda Street. If you want to compare, the places to check out are Kachins, Raymond, Santobar, and Lobo (very high end and fantastic!) to get a good range of prices. If you are in Satwa, then try Whistle and Flute near Plant Street (04 342 9229) - it's tricky first time round to find but worth it if you have the time and money to get the best suit possible. Call them for specific directions. Another great bet is Royal Fashion at the Jumeirah Beach Hotel. And recently, we have tried Made to Measure (M2M) They are in Jumeirah 3 Opposite Sunset Mall +971.04.3942244.

Many come to Dubai looking for Indian clothes, in which case Tia Fashion in Mina Bazaar is the place to go. For something a little lower end is Sheetals. Other places for Indian clothes include Roopam and Ratti, where you can get your material and then go to one of the tailors for stitching. For something a little more reasonable, "She" is a good option. For a place to stitch your fabrics into your own creation within a couple of days go to Dream Girl or Grace Taylors. If making clothing is your thing, then Satwa, which feels like a town square is worth going to, if you have the time.

Tips on Tailoring clothes

If you want to design something from scratch, it makes sense to bring a magazine with you to demonstrate what you want.

If the tailor does not speak English, then they are not going to understand what you want. Go elsewhere.

Consider getting an extra pair of trousers if getting a suit done.

Only put down a maximum deposit of 50%

Be aware that shops close in the afternoon for a break

You probably will not be able to get much more of a discount than the figures quoted unless you order a number of items

If you think you will wear a waistcoat, you are in the minority

There are so many options with suits, so try and come with a picture of what you want. Options to consider on a jacket are: a two part back, single or double breasted, two or three buttons, height of lapel, any extra inside pockets for mobiles etc, how many buttons on the arm, a hook, the colour of the lining.

With trousers, consider: whether you will want lining if you are from a colder country, pleats or no pleats, number of belt hooks, number of back pockets, money pocket.

With shirts, consider: the type of collar, the hardness of the collar, single or double cuffs, whether you want a pocket, initials on the cuff, stitching next to the buttons, a slightly looser cuff for the side you wear your watch.

And finally, make sure you get what you asked for, and do not pay until it is perfect, but most of all, wear your clothes with pride - and tell your tailor that you heard about them from here. We send so much business their way!

SOUKS OUTSIDE DUBAI

Other Souks outside Dubai worth checking out:

The Blue Souk in Sharjah sells traditional objects in a different environment with big discounts on carpets and furniture. It's focus is on regional arts and crafts and is the place to buy a carpet.

The Fujairah Market is almost a step back in history and you can see how markets probably operated back in the day

The Souk Al Arsah in Sharjah is as traditional as it comes, having been rebuilt exactly to specification – it's worth checking out if making a trip to Sharjah Museum.

The New Souk at Khor Fakkan overlooks the gulf and would be one of the places you would visit if you traveled here. An eye catching and charismatic little spot.

In Abu Dhabi, the Central Market Abu Dhabi is another trendy Nouveau Souk as well as the Souk at Bab Al Bahr, behind the

Shangri La is worth a peak if you are there. Sometimes you could get lucky at the Iranian souk in Abu Dhabi at the Mina Port with Iranian hand painted goods, but you may just end up looking through plastic tat.

SHOPPING FESTIVALS & OTHER MARKETS

Of all the markets in Dubai, there are only two worth mentioning and worth considering – Covent Garden Market and Global Village. There are others which pop up all the time, so it's worth checking with your concierge what's on. Only in Dubai will you have festivals associated with shopping.

DUBAI SHOPPING FESTIVAL (DSF) & DUBAI SUMMER SURPRISES (DSS)

Dubai Shopping Festival is an annual shopping fest normally held for a month during December/January or February and almost always running alongside the Global Village festivities. It's to push further sales during the busiest holiday season of the year. Dubai Summer Surprises is the equivalent held in June and July, but to get people to visit Dubai during the down (hot!) season.

If you are a shopaholic or "value shopper", these times of year are perfect for you. All the shopping malls, independent shops, supermarkets, electronic stores take part in explosive promotions offering as much as 75% off the regular retail price. Some argue the festival is just over hyped nonsense, but we've picked up pretty good bargains in the past. As well as shopping, lots of entertainment and fun actvities for the kids take place to alleviate any kiddie stress from their parents shopping binges!

During DSF, you should also pop into the Global Village which normally runs from 4pm till late (check out our section on Global Village for more detail). Here you'll find more in the way of entertainment, live performances and acts with themes ranging from around the globe. Unique items will be on sale and there's a large range of international food to sample. Kids will love the buzz.

Please note that if you are booking a holiday around the Dubai Shopping Festival, room rates will be higher and busier then in other months, but generally this is the most popular time to visit UAE as the weather is at its coolest.

Points of note

If you are thinking of planning a trip around Dubai Shopping Festival, book your air tickets or hotels well in advance. The Festival starts with a bang on the first few nights with fireworks and big name acts appearing on stage so if you are big on entertainment, aim to visit at the beginning of the festival. Although if you are a real bargain hunter, going toward the end of the festival may give you even better savings, but maybe less choice?

Dates of Dubai Shopping Festival are normally mid Jan to mid February. The 2011 festival was on 20th January to 20th February.

Take a jumper. It can get chilly in the evenings during January and February.

Big name acts are contracted to make appearances at the event.

Look out for Modhesh – the mascot of DSS – a sort of weird yellow bouncy creature that the Dubai public have a love hate relationship with. Modhesh World, held at Dubai World Trade Centre, is a quasi theme park of sorts which will keep kids occupied while you plan your next conquest.

The only other shopping festival of sorts that rival these is during Ramadan where shops are open late and there are offers in advance of the Eid festival. This is when you can get dates by the barrel load.

When – Dubai Shopping Festival runs for one month during mid January and mid February. Dubai Summer Suprises runs from mid June to mid July. For exact dates, please check their website below. Opening times are usually in line with mall opening hours so check out the individual stores

How long – This is totally down to how much shopping you can take!

Location – The whole of Dubai is under Dubai Shopping Festival Fever, the shops who don't partake in promotions are party poopers.

Cost – The sky is high. or just go for the free entertainment

More info – dubaievents.ae

JBR THE WALK & COVENT GARDEN MARKET

The Walk at Jumeirah Beach Residence opened in 2008 and is an ocean facing promenade of nearly 2 kilometres with around 300 stores, restaurants and cafes. When it is not too hot, the Jumeirah Walk is a pleasant experience as apart from providing beautiful and refreshing views of the Arabian Sea it offers plenty of opportunities for splashing your cash as well.

The Jumeirah Beach Walk was initially designed to meet the needs of the residents of some 40 towers, the majority being residential apartments and a few hotels. But it soon evolved to being a cool place to hangout and now houses some amazing outdoor shopping boutiques such as Saks Fifth Avenue Outlet Store and Boutique 1 (one of our favourites), art galleries, sports shops, cultural artefacts as well as casual food and drink outlets to the chic world renowned chains such as Frankies, BiCE and Ruby Tuesdays. All this choice with a location that feels like you are sitting on the Mediterranean is just the prefect setting for a relaxing evening.

The highlight of The Walk at the Jumeirah Beach Residence is the Covent Garden Market. Not akin to the Covent Garden in London, but it does have some great stalls, and during the non Summer months it's a great place to come to sample the atmosphere. Great for kids, there are sometimes clowns, artists and a few stalls, so it's great to spend an evening or weekends. Originally for the residents at JBR, the Market now does draw a crowd and sometimes holds small festivals and themed functions.

Points of note –

Parking is a problem because of the crowds and especially in the evenings when traffic moves along at snail's pace.

It is advisable to be properly dressed so as not to attract attention and maintain the law of the land at all times.

Marina Walk is a different walk so don't let you taxi river get confused!

When –Evening is the best time to visit but worth visiting at other times to avoid the crowds. The official timings are 10 am -12 midnight (Daily) and on Thurs-Fri it is 10 pm - 1 am (after midnight). (The Covent Garden Market is from 10am to Midnight October to April, Wednesday, Thursday, 5pm -9pm Friday and Saturday)

How long –It depends totally on you whether you wish to spend 5 minutes, 5 hours or 5 days.

Location –Opposite Jumeirah Beach. The official address is Jumeirah, Al Sufouh Rd, next to Ritz Carlton Hotel and this hotel can serve as a landmark to give directions to the taxi driver. (The Covent Garden Market is located between Hilton Dubai Jumeirah Resort and the Sheraton Jumeirah Beach Resort & Towers)

Cost –There is no entry ticket here and it is open to all.

More info – facebook.com/thewalkatjbr

GLOBAL VILLAGE DUBAI

Global village in Dubai is a huge event running alongside Dubai Shopping Festival during the cooler months between October and March. Essentially it's a mini expo of Eastern and Middle Eastern Countries hosting a number of pavilions. Each one sells goods associated to its country. It has moved around over the years and now has a more permanent area in Dubailand. Dubailand was supposed to be a huge theme park but plans for this got shelved during the downturn and although plans for this seem to be back on, it will be a lot more modest affair.

The main aim of Global Village is to bring cultures and customs together. There are creative local items for sale, fabulous international food to sample and entertaining dances and performances. Additionally the Global Village experience has a carnival feel and there are plenty of amusement rides and games to keep kids and adults of all ages entertained and busy for hours. With the rising popularity of Dubai Shopping Festival and Dubai as a general hotspot to visit during the western winter season, Global Village has seen its visitor number increase every year and now welcomes over 4 million visitors annually.

Each year the Global Village hosts an annual carnival; this starts with the Dubai shopping festival but progresses onwards to include many other varied activities as well, some of the noteworthy events being the World Cultural stage, 'Beach Adrenalin' Jet-Ski show and the Lantern Festival featuring the Chinese lanterns. 30 different countries sell their traditional or typical products from China to Yemen to India and Lebanon. It really is a great idea, and if you are bringing your kids along, the rides will keep them busy.

Points of note

Global Village was always a mini precursor to being part of Dubailand - but the money has dried up a little for Dubai to invest in such a huge undertaking. So, Global Village remains on its own. almost

Take a jumper. It can get chilly in the evening.

Sometimes the fireworks in the desert can rival Disney's

Yemeni Honey is available here (Hint – it's the best honey in the world!)

When – Monday is the only family day in a week, which means only families are allowed. The timings are from 4pm till 12 am on Mondays as well as on Saturdays, Sundays, Tuesdays and Wednesdays. On Thursdays and Fridays the Global Village is open from 4 pm till 1 am. Global Village is only opene mid November to end of February/early March. Check their site for more information.

How long – This depends on how much time you want to spend inside the Global village indulging in shopping, dining and going for rides. A typical visit usually lasts for 3-4 hours, but it isn't hard to kill time in this place!

Location – The Dubai Global Village is located on the Emirates Road in Dubailand. Cost – The entry ticket costs 10 AED. You can also opt for VIP packages if these are available, these usually includes entry tickets, VIP car pass and some fun fair coupons which are meant for rides.

Booking – No booking required, visit the Global Village during the working hours whenever you like.

More info – globalvillage.ae and 04 3624114

SOUVENIRS

It's a question we get all the time - what should you buy from Dubai and where should you buy it from? Everyone wants to take a taster back of Dubai either for themselves – or for loved ones. It's simply not good enough to get the fake t-shirt any more. But there's no need to worry as the Dubai souvenirs are unique and plentiful and we tell you where you can get them from.

First things first, don't leave it too late. If you wait until you get to the airport, you will be left with not a great selection and you may be paying over the odds. In this section we have also included some other things worth buying, such as gold or getting some clothes tailored. That said, those of you trigger happy at spending cash will find it very easy at the malls and probably don't need to read this. After all, Dubai is for shopping!

DATES

Dates are possibly one of the more authentic purchases you can get from the UAE. And the dates here are some of the best you can get anywhere. The Bedouin used to live on the date – and, to a degree, the local Emirati still do – dates are used in gifting, hospitality and simply to indulge. There is one date you must try and that is from Bateel dates. Bateel, is beyond question the best date shop for this. The question really remains – whether you wish to indulge for yourself or pass these fine dates to friends. Go into the first Bateel you see on your trip and try a selection before buying. Our favourites are Khidri with orange or lemon peel, khidri with caremalized pecan or almond - and make sure you buy some agwa, which although a little expensive, in comparison, are the best and are said to be blessed by the Prophet, back in the day. The best dates are Kholas, Khidri and Agwa, in ascending order. The price ranges from 100 to 250 Dhs per kilo, but you could buy a small box and mix 300g worth. You will see, in the shops, the various displays which are often gifted on occasions such as Eid, when people do spend up to Dhs 30,000! Dates are such a prominent part of UAE society, that you will find them all over, and a great way to get a large bunch of gifts is to go to any one of the supermarkets, such as Choithram or Carrefour, who sell boxes of preboxed dates for Dhs10 upwards. Perfect presents, if you have no time – or even if you do, but can't be bothered!

Bateel – Dubai Mall

Bateel – Atlantis

Bateel – Burjuman Centre

Bateel – Deira City Centre

CHOCOLATES

The big secret of the Middle East is they have some of the best chocolates in the world. It's big business. You may have heard of Patchi. Well, there's a branch here, but our favourite chocolate – and something unique to take back with you is the camel milk chocolate from Al Nassma. The chocolate is premium end and tastes amazing, actually capturing the taste of Arabia. And is actually more healthy than regular chocolate. We recommend it highly.

Since chocolate is big thing here, you will find lots of chocolate shops here, all the premium chocolatiers from Europe all have shops here. You'll find shops like Godiva and Galler. But we like the UAE specific ones. Our secret special tipple around the UAE is a company called Fuala. They're not in the major malls, but believe you me, these are the best chocolates in the UAE. This is where the local Emirati get their chocolates. Another chocolate shop which comes highly recommended and we have been gifted is ChoCo'a which is a Lebanese chocolate shop. Again, not in the malls there is one shop in Dubai which is worth visiting if you are in the vicinity.

The other novelty worth considering if you are going for tea at the Burj al Arab is to ask the chocolate cake. There is a reason why it is so expensive – it's finished off with a 24-carat gold leaf.

The best thing is to go in and try one or two for taste. The chocolates look and taste amazing. Also, because the UAE is close to Iran, you will get some great Bakhlava (pastry type sweets) either in these shops or in the supermarkets. Calorific!

A final word of advice – for those of you with nut allergies, be very careful, many of the chocolates here contain nuts in plenty, even when you don't expect them!

Al Nassma Camel Chocolate (al-nassma.com)- Mall of the Emirates, Burj Khalifa's "At the Top", Dubai Mall, hotels such as Burj al Arab and Madinat Jumeirah Jumeirah Hotel and dotted around premium venues in Dubai.

Patchi – Burjuman, Mall of the Emirates, Mercato Mall, Dubai Festival City

Choco'a – (chocoa.ae) near Mall of the Emirates

Fuala – (fuala.ae) Jumeirah Road and Al Mamzar Road

GOLD BAR FROM AN ATM

If gold jewellery is not to your liking, you can still take home your own piece of bling in the form of a gold bar. You have no doubt read the news stories of the gold ATMs that you can get in the UAE. It first started off in the Emirates Palace in Abu Dhabi, but you can now buy your own bar of gold as a memento of your trip from one of the ATMs in Dubai. The most prominent ones are at the Atlantis and at Burj Khalifa.

You can get the bars in different sizes – at 1, 5 or 10g. All you need to do is enter cash into the ATM to get your small little bar. The gold price is updated minute by minute, but you will need to spend about 200 AED plus the smallest bar. Now you can even use credit cards. And the good thing about this souvenir is that it retains its value – or even increase! But, don't be fooled – if you are thinking this is a quick way to launder money – think again. With the strict anti laundering checks in place this is not the way to cover your tracks!

TRADITIONAL ARABIC GOODS

There are whole heap of gifts that you could get in Arabia and people always like to pick up a few ornaments for their home. There are many things that you can get. Some of them are not really from the UAE, but from all over the region, so don't feel you that you have to buy the uber-kitsch 7 sands of the Emirates or tat like a glowing Burj al Arab. Things you could buy include lamps, shishas, wood carvings, prayer beads, silver, the traditional dagger, Iranian carpets, pashminas and trinket boxes. That's a good selection but there are many other things available in the stores. We find that the ladies love the pashminas as gifts, simply for the quality you can purchase.

Although there are many places to pick up your Arabian souvenirs, there are the ones checking out to buy your knick knacks. Firstly, if you are in Dubai Mall, you need to cross over to Souk Al Bahar, where you will find one of the many branches of Al Jaber Gallery. Most of the things you'll want as a tourist are there, but on the way there you will see places like Emad Gallery which sell some great pashminas and carpets as well as a host of stores selling things like

Moroccan lamps. All of these are available at all the souks, but you can do it in one go at Souk Al Bahar.

OTHER SOUVENIRS

Among the other novel gift purchases and mementos here are some other unique ones worth mentioning:

Arabic Calligraphy - Another great souvenir is to take back some modern calligraphy. For this we recommend G1 Gallery (g-1.com) which sell canvas prints and fine art – and which has numerous stores in Dubai.

Stuffed Camel - The shop for a quick gift for kids is to get a stuffed camel from the camel company (camelcompany.ae). These are perfect for the little ones.   Some of the t-shirts are quite cool and less tacky than you might think. Again, the camel company can be found in the main souks and large malls.

Allah Din Shoes – although not strictly traditional Emirati, this little stall, based on the 1001 nights sells the very tempting curly toed shoes. If you buy them, you may end up wearing them for fancy dress. The Shoe stall - you can't miss it – is located at the Bur Dubai Abra Station just as you get on or get off the Abra on the Bur Dubai side.

Arabic incense – buy an oil burner and some oud to infuse your home on your return. The best place for this is from Ajmal (ajmalperfume.com), in many of the malls but also in places like the Gold Souq. You can buy some of the most amazing Medhans (oil burner) and either Oud or Bukhoor to burn. Try before you buy – and consider whether you want your Medhan to be coal burning or to be heated using a plug. You can buy fast burning coals and igniters as well, but if you think you will be using the medhan on a regular basis to make your house smell super Arabian, then we recommend going for the plugged version.

Traditional Dress – While we wouldn't suggest wearing traditional dress while you are on holiday, it does make a nice memento – and you can pick up your kandoura or abaya for a reasonable price at Carrefour or at some of the mega markets. If you want a selection to choose from off the peg, go to Deira City Centre Mall where there are many different choices and options including Gift Village which is upstairs.

Yemeni Honey – Honey, from Arabia, is some of the best in the world. We like the Yemeni blends ourselves, but all from Arabia are good. Occasionally specialist shops pop up and close down, so look out for them, but we know you can get pots at the Carrefour in Deira City Centre Mall or most other supermarkets including Choithram & Geant. Spinneys, which is a higher end expat supermarket, don't usually hold local honey.

WHERE TO STAY

With every passing day, and every new hotel that opens in Dubai, the competition to grab the traveller's dollars gets harsher and harsher and for you that means more hotels to choose from – and, to a degree, more confusion!

The elusive question is this: which is the best hotel in Dubai to stay at for me? Dubai has set itself up as an upmarket destination that caters to all niches, but it's difficult to pick out the great ones from the average ones, so what we have done here is put together our recommended hotels that we believe are the best hotels and the ones you should aim to stay at. After all, if you are visiting Dubai – you only want the best. More importantly, we want to help you find the best hotel in Dubai that matches your individual need. Indeed, the very best hotels in Dubai are world class and sometimes it is difficult to differentiate from the very best hotels due to their very high ratings. Everyone has their favourites from the various 5 star hotels (and sometimes 7 star!), and some hotels have always been common to the top ten, but this is starting to change. It is now more difficult than ever before to pick those top ten and identify the best hotels in Dubai and so we have we have given you some clarity than just giving you a list. There may be divided opinion as to which is actually the best – it depends on what best means! – but we are confident in the hotels that we have recommended are good ones.

Here are some facts that we find ourselves often providing clarifciation on: hydropolis, the supposed underwater hotel, never got built; the Armani Hotel is not the tallest hotel in Dubai – it just happens to be in the tallest building; the JW Marriott Marquiss, which opened in 2013, is the tallest hotel in the world; and the Versace hotel is forever "opening soon" - we think that means 2014 sometime.

In years gone by we would have just had one list for the best hotels, but we have split down the hotels based on certain areas as well as providing our view on some other categories:

Best Hotels in Dubai

The Grapeshisha Choice Hotels

Best Hotels in Dubai for Families

Best Hotels in Dubai for Business

Affordable Hotel Alternatives

Budget Hotels

Hotel Apartments

Hotels on the Palm

Hotels in "Old Dubai"

Hotels on Sheikh Zayed Road

Hotels near the Burj Khalifa – "Downtown Dubai"

Hotels in Greater Jumeirah

Hotels on Dubai Marina and on the Walk

Hotels in the desert and Out of town

For the details of all the hotels, see our Hotel Appendix at the end of this section which has all the details of the hotels that we have highlighted

BEST HOTELS IN DUBAI

The ultimate list of hotels in Dubai is a competitive one. With nearly 20 super high end hotels on this list, these are the hotels which are far and above the best hotels in Dubai. You may not agree with our list and our view, but we would almost guarantee these to be almost faultless. You pay for this quality, but you live like a king, queen, sheikh or sheikha!

(in no particular order)

Jumeirah Zabeel Saray

One and Only the Palm

One and Only Royal Mirage

The Atlantis Dubai

The Waldorf Astoria Dubai Palm Jumeirah

Park Hyatt

Ritz Carlton

The Address Downtown Dubai

Madinat Jumeirah

Raffles

Beit Al Bahar (Jumeirah Beach Hotel)

Westin Dubai Mina Seyahi Beach Resort & Marina

Jumeirah Emirates Towers

Grosvenor House Hotel

The Oberoi Dubai

Burj Al Arab

Armani Hotel

Hilton Dubai Creek

Kempinski Hotel & Residences Palm Jumeirah

Ritz Carlton DIFC

THE GRAPESHISHA CHOICE HOTELS

These hotels are the ones we love to stay in. They are wholly subjective, and they are not necessarily the most expensive, but we feel they are the ones we would pay for if we were just passing through or in need of a break.

(in no particular order)

Park Hyatt

One and Only Royal Mirage

Westin Dubai Mina Seyahi Beach Resort & Marina

Jumeirah Zabeel Saray

Le Meirdien Mina Seyahi

Hilton Dubai Creek

Desert Palm

Arabian Courtyard

Madinat Jumeirah Al Qasr

Media One hotel Dubai

Sofitel Jumierah Beach

XVA

Fairmont Dubai

Orient Guest House

Le Royal Meridien

BEST HOTELS IN DUBAI FOR FAMILIES

Many come to Dubai for the ultimate family holiday and all it offers. And it is a great destination for that, but it helps to have a hotel that caters to your kids as well. The Atlantis is built just for this, but may not be for everyone especially if your kids are shorter than 1.4m. But Dubai is not just about the Atlantis. These hotels are great for families and kids:

(in no particular order)

The Atlantis Dubai

Westin Dubai Mina Seyahi Beach Resort & Marina

Le Royal Meridien

Dubai Marine

Jumeirah Beach Hotel

Palm Tree Court and Spa

Le Meridien Mina Seyahi

Sheraton Jumerah Beach

One and Only Royal Mirage

Madinat Jumeirah Mina A Salam

Hilton Dubai Jumeirah

BEST HOTELS IN DUBAI FOR BUSINESS

The business traveller is spoilt for choice in Dubai. Whether you are maxing your expenses, scouting for partnerships or exhibiting at one of the many conventions, these are the hotels that do the obvious for you and then some, so that you can focus on doing what you need to seal the deal:

(in no particular order)

Grosvenor House

Ritz Carlton

Jumeirah Emirates Towers

The Address Downtown Dubai

Fairmont Dubai

JW Marriott Marquis Hotel Dubai

Rose Rayhaan

Intercontinental Dubai Festival City

The Monarch

Novotel WTC

Shangri-La

Dusit Thani

Chelsea Towers

JW Marriott Marquis

Ritz Carlton DIFC

AFFORDABLE HOTEL ALTERNATIVES

Dubai is expensive for many and the drop to three star is too exponential a drop. These hotels are our list of those great value hotels. Bang for your buck great quality but also those hotels that sometimes drop their rates, giving you a 5 star hotel at much reduced rates. Getting a deal in Dubai makes you feel a little smug, and it feels good.

(in no particular order)

Amwaj Rotana Jumeirah Beach

Crowne Plaza Dubai

Dhow Palace Hotel

Arabian Courtyard

Novotel WTC

Towers Rotana

Four Points Sheraton

The Address Dubai Marina

Al Manzil Hotel

Traders Hotel Deira

Grand Hyatt

Sheraton Jumeirah Beach

Qamardeen Hotel

Taj Palace Hotel

Pullman Dubai Mall of the Emirates

BUDGET HOTELS

If all you need is a clean bed in a good location, they you should pick one of our budget hotels. They aren't strictly budget, but Dubai isn't a budget location. The downside of some budget hotels in Dubai is that they really aren't very good – noisy, dirty, and none of things that you would expect of the equivalent budget hotel elsewhere. These are the good quality budgets in Dubai, but beware! The rooms get snapped up!

(in no particular order)

Byblos Hotel Dubai

Villa 47

XVA

Orient Guest House

Ibis WTC

Majestic Hotel

Al Hijaz Motel

HOTEL APARTMENTS

Sometimes it makes more sense to stay in a hotel apartment in Dubai, especially when you are travelling in a large party or are staying for a longer period of time. There are apartment hotels all across Dubai. In the past, there used to be many in Deira and Bur Dubai, places like Golden Sands. There are somewhat run down and now likely to be taken up by bachelors on shorter term contracts. Our recommendations for hotel apartments are located on Dubai Marina and on Sheikh Zayed Road, both locations that give access to Dubai.

(in no particular order)

Radisson Blu Residence Dubai Marina

Oasis Beach Tower Apartments

Hilton Dubai Jumeirah Residences

Fraser Suites Dubai

Chelsea Tower Hotel Apartments

HOTELS ON THE PALM

There aren't actually that many hotels on the Palm. The Atlantis is the most well known, but Jumeirah Zabeel Saray and One and Only the Palm are great honeymoon destinations. There are a few major hotels under construction which should be complete within the next couple of years and will definitely be battling to be the place you need to stay. Just bear in mind that staying on the Palm means that you are 20-30 minutes away from the rest of Dubai, if you were looking for a mix of tourism and shopping for your stay.

(in no particular order)

The Atlantis Dubai

One and Only the Palm

Jumeirah Zabeel Saray

Anantara Dubai the Palm

Waldorf Astoria Dubai Palm Jumeirah

Kempinski Hotel and Residences Palm Jumeirah

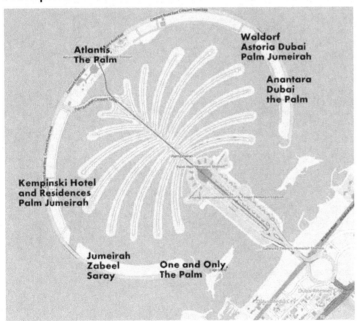

Hotels on the Palm, Copyright OpenStreetMap contributors, CC BY-SA, Grapeshisha

HOTELS IN "OLD DUBAI"

Old Dubai represents the areas of Deria and Bur Dubai, the two areas that used to encompass the whole of Dubai. Things have changed though, and so now Dubai either side of the creek is considered old to the glam of New Dubai. But amongst the hubbub are some great hotels and definitely worth considering if you want to be closer to the heart of real Dubai.

(in no particular order)

Arabian Courtyard

Hilton Dubai Creek

Jumeirah Creekside Hotel

Raffles

Grand Hyatt

Intercontinental Dubai Festival City

Park Hyatt

Sheraton Dubai Creek

Majestic hotel

Barjeel Heritage Guest House

XVA

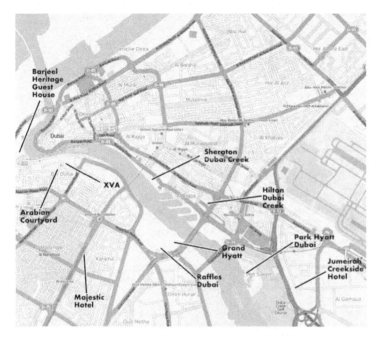

Hotels in Old Dubai, Copyright OpenStreetMap contributors, CC BY-SA, Grapeshisha

HOTELS ON SHEIKH ZAYED ROAD

You'll definitely pass through the SZR during your time in Dubai, and it's worth considering as a place to stay if you need to be centrally located. And if you need to be close to DIFC, then this is probably as good a location as any. Be amongst the skyscrapers – and make sure you ask for a room high up to get the views.

(in no particular order)

Fairmont

Jumeirah Emirates Towers

Shangri-La

Ritz Carlton DIFC

Dusit Dubai

Monarch Dubai

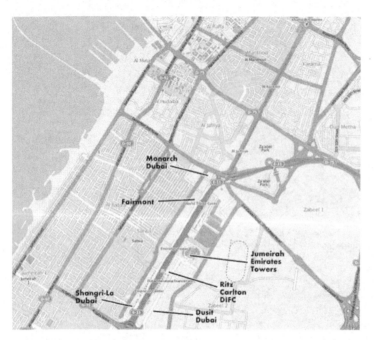

Hotels on Sheikh Zayed Road, Copyright OpenStreetMap contributors, CC BY-SA, Grapeshisha

HOTELS NEAR THE BURJ KHALIFA – "DOWNTOWN DUBAI"

Burj Khalifa is such a central spot in Dubai, predominantly due to the Dubai Mall that many stay close by, and you are possibly spoiled with one of the most unique hotels in the World, the Armani Hotel. But there are a variety of other options including the multiple Address hotels.

(in no particular order)

Armani

The Palace Hotel The Old Town

The Address – Downtown Dubai

The Address – Dubai Mall

The Oberoi, Dubai

JW Marriott Marquis Dubai

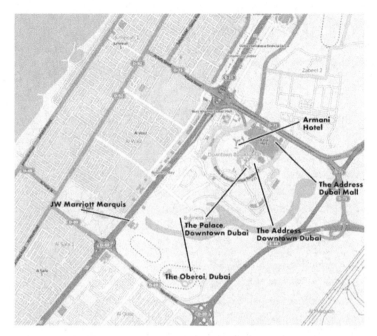

Hotels near Burj Khalifa, Copyright OpenStreetMap contributors, CC BY-SA, Grapeshisha

HOTELS IN GREATER JUMEIRAH

For us, Greater Jumeirah is the area of the beach past Umm Suquiem all the way to the palm Jumeirah. It's prime beach space and holds the legend of Burj Al Arab, probably the most expensive hotel in the world, but resorts like Madinat Jumeirah which holds 3 separate hotels, provide an amazing destination hotel close to the coast.

(in no particular order)

Jumeirah Beach Hotel

Burj Al Arab

Madinat Jumeirah Dar Al Masyaf

Madinat Jumeirah Mina A Salam

Madinat Jumeirah Al Qasr

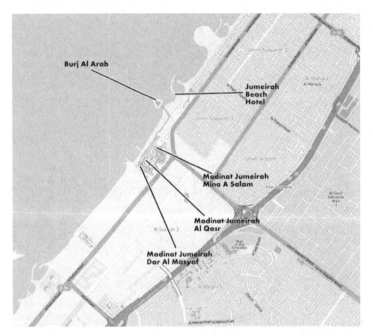

Jumeirah Hotels, Copyright OpenStreetMap contributors, CC BY-SA, Grapeshisha

HOTELS ON DUBAI MARINA AND ON THE WALK

Jumeirah extends down the coast into new Dubai where a major amount of construction has been undertaken over the last 10 years. And now the area is a real pull with some niche hotels overlooking the coach. It's now a great place to stay. We still love the One and Only, but maybe we're a little biased. The rest are all top quality!

(in no particular order)

Westin Dubai Mina Seyahi Beach Resort & Marina

One and Only Royal Mirage

Sofitel Jumeirah Beach

Sheraton Jumeirah Beach

Ritz Carlton

Le Royal Meridien

Movenpick Jumeirah Beach

Hilton Dubai Jumeirah

Le Meridien Mina Seyahi

The Address Dubai Marina

Habtoor Grand Resort and Spa

Hilton Dubai Jumeirah

Grosvenor House

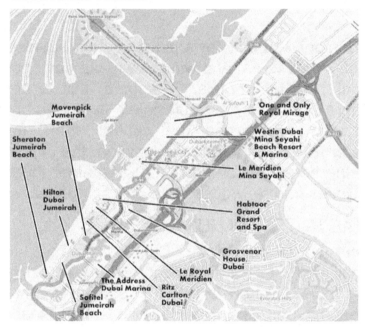

Hotels in Dubai Marina, Copyright OpenStreetMap contributors, CC BY-SA, Grapeshisha

HOTELS IN THE DESERT AND OUT OF TOWN

If the city life is not for you on your break, there are some niche alternatives. Al Maha and Desert Palm Dubai are great places in the desert and worthy of the experience of being away from everything. But it may be worth combining two stops on this type of trip with one closer to central Dubai or elsewhere.

(in no particular order)

Al Maha

Desert Palm Dubai – Polo

Banyan Tree Al Wadi in RAK

Kempinski Hotel in Amman

The Meydan – Horse Racing

Al Sahra Desert Resort

Bab Al Shams

HOTEL APPENDIX

Since hotels are a central spot, not only for a place to stay, but also provide some of the best places to eat and wind down, we have put together a sort of biodata of 100+ hotels. Of course, this is not comprehensive since there are more than 500 hotels in Dubai, but these cover a plethora of types and the central spots for entertainment. We have provided the name, the location, the official star rating, our view on the hotel, numbers of rooms, whether there is a beach pool or spa, closest metro, website and phone number.

RECOMMENDED 5 STAR HOTELS IN DUBAI

The Address – Downtown Dubai,5 Star, Burj Khalifa,The tall building next to Burj Khalifa,Great central location with an amazing Inifinity pool overlooking the Burj and the Dubai Fountain, Rooms: 196, Burj Khalifa,No Beach, Pool, Spa, Near Sheikh Zayed Road, Metro: Burj Dubai ,Burj Dubai, Website: www.theaddress.com, Phone: (04) 4368888

The Address – Dubai Mall,5 Star, Burj Khalifa,The hotel for shopaholics,Great location for quick access to Dubai Mall ,Rooms: 244,Burj Khalifa,No Beach, Pool, Spa,"Near Sheikh Zayed Road, connected to Dubai Mall", Metro: Burj Dubai, Website: www.theaddress.com, Phone: (04) 4388888

The Address - Dubai Marina,5 Star, Dubai Marina,The business hotel close to Media City,Great service focused business hotel ,Rooms: 200,Dubai Marina,No Beach, Pool, Spa, Next to Marina

Mall, Metro:Jumeirah Lake Towers, Website: www.theaddress.com, Phone: (04) 4367777

Al Qasr Hotel (Madinat Jumeirah),5 Star, Jumeirah,One of the best resorts in Dubai,Al Qasr is a great hotel with all the benefit that madinat offers and being as central as you can get within Jumeirah ,Rooms: 292,Jumeirah,Beach, Pool, Spa, Near to Burj Al Arab, Metro: Mall of the Emirates, Website: www.jumeirah.com, Phone: (04) 3666574

Anantara Dubai the Palm, 5 Star,Palm Dubai,Thai paradise in Dubai,Idyllic serenity away from the Dubai chaos ,Rooms:293,Beach, Pool, Spa,Far East end of the Palm overlooking the Burj Al Arab, Metro: Palm Monorail Website: www.anantara.com, Phone: (04) 567 8888

Armani Hotel, 5 Star, Burj Khalifa,Sophistication in the tallest building in the world,You'll need to be able to dress up to dress down if you are cool enough to stay here ,Rooms: 160,Burj Khalifa,No Beach, Pool, Spa, Inside Burj Khalifa, Metro: Burj Dubai, Website: www.armanihotels.com , Phone: (04) 8883888

Atlantis Dubai, 5 Star, Palm Jumeirah,The epitome of Dubai at the end of the Palm,Atlantis is a holiday in itself and you probably wont get time to do the toursim in Dubai with all that is offered here - perfection in family holidays doesn't get much better than this, Rooms: 1539,Palm Jumeirah,Beach, Pool, Spa, At the furthest end of the Palm, Metro: Palm Monorail, Website: www.atlantisthepalm.com , Phone: (04) 4260000

Beit Al Bahar (Jumeirah Beach Hotel), 5 Star, Jumeirah,The exclusive area of Jumeirah Beach Hotel,Great location for those who can snap up the few rooms available, Rooms: 19,Jumeirah,Beach, Pool, Spa, Next to Burj Al Arab, Metro: Mall of the Emirates, Website: www.beitalbahar.com , Phone: (04) 4068399

Burj Al Arab, 7 Star,Jumeirah,"The 7 star, golden, most expensive hotel in the world","Staying at the Burj is something one should do once in a lifetime, if you can afford it." ,Rooms: 202,Jumeirah,Beach, Pool, Spa,Next to Jumeirah Beach Hotel on the coast, Metro: Mall of the Emirates, Website: www.burjalarab.com , Phone: (04) 3017777

Dar Al Masyaf (Madinat Jumeirah),5 Star, Jumeirah,The exclusive hotel of Madina Jumeirah with private pools with villas, The most exclusive of the Madinat properties - this is where chiefs of state stay, Rooms: 290,Jumeirah,No Beach, Pool, Spa, Near to Burj Al Arab, Metro: Mall of the Emirates , Website: www.jumeirah.com , Phone: (04) 3666574

Dubai Marine Beach Resort and Spa,5 Star,Jumeirah,The mainstay hotel of Dubai pre building boom, Great entertainment and amenities while being close to old dubai and new dubai, Rooms: 195,Jumeirah,Beach, Pool, Spa,Next to Dubai Diving Centre, Metro: World Trade Centre, Website: www.dxbmarine.com , Phone: (04) 3461111

Dusit Thani,5 Star, Sheikh Zayed Road,Thai iconic building on the Sheikh Zayed Road, Great business hotel where service can't be faulted ,Rooms: 321,Sheikh Zayed Road, No Beach, Pool, No Spa, Opposite Shangri-La Hotel, Metro: Financial Centre , Website: www.dusit.com , Phone: (04) 3433333

Fairmont Dubai,5 Star, Sheikh Zayed Road,The coolest hotel on Sheikh Zayed Road,"Convenient, cool and well positioned, the Fairmont is the best hotel on SZR, especially if you can get into Fairmont Gold" ,Rooms: 394,Sheikh Zayed Road, No Beach, Pool, Spa, Opposite Dubai Convention Centre, Metro: World Trade Centre , Website: www.fairmont.com , Phone: (04) 3325555

Grand Hyatt,5 Star, Bur Dubai, The mammoth business hotel of Dubai, Business type hotel which does everything you need it to do. Closer to the older part of Dubai and located well for access to both halves of Dubai., Rooms: 674,Bur Dubai,No Beach, Pool, Spa, Next to Wafi Shopping Mall, Metro: Dubai Healthcare City , Website: dubai.grand.hyatt.com/hyatt/hotels/ , Phone: (04) 3171234

Grosvenor House Dubai,5 Star, Dubai Marina,Super trendy business hotel that contains Buddha Bar and Rhodes Mezzanine, This is the perfect business hotel residence to expense to your clients or boss, Rooms: 422,Dubai Marina,No Beach, Pool, Spa, Near to Habtoor Grand, Metro: Dubai Marina , Website: www.grosvenorhouse-dubai.com , Phone: (04) 3998888

The H Hotel Dubai,5 Star, Sheikh Zayed Road,"Specialist Business Hotel at 1 Sheikh Zayed Road, formally known as The Monarch",Great business focused rooms with great views of the Sheikh Zayed Road ,Rooms: 236,Sheikh Zayed Road, No Beach, Pool, Spa,"At the beginning of Sheikh Zayed Road, next to the WTC", Metro: World Trade Centre , Website: www.themonarchdubai.com , Phone: (04) 5018888

Habtoor Grand Beach Resort and Spa,5 Star, Dubai Marina,Party central on Jumeirah Beach,Trendy hotel for the wealthy thirty somethings without kids, Rooms: 446,Dubai Marina, Beach, Pool, Spa, Al Sofoh Street, Metro: Nakheel , Website: grandjumeirah.habtoorhotels.com , Phone: (04) 3995000

Hilton Dubai Creek,5 Star, Deira,Amazing lobby and interiors, This was one of the first landmark hotels in Dubai and it retains its charm and superiority. A great hotel, Rooms: 150,Deira,No Beach, Pool, Spa, Baniyas Road close to City Centre Shopping Mall, Metro: Union ,Union, Website: www.hilton.com , Phone: (04) 2271111

Hilton Dubai Jumeirah,5 Star, Dubai Marina,Fabulous family hotel on the Marina, "Lovely hotel on the Walk, making a perfect holiday destination", Rooms: 389,Dubai Marina, Beach, Pool, Spa,Al Sufuoh Road next to Jumeira Beach Residence, Metro: Jumeirah Lake Towers ,Jumeirah Lake Towers, Website: www.hilton.com , Phone: (04) 3991111

Intercontinental Dubai Festival City,5 Star, "Deira, Dubai Festival City",Business Hotel close to the airport,"A little further out of central Dubai, the Intercon is worth it for the larger rooms." ,Rooms:

498,"Deira, Dubai Festival City",No Beach, Pool, Spa,Bottom end of the creek, Metro: Emirates , Website: www.intercontinental.com , Phone: (04) 7011111

Jumeirah Beach Hotel,5 Star, Jumeirah,The wave to the Burj Al Arab's sail.,"Legendary Dubai hotel although probable feeling a little dated, but great for families with access to wild wadi." ,Rooms: 617,Jumeirah,Beach, Pool, Spa,Next to Burj Al Arab, Metro: Mall of the Emirates , Website: www.jumeirah.com , Phone: (04) 3480000

Jumeirah Emirates Towers,5 Star, Sheikh Zayed Road,Iconic twin towers at the beginning of Sheikh Zayed Road,Great business hotel where you will occasionally see His Highness Sheikh Mohamed., Rooms: 400,Sheikh Zayed Road,No Beach, Pool, Spa,Next to DIFC, Metro: Emirates Tower, Website: www.jumeirah.com , Phone: (04) 3300000

Jumeirah Zabeel Saray,5 Star, Palm Jumeirah,Boutique hotel on the Palm,Fab holiday for couples or families with young children, Rooms: 405,Palm Jumeirah,Beach, Pool, Spa,On the West Crescent, Metro: Palm Monorail, Website: www.jumeirahzabeelsaray.com , Phone: (04) 4530000

JW Marriott Marquis Hotel,5 Star, Sheikh Zayed Road,Tallest Hotel in the World,"Massive, busy and business focused" ,Rooms:1350,No Beach, Pool, Spa, Sheikh Zayed Road between the Burj and the Palm, Metro: Business Bay,Website: www.marriott.co.uk Phone: (04) 4140000

Kempinski Hotel and Residences the Palm,5 Star, Palm Dubai,Large rooms with hand to toe service, You won't want to leave ,Rooms:244,Beach, Pool, Spa,West Frond of the Palm, Metro: Palm Monorail,Website: www.kempinski.com Phone: 04 444 2000

Le Meridien Mina Seyahi,5 Star, Jumeirah,Beachfront hotel famous for the Barasti beach bar, beach focused hotel favourite, Rooms: 211, Jumeirah,Beach, Pool, Spa,Overlooking the Palm behind Dubai

Media City, Metro:Nakheel, Website: www.lemeridien-minaseyahi.com , Phone: (04) 3993333

Le Royal Meridien Beach Resort and Spa,5 Star, Dubai Marina,The beach resort with Rhodes Twenty10 inside, Fabulous beach hotel and one of our faves, Rooms: 500,Dubai Marina,Beach, Pool, Spa,Between Ritz Carlton and the Habtoor Grand, Metro:Nakheel, Website: www.leroyalmeridien-dubai.com, Phone: (04) 3995555

Mina A Salam (Madinat Jumeirah),5 Star, Jumeirah,Great resort hotel with picture perfect views of Burj Al Arab,"We love Mina A'Salam blended into the exclusiveness of Madinat, and kids will love the turtle farm." ,Rooms: 292,Jumeirah,Beach, Pool, Spa, Near to Burj Al Arab, Metro: First Gulf Bank ,First Gulf Bank, Website: www.jumeirah.com , Phone: (04) 3666574

The Oberoi Dubai,5 Star,Business Bay,Boutique Indian Perfection,Modern 5 star with excellent service ,Rooms:252,No Beach, Pool, Spa,Business Bay behind SZR, Metro: Business Bay,,Website: www.oberoihotels.com/hotels-in-dubai/ , Phone: 04 444 1444

One and Only Royal Mirage,5 Star, Jumeirah,Serenity in Dubai,"Our favourite hotel, even with the views of the Palm" ,Rooms: 451,Jumeirah,Beach, Pool, Spa,Overlooking the Palm, Metro:Nakheel, Website: www.oneandonlyroyalmirage.com , Phone: (04) 3999999

One and Only the Palm,5 Star, Palm Jumeirah,Paradise on the Palm,Honeymoon retreat away from Dubai ,Rooms: 94,Palm Jumeirah,Beach, Pool, Spa, On the West Crescent, Metro: Palm Monorail,Palm Monorail,Website: www.oneandonlythepalm.com , Phone: (04) 4401010

The Palace Hotel The Old Town (The Address),5 Star, Burj Khalifa,Palatial surroundings close to Burj Khalifa,Darkened Arabian furnishings give this hotel an authentic feel despite its almost unauthentic location, Rooms: 242,Burj Khalifa,No Beach, Pool, Spa,Overlooking the Dubai Fountain, Metro:Burj Dubai, Website: www.theaddress.com , Phone: (04) 4287888

Park Hyatt,5 Star, Deira,Creekside perfection that does the perfect Friday brunch,The best hotel on Dubai Creek ,Rooms: 225,Deira,No Beach, Pool, Spa,"Along Baniyas Road, on the Creek", Metro:Deira City Centre, Website: dubai.park.hyatt.com, Phone: (04) 6121234

Raffles Dubai,5 Star,,Bur Dubai,The Egytian Pyramid that could appear cheesey but isnt.,"Surprisingly great hotel in an odd location for a Raffles, with some amazing restaurants including The Noble House at the top of the pyramid." ,Rooms: 246,Bur Dubai,No Beach, Pool, Spa,Sheikh Rashid Road connected to Wafi Mall, Metro:Dubai Healthcare City, Website: www.raffles.com , Phone: (04) 3246000

Ritz Carlton,5 Star,Jumeirah,Classy high end with an old school type charm,This hotel might be classed as the best in other cities in the world ,Rooms: 138,Jumeirah,Beach, Pool, Spa,Next to Jumeirah Beach Residence, Metro:Dubai Marina, Website: www.ritzcarlton.com dubai, Phone: (04) 3994000

Ritz Carlton DIFC,5 Star,Sheikh Zayed Road, The new Ritz,Business focussed for the richest bankers and wheeler dealers., Rooms: 341,Sheikh Zayed Road,No Beach, Pool, Spa,Sheikh Rashid Road connected to Wafi Mall, Metro:Financial Centre, Website: www.ritzcarlton.com/dubaifc , Phone: (04) 3722222

Shangri-La,5 Star,Sheikh Zayed Road,Sheikh Zayed Road's best dim sum,"Another business hotel on the SZR, competing with The Fairmont as the street's best. Recommended.", Rooms: 302,Sheikh Zayed Road,No Beach, Pool, Spa,Next to Crown Plaza opposite Dusit Thani, Metro: Financial Centre, Website: www.shangri-la.com , Phone: (04) 3438888

Sheraton Dubai Creek,5 Star,Deira,Mainstay hotel on the creek,"Great creek views, but look for a deal", Rooms: 262,Deira,No

Beach, Pool, Spa,Baniyas Road opposite Etisalat, Metro: Baniya, Website: www.sheraton.com/dubai , Phone: (04) 2281111

Sheraton Jumerah Beach Resort and Towers,5 Star,Dubai Marina,Family Hotel on the Marina,Premium Sheraton with a focus on the family ,Rooms: 256,Dubai Marina,Beach, Pool, Spa,on Marina Walk, Metro: Jumeirah Lake Towers, Website: www.sheratonjumeirahbeach.com , Phone: (04) 3995533

Sofitel Dubai Jumierah Beach,5 Star, Dubai Marina,Frenchness on the beach,Lovely marina hotel on the walk - with almost perfect service. ,Rooms: 438,Dubai Marina,No Beach, Pool, Spa,Next to Jumeirah Beach Residence, Metro: Jumeirah Lake Towers , Website: www.sofitel.com , Phone: (04) 4484848

Taj Palace Hotel,5 Star, Deira,"Indian style, dry hotel","Doesn't get the prominence because it is alcohol free, but popular amongst Indians and GCC travelers. Probably due a refurb." ,Rooms: 249,Deira,No Beach, Pool, Spa,between Al Rigga and Al Maktoum Streets, Metro: Al Rigga Website: www.tajhotels.com , Phone: (04) 2232222

Westin Dubai Mina Seyahi Beach Resort & Marina,5 Star, Jumeirah,New family hotel on the Marina,A nice private beach and water sports makes for a pleasnt holiday if you can get a good deal. ,Rooms: 294,Jumeirah,Beach, Pool, Spa,Al Soufouh Street overlooking Dubai Media City, Metro: Nakheel , Website: www.westin.com/dubaiminaseyahi , Phone: (04) 3994141

Waldorf Astoria Dubai Palm Jumeirah,5 Star, Palm Jumeirah,One of the best new hotels in Dubai,"Palatial, airy and elegant all in one" ,Rooms: 319,Beach, Pool, Spa, East crescent of the Palm, Metro: Palm Monorail ,Website: www.waldorfastoria.com/dubaipalm , Phone: 04 818 2222

RECOMMENDED 5 STAR DESERT RESORTS IN DUBAI

Al Maha Desert Resort and spa,5 Star, Outskirts of Dubai,The best desert resort in the UAE,Perfect for a retreat away from the bling ,Rooms: 42,Outskirts of Dubai,No Beach, Pool, Spa,"Al Ain Road, after exit 50", Metro: n/a,Website: www.al-maha.com , Phone: (04) 8329900

Bab Al Shams Desert Resort & Spa,5 Star, Outskirts of Dubai,The location of Al Hadheerah show/restaurant,"If you want to experience desert living, this is the place to come. For info - Bab al Shams means Gate of the Sun." ,Rooms: 113,Outskirts of Dubai,No Beach, Pool, Spa,Emirates Road, Metro: n/a,Website: www.meydanhotels.com , Phone: (04) 8096100

Desert Palm,5 Star, Outskirts of Dubai,Boutique Hotel in the desert,"Perfect as part of honeymoon retreat, especially if you like polo." ,Rooms: 38,Outskirts of Dubai,No Beach, Pool, Spa,"Al Awir Road, Near Dragon Mart", Metro: n/a,Website: www.desertpalm.ae , Phone: (04) 3238888

The Meydan,5 Star, Outskirts of Dubai,A horse lover's fantasy location,"Somewhat of an event hotel, this is the hotel of the most expensive horse race in the world." ,Rooms: 279,Outskirts of Dubai,No Beach, Pool, Spa,Nad al Shiba Street, Metro: n/a,Website: www.meydanhotels.com , Phone: (04) 3813333

OTHER NOTABLE 5 STAR HOTELS IN DUBAI

Al Bustan Rotana Hotel,5 Star, Deira,"Airport Hotel, Rotana style",Business hotel near the airport with some top end restaurants - Benihana and Blue Elephant ,Rooms: 275,Deira,No Beach, Pool, Spa,Al Garhoud Bridge, Metro: GGICO ,GGICO, Website: www.rotana.com , Phone: (04) 2820000

Al Murooj Rotana Hotel,5 Star,Sheikh Zayed Road,Walking distance from Dubai Mall,Dependable 5 star hotel ,Rooms: 247,Sheikh Zayed Road,No Beach, Pool, Spa, Near Dubai Mall, Metro: Burj Dubai , Website: www.rotana.com , Phone: (04) 3073410

Asiana Hotel,5 Star, Deira,New hotel in Deira,Can get amazing rates for this 5 star - good if you need to be in Deira ,Rooms: 136,Deira,No Beach, Pool, Spa,Salah Al Din Road next to Al Reef mall, Metro: Al Rigga , Website: www.asianahoteldubai.com, Phone: (04) 2387777

Auris Plaza Hotel,5 Star, Al Barsha,New 5 star near Mall of the Emirates,Too new to review ,Rooms: 337,Al Barsha,No Beach, Pool, Spa,Behind Mall of the Emirates, Metro: Sharaf DG , Website: www.auris-hotels.com , Phone: (04) 4554800

Bonnington Hotel Jumeirah Lakes Tower,5 Star, Dubai Marina,Polished 5 star in JLT,"Hotel is new and pretty good, but the area around is still in process, so bear in mind." ,Rooms: 208,Dubai Marina,No Beach, Pool, Spa,"Sheikh Zayed Road, Jumeirah Lakes Towers", Metro: Jumeirah Lake Towers, Website: www.bonningtontower.com , Phone: (04) 3560000

The Conrad Dubai,5 Star, Sheikh Zayed Road,Well located Business hotel,Perfect for WTC Conferences ,Rooms:555, No Beach, Pool, Spa,Sheikh Zayed Road next to the Fairmont, Metro: World Trade Centre ,Website: http://www.conradhotels.com , Phone: (04) 4447444

Crowne Plaza - Dubai Festival City,5 Star,316,"Deira, Dubai Festival City",Stopover 5 star close to the airport.,Can get a good discount while enjoying the benefit of the Intercon next door. ,Rooms: 316,"Deira, Dubai Festival City",No Beach, Pool, Spa,Bottom end of the creek, Metro:Emirates, Website: www.crowneplaza.com , Phone: (04) 7012222

Crowne Plaza - Deira,5 Star, Deira,Spice Island restaurant,"4 star quality at 5 star prices, there are better 5 stars in Dubai" ,Rooms: 142,Deira,No Beach, Pool, Spa,Salah Al Din Street, Metro:Abu Baker Al Siddique, Website: www.crowneplaza.com , Phone: (04) 2625555

Crowne Plaza - Dubai, Sheikh Zayed Road,5 Star, Sheikh Zayed Road,Staple hotel on the SZR,Great location but a little dated. ,Rooms: 572,Sheikh Zayed Road,No Beach, Pool, Spa,Al Nahyan Street, Metro:Emirates Towers, Website: www.crowneplaza.com , Phone: (04) 3311111

Fairmont Palm Hotel ,5 Star, Palm Dubai,Yet another Palm extravaganza,"Great, but least great of the greats on the Palm" ,Rooms:381,Beach, Pool, Spa,Initial trunk of the Palm, Metro: n/a,,Website: http://www.fairmont.com/palm , Phone: 04 4573388

Grand Millennium Hotel Dubai,5 Star, Al Barsha,Media City 5 star hotel ,Worth staying here if you have meetings or events to attend near by. Bar that it's a little too far for the generalist. ,Rooms: 343,Al Barsha,No Beach, Pool, Spa,Between Mall of the Emirates and Ibn Battuta city Centre, Metro: Dubai Internet City, Website: www.grandmillenniumdubai.com , Phone: (04) 4299999

Hyatt Regency Dubai,5 Star, Deira,Perfect for the gold and gold souk lovers,Signature Hyatt hotel in Deira ,Rooms: 414,Deira,No Beach, Pool, Spa,Al Khaleej Road, Metro: Palm Deira , Website: dubai.regency.hyatt.com, Phone: (04) 2091234

Ibn Battuta Gate Hotel,5 Star,Jebel Ali,Another mall named hotel,"So far out, without anything to show for" ,Rooms: 396,Jebel Ali,No Beach, Pool, Spa,Jebel Ali, Metro: Ibn Battuta, Website: moevenpick-dubai-ibnbattuta.com, Phone: (04) 4440000

Jumeirah Creekside Hotel,5 Star, Deira,Stopover hotel done by Jumeirah,"Not bad as a stopover or for a business trip, but not really a holiday location" ,Rooms:292,No Beach, Pool, Spa,Dubai Creek next to Century Village and the Irish Village, Metro: GGICO , Website: www.jumeirah.com , Phone: (04) 2308555

JW Marriott Hotel,5 Star, Deira,Old school charm amongst the hustle and bustle,Mainstay that feels grander than it actually is ,Rooms: 351,2624444,,Deira,No Beach, Pool, Spa,Abu Baker Al

Siddique Road, Metro:Abu Baker Al Siddique, Website: www.jwmarriottdubai.com , Phone: (04) 2624444

Kempinski Hotel Mall of the Emirates,5 Star, Al Barsha,Ski lovers fantasy,"Slightly confusing hotel trying to cater for everyone, but good for business if meeting are nearby" ,Rooms: 393,Al Barsha,No Beach, Pool, Spa,Connected to Mall of the Emirates, Metro: Mall of the Emirates, Website: www.kempinski-dubai.com , Phone: (04) 3410000

Kempinski Hotel & Residences Palm Jumeirah,5 Star, Palm Jumeirah,Another addition to the Palm crowd of hotels,Kempinski quality on the Palm ,Rooms: 234,Palm Jumeirah,No Beach, Pool, Spa,Eastern Crescent, Metro: Palm Monorail Website: www.kempinski.com/en/palmjumeirah , Phone: (04) 4442444

Le Meridien Dubai,5 Star, Deira,5 star airport hotel,Great restaurants for airport business meetings ,Rooms: 383,Deira,No Beach, Pool, Spa,Airport Road, Metro: Airport Terminal 1, Website: www.lemeridien-dubai.com , Phone: (04) 2170000

Media Rotana Dubai,5 Star, Al Barsha,DMC/DIC business hotel,The downside of having to be located close to DMC are cancelled out by being close to the metro ,Rooms: 459,Al Barsha,No Beach, Pool, Spa, Near Millenium Hotel, Metro: Dubai Internet City , Website: www.rotana.com Phone: (04) 4350000

Metropolitan Palace Hotel,5 Star, Deira,Bland 5 star in Deira,Overpriced 4 star dressed up with chandaliers and a 5 star mantle ,Rooms: 212,Deira,No Beach, Pool, Spa,Maktoum Street next to Al Dana Centre, Metro: Al Rigga , Website: www.habtoorhotels.com , Phone: (04) 2270000

Millennium Plaza Hotel,5 Star, Sheikh Zayed Road,Another new hotel in Deira,Dry hotel with larger rooms ,Rooms: 204,Sheikh Zayed Road,No Beach, Pool, Spa,"After Khalid Al Attar Tower, opposite Emirates Grand Hotel", Metro: Emirates Towers , Website: www.millenniumhotels.com Phone: (04) 3877777

Moevenpick Bur Dubai,5 Star, Bur Dubai,Swiss Business Hotel,"Good Service, and a more interesting choice of location for the SZR executive" ,Rooms: 255,Bur Dubai,No Beach, Pool, Spa,19th Street Oud Metha, Metro: Al Karama, Website: www.moevenpick-burdubai.com , Phone: (04) 3366000

Moevenpick Hotel Deira,5 Star, Deira,"Airport Hotel, with a twist of Moevenpick",Onlu 10 minutes from the airport - worth the journey for the relaxation if you need it. ,Rooms: 216,Deira,No Beach, Pool, Spa,Corner of Abu Baker Al Siddique and Al Sallahuddin Road, Metro: Abu Baker Al Siddique , Website: www.moevenpick-hotels.com , Phone: (04) 4401111

Moevenpick Jumeirah Beach,5 Star, Jumeirah,Remarkably non bling 5 star in the centre of blingness,Perfectly competent 5 star resort ,Rooms: 294,Jumeirah,No Beach, Pool, Spa,At Jumeirah Beach Residence, Metro: Dubai Marina , Website: www.moevenpick-jumeirahbeach.com Phone: (04) 4498888

Palazzo Versace Hotel,5 Star, Culture Village Dubai Creek,Versace with the refrigerated beach,"Too new to rate, but it will be great" ,Rooms:251,Beach, Pool, Spa,On the Creek between the bridges, Metro: Creek Metro 1,Website: www.palazzoversace.com , Phone: (04) 4092900,,,

Park Regis Kris Kin Hotel,5 Star, Bur Dubai,Best city hotel in its area.,Great views of new and old Dubai from afar. ,Rooms: 390,Bur Dubai,No Beach, Pool, Spa,Shaikh Khalifa Bin Zayed Stree opposite Burjuman Centre, Metro: Khalid bin Al Waleed,Website: www.parkregisdubai.com , Phone: (04) 3771111

Radisson Royal Hotel,5 Star, Sheikh Zayed Road,Superior Radisson city hotel,Location of Mo Vida Nightclub ,Rooms: 471,Sheikh Zayed Road,No Beach, Pool, Spa,across from Dubai WTC and DIFC, Metro: World Trade centre, Website: www.radissonblu.com , Phone: (04) 3080000

Rixos the Palm Dubai,5 Star,Palm Jumeirah,Turkish Hotel on the Palm,More affordable Palm location ,Rooms: 233,Palm Jumeirah,No Beach, Pool, Spa,East Crescent, Metro: Nakheel, Website: www.rixos.com , Phone: (04) 4575555

Samaya Hotel Deira,5 Star, Deira,New hotel in Rigga,Good hotel to soak up old Dubai ,Rooms: 213,7033333,,Deira,No Beach, Pool, Spa,"Rigga, Al Buteen Street, opposite the Dubai Chamber", Metro: Al Rigga , Website: www.samayahotel.com , Phone: (04) 7033333

The Address Montgomerie Dubai,5 Star, Sheikh Zayed Road,Boutique hotel for the golf lover,"The Montgomerie is a lovely small hotel with oodles of charm, but you have to be a golf lover to be here" ,Rooms: 21,,Sheikh Zayed Road,No Beach, Pool, Spa,Emirates Hill Interchange 5, Metro: Dubai Marina , Website: www.theaddress.com , Phone: (04) 3905600

RECOMMENDED 4 STAR HOTELS IN DUBAI

Al Manzil Hotel,4 Star, Sheikh Zayed Road,Excellent 4 star close to the Burj,Sister hotel to the Qamardeen and almost equivalent in style and appearance ,Rooms: 197,Sheikh Zayed Road,No Beach,No Pool,No Spa,Next to Burj Khalifa, Metro: Burj Khalifa , Website: www.al-manzil-hotel-dubai.com , Phone: (04) 4285888

Amwaj Rotana Jumeirah Beach,4 Star, Jumeirah,4 star on the Walk,"Great views of the sea, and well located for all the food joints on the walk." ,Rooms: 301,Jumeirah,No Beach, Pool, Spa,Al Safouh Road Jumeirah Beach Residence Area, Metro: Dubai Marina ,Website: www.rotana.com Phone: (04) 4282000

Arabian Courtyard,4 Star, Bur Dubai,Authenticity on a larger scale,This hotel feels how you would have seen hotels evolve in the UAE if there wasn't the bling injection ,Rooms: 173,Bur Dubai,No Beach, Pool, Spa,"Al Fahidi Street, Opposite Dubai Museum", Metro: Al Fahidi ,, Website: www.arabiancourtyard.com , Phone: (04) 3519111

Byblos Dubai Hotel,4 Star, Al Barsha,Hip hotel near DMC and the Marina,Close to the metro and good for singleton's on business in Dubai ,Rooms: 151,Al Barsha,No Beach, Pool, Spa,Al Barsha Tecom Area, Metro:Dubai Marina, Website: www.bybloshoteldubai.com , Phone: (04) 4488000

Dhow Palace Hotel,4 Star, Bur Dubai,4 star of days gone bye,"a famous hotel, that is perfectly fine, but a little wethered, perhaps from too many party people recovering" ,Rooms: 282,Bur Dubai,No Beach, Pool, Spa,"Kuwait Road, close to Burjuman", Metro: Al Fahidi ,Al Fahidi, Website: www.dhowpalacedubai.com , Phone: (04) 3599992

Four Points Sheraton Bur Dubai,4 Star, Bur Dubai,Staple location for the Mina Bazaar fanatic,Good value 4 star hotel close to the older area of Dubai ,Rooms: 125,Bur Dubai,No Beach,Pool,No Spa,"Khalid bin Walid Street, close to Burjuman", Metro: Al Fahidi , Website: www.fourpoints.com/burdubai , Phone: (04) 3977444

Media One hotel Dubai,4 Star, Al Barsha,Cool hotel for the young execs,Trendy hotel for business on a budget. Not really for families. ,Rooms: 260,Al Barsha,No Beach,Pool,No Spa,"Behind Shatta towers, Dubai Media City", Metro: Nakheel , Website: www.mediaonehotel.com , Phone: (04) 4271000

Novotel WTC,4 Star,Sheikh Zayed Road,Great value near WTC,"This hotel is great for having a central location that's clean. It's a solid 4 star, but you can get good deals which means it's place to view Dubai from on a discount." ,Rooms: 412,Sheikh Zayed Road,No Beach,Pool,No Spa,Zabeel Street in the WTC complex, Metro: World Trade Centre , Website: www.novotel.com , Phone: (04) 3320000

Pullman Dubai Mall of the Emirates,4 Star, Al Barsha,The other hotel on the Mall of the Emirates,"If MOE is the location you want to stay at, this is great - it's close to the metro and, of course, all the eateries of the mall...and the ski slope." ,Rooms: 481,Al Barsha,No

Beach, Pool, Spa,connected to MOE, Metro: Mall of the Emirates , Website: www.pullmanhotels.com , Phone: (04) 3772000

Qamardeen Hotel,4 Star, Sheikh Zayed Road,4 star perfect location for Dubai Mall lovers,"With all that is around, this is a pretty good 4 star if you want to tour Dubai." ,Rooms: 186,Sheikh Zayed Road,No Beach,Pool,No Spa,Next to Burj Khalifa, Metro: Burj Khalifa , Website: www.southernsunme.com/qamardeen , Phone: (04) 4286888

Rose Rayhaan,4 Star, Sheikh Zayed Road,Tallest hotel in the world,Dry hotel targeted at the GCC business traveller ,Rooms: 462,Sheikh Zayed Road,No Beach, Pool, Spa,Dubai Financial Centre, Metro:Financial Centre, Website: www.rotana.com , Phone: (04) 3230111

Towers Rotana,4 Star, Sheikh Zayed Road,Nice stopover 4 star hotel on SZR with rooftop pool,"We stay here because it's convenient, has parking and has teatro downstairs." ,Rooms: 360,Sheikh Zayed Road,No Beach,Pool,No Spa,Opposite WTC, Metro: Financial Centre , Website: www.rotana.com , Phone: (04) 3435111

Traders Hotel Deira,4 Star, Deira,Quality 4 star business hotel ,Popular and unassuming business hotel in Deira ,Rooms: 250,Deira,No Beach, Pool, Spa,Salah Al Deen Street, Metro: Abu Baker Al Siddique , Website: www.tradershotels.com , Phone: (04) 2659888

OTHER NOTABLE 4 STAR HOTELS IN DUBAI

Al Hamra Hotel,4 Star, Deira,New Deira Hotel,Small new hotel in Deira ,Rooms: 54,Deira,No Beach,Pool,No Spa,Abu Baker Siddique Road, Metro: Al Rigga, Website: www.alhamrahoteldubai.net , Phone: (04) 2609000

Al Jawhara Gardens,4 Star, Deira,"Bland, functional 4 star","Dry, clean hotel, close to city centre mall" ,Rooms: 114,Deira,No

Beach,Pool,No Spa,Port Saeed Area Opposite City Centre Mall, Metro: GGICO , Website: www.jawhara.ae , Phone: (04) 2107777

Arjaan by Rotana,4 Star, Dubai Marina,Close to DMC and Mall of the Emirates,Good for business and business long stays on expenses ,Rooms: 167,Dubai Marina,No Beach,Pool,No Spa,, Metro:Nakheel, Website: www.rotana.com , Phone: (04) 4360000

Avari Dubai, 4 Star, Deira,Older building recently upgraded to a nearly 4 star,Convenient as a passing through Dubai hotel ,Rooms: 179,Deira,No Beach, Pool, Spa,"Adjacent to Al Rigga Post Office, near the clock tower", Metro: Abu Baker Al Siddique ,Website: www.avari.com, Phone: (04) 2956666

Boutique7, Hotel and Suites,4 Star, Al Barsha,Smaller 4 star close to DIC/DMC,Good for business week stays ,Rooms: 79,Al Barsha,No Beach, Pool, Spa,"Tecom, opposite DMC", Metro: Dubai Internet City , Website: www.boutique7.ae , Phone: (04) 4345555

City Centre Hotel and Residence,4 Star, Deira,The other Pullman Hotel at MOE,Smart 4 star next to the metro ,Rooms: 317,Deira,No Beach,Pool,No Spa,Adjacent to City Centre Shopping Mall, Metro: Deira City Centre , Website: www.accorhotels.com , Phone: (04) 2941222

Coral Deira Hotel,4 Star, Deira,Basic hotel in Deira,"More 3 star then 4 star, you could get a discount rate if you need to stay in Deira" ,Rooms: 140,Deira,No Beach,Pool,No Spa,Al Muraqqabt Street, Metro: Salah Al Din , Website: www.coral-deira.com , Phone: (04) 2248587

Courtyard by Marriott Green Community Dubai,4 Star, Jebel Ali,Famous for being located in a resedential area,"A little far out for most things, but offers great service and relaxation" ,Rooms: 165,Jebel Ali,No Beach,Pool,No Spa,Dubai Park Greens Community near Choithram, Metro: n/a,Website: www.cydubaigreencommunity.com , Phone: (04) 8852222

Dubai Marriott Harbour Hotel and Suites,4 Star, Jumeirah,Dubai Marina quality at 4 star prices,Very good 4 stay overlooking the palm ,Rooms: 232,Jumeirah,No Beach, Pool, Spa,Al Sufouh Road, Metro:Dubai Marina, Website: www.marriott.com , Phone: (04) 3194000

Iberotel Emirates Grand Hotel,4 Star, Sheikh Zayed Road,Another pair of twin towers on Sheikh Zayed Road,Overpriced aparthotel on SZR ,Rooms: 409,Sheikh Zayed Road,No Beach, Pool, Spa,Close to DIFC, Metro:Financial Centre, Website: www.emiratesgrandhotel.com , Phone: (04) 3230000

Flora Grand Hotel,4 Star, Deira,"Somewhat soulless due to the area, but good enough",Good older 4 star on Al Rigga ,Rooms: 200,Deira,No Beach, Pool, Spa,Al Rigga Street, Metro: Al Rigga , Website: www.florahospitality.com , Phone: (04) 2233344

Four Points Sheraton Sheikh Zayed Road,4 Star, Sheikh Zayed Road,4 points quality on SZR,Immaculate business residence hotel on SZR ,Rooms: 384,Sheikh Zayed Road,No Beach,Pool,No Spa,next to Crown Plaza, Metro: Financial Centre , Website: www.fourpointssheikhzayedroad.com , Phone: (04) 3230333

Holiday Inn Al Barsha Hotel,4 Star, Al Barsha,Good value hotel,"mid way beteen two metro stops, this is good for commuting business" ,Rooms: 310,Al Barsha,No Beach,Pool,No Spa,next to MOE, Metro: Baniyas Square , Website: www.hialbarshadubai.com , Phone: (04) 3234333

Jumeira Rotana Hotel,4 Star, Bur Dubai,Mid range hotel near Diyafah Street,"Professional, but busy hotel - thought you can often get a good deal" ,Rooms: 114,Bur Dubai,No Beach, Pool, Spa,"Al Diyafah Street, beside Dune Centre Building", Metro: World Trade Centre , Website: www.rotana.com , Phone: (04) 3455888

Landmark Grand Hotel,4 Star, Deira,One of many landmark hotels in the area and Dubai,new 4 star in a refreshing spot. ,Rooms: 174,Deira,No Beach,Pool,No Spa,"Rigga Road, Opposite Al Ghurair

Shopping Centre", Metro:Union, Website: www.landmarkhotels.net , Phone: (04) 2501111

Landmark Hotel-Riqqa,4 Star, Deira,"Close to Al Rigga street, and quality 4 star standards",Great location for both metro lines ,Rooms: 84,Deira,No Beach,Pool,No Spa,"Al Jazira Street, between al ghurair and reef mall", Metro:Baniyas Square, Website: www.landmarkhotels.net , Phone: (04) 2946556

Le Meridien Fairway,4 Star, Deira,"City type resort, close to the airport","Nice enough hotel, in a bizarre location" ,Rooms: 58,Deira,No Beach, Pool, Spa,Al Garhoud Road, Metro: Airport Terminal 1 , Website: www.lemeridien.com/fairway , Phone: (04) 6085000

Mercure Gold Hotel,4 Star, Bur Dubai,Average hotel near Jumeira,somewhat lacking for a 4 star hotel ,Rooms: 184,Bur Dubai,No Beach,Pool,No Spa,Al Mina Road, Metro: World Trade Centre , Website: www.mercure-gold-hotel-dubai.com , Phone: (04) 3019888

Novotel Deira City Centre,4 Star, Deira,Good value near city centre mall,Novotel quality 4 star ,Rooms: 188,Deira,No Beach,Pool,No Spa,"In front of City Centre Mall, Port Saeed Area", Metro: Deira City Centre, Website: www.accorhotels.com , Phone: (04) 2925200

Radisson Blu Dubai Deira Creek,4 Star, Deira,Popular busy hotel on the creek,Somewhat dubious reputation for the bar ,Rooms: 476,Deira,No Beach, Pool, Spa,"baniyas Street, next to Dubai Municipality, opposite Dubai Creek", Metro: Union Square, Website: www.radissonblu.com/hotel-dubaideiracreek , Phone: (04) 2227171

Ramada Jumeirah Hotel,4 Star, Jumeirah,Great value hotel without the excess,Perfect for exhibition visitors ,Rooms: 252,Jumeirah,No Beach, Pool, Spa,"Al Mina Road, near Union House building", Metro:Al Jafiliya, Website: www.ramadajumeirah.ae , Phone: (04) 7027000

Rihab Rotana,4 Star, Deira,More apartment hotel than standard hotel,Dry airport hotel by Rotana ,Rooms: 134,Deira,No Beach,Pool,No Spa,Off Sheikh Rashi Road, Metro:Deira City Centre, Website: www.rotana.com , Phone: (04) 2940300

Rimal Rotana,4 Star, Deira,Good quality hotel for families,Great hotel for Al Rigga ,Rooms: 124,Deira,No Beach,Pool,No Spa,Close to Al Rigga, Metro:Al Rigga, Website: www.rotana.com , Phone: (04) 2688000

Riviera Hotel,4 Star, Deira,Older hotel on the Creek,"Close to the souks and the abras, so perfect for the heart of old dubai" ,Rooms: 109,Deira,No Beach,No Pool,No Spa,Baniyas Street , Metro:Baniyas Square, Website: www.rivierahotel-dubai.com , Phone: (04) 2222131

Villa Rotana,4 Star, Sheikh Zayed Road,A staple SZR 4 star,Good for the medium stay executive unsure on length of project ,Rooms: 118,Sheikh Zayed Road,No Beach,Pool,No Spa,Next to safest way, Metro: Business Bay ,Website: www.rotana.com , Phone: (04) 3216111

RECOMMENDED LOWER STAR HOTELS IN DUBAI

Al Hijaz Motel,3 Star, Deira,5 room 2 star,Small hotel based in the Heritage House Museum ,Rooms: 5,Deira,No Beach,No Pool,No Spa,Al Ahmadiya Street, Metro: Al Ras ,Website: www.alhijazmotel.com , Phone: (04) 2250085

Ibis WTC,2 Star, Sheikh Zayed Road,The cleanest cheapest 2 star in Dubai,With Ibis you know you are getting a clean bed and bathroom ,Rooms: 210,Sheikh Zayed Road,No Beach,No Pool,No Spa,next to the World Trade Centre, Metro: World Trade Centre , Website: www.ibishotel.com , Phone: (04) 3324444

Orient Guest House,3 Star, Bur Dubai,Being one of the only authentic Arabian Hotels in Dubai,"If you are not too fussed for the bling of Dubai and are more of traveller, book early to get a room at the Orient" ,Rooms: 10,Bur Dubai,No Beach,No Pool,No Spa,"Bastakiya, near Dubai Museum", Metro: Al Fahidi , Website: www.orientguesthouse.com , Phone: (04) 3519111

Villa 47,2 Star, Deira,Simple b&b with your new best friend Ancy,Perfect 2nd home 5 mins from the airport ,Rooms: 2,Deira,No Beach,No Pool,No Spa, Near Choithram Deira, Metro: GGICO , Website: www.villa47.com, Email,ancypottenkulam@gmail.com

XVA,3 Star, Bur Dubai,Bastikiya boutique hotel,"The rooms were all originally designed, giving each of the seven spots a unique feel within this Arabian secret spot. Worth fighting for a room if you love the authentic way to travel." ,Rooms: 7,Bur Dubai,No Beach,No Pool,No Spa,Bastakiya, Metro: Al Fahidi , Website: www.xvahotel.com , Phone: (04) 3535383

RECOMMENDED HOTEL APARTMENTS IN DUBAI

Chelsea Tower Hotel Apartments,5 Star Hotel Apartments,Sheikh Zayed Road,huge skyscraper on SZR,Best amount of space from this newish high rise, Rooms: 281,Sheikh Zayed Road,No Beach, Pool, Spa,Opposite DIFC, Metro: Financial Centre , Website: www.chelseatowerdubai.com, Phone: (04) 3434347

Flora Park Hotel Apartments,5 Star Hotel Apartments,Deira,Clean and functional in Deira,Good for larger groups on a budget ,Rooms: 118,Deira,No Beach, Pool, Spa,Port Saeed Road near City Centre Mall, Metro:Deira City Centre, Website: www.florahospitality.com , Phone: (04) 2309595

Fraser Suites Dubai,5 Star Hotel Apartments ,Sheikh Zayed Road,Good value suites,Added bonus of a view of the palm ,Rooms: 158,4401400,,Sheikh Zayed Road,No Beach, Pool, Spa, Near Wellington School, Metro: Dubai Internet City , Website: www.frasershospitality.com , Phone: (04) 4401400

Hilton Dubai Jumeirah Residences,5 Star Hotel Apartments, Dubai Marina,Perfect holiday spot for large families,"Nearly a 5 star equivalent, but with some definite 5 star qualities" ,Rooms: 364,Dubai Marina,No Beach,Pool,No Spa,"Near the Walk, next to JBR", Metro: Jumeirah Lake Towers, Website: www.hilton.com , Phone: (04) 3991111

Oasis Beach Tower Apartments,5 Star Hotel Apartments,Dubai Marina,Perfect for beach loving families,Nice apartments close to the beach ,Rooms: 180,Dubai Marina,No Beach, Pool, Spa,On the walk between Ritz Carlton and Hilton Jumeirah, Metro: Jumeirah Lake Towers , Website: www.oasisbeachtower.com , Phone: (04) 3994444

Radisson Blu Residence Dubai Marina,4 Star Hotel Apartments, Dubai Marina,Basic apartments,Perfect for crashing for the night ,Rooms: 152,Dubai Marina,No Beach,Pool,No Spa,Before Marina Mall, Metro: Jumeirah Lake Towers, Website: www.radissonblu.com/hotel-dubaimarina , Phone: (04) 4355000

Dusit Residence Dubai Marina,5 Star Hotel Apartments, Dubai Marina,Good price at the downside of location and no beach,"Not as good as the original Dusit, but top quality all the same" ,Rooms: 146,Dubai Marina,No Beach,Pool,No Spa,"off Jumeirah Beach Road, near Grosvenor House", Metro: Dubai Marina , Website: www.dusit.com/drdm , Phone: (04) 4259999

Grand Midwest Tower Hotel Apartments,4 Star Hotel Apartments, Bur Dubai,Standard hotel apartments on the sheikh Zayed Road,4 star equivalent rooms ,Rooms: 84,3511114,,Bur Dubai,No Beach,Pool,No Spa,Behind Bank Street near Burjuman Centre, Metro: Khalid bin Waleed , Website: www.grandmidwest.com , Phone: (04) 3511114

Moevenpick Hotel & Apartments Bur Dubai,5 Star Hotel Apartments, Bur Dubai,One of the better Bur Dubai Apartment hotels,Good for families and execs ,Rooms: 57,3366000,,Bur Dubai,No Beach, Pool, Spa,"Oud Metha Road, Opposite American

Hospital", Metro: Oud Metha , Website: www.moevenpick.com , Phone: (04) 3366000

Xclusive Hotel Apartments,4 Star Hotel Apartments, Bur Dubai,"Not exclusive, but half decent apartments, despite the exterior","In comparison to other 3 star apartments in Bur Dubai, this is actually quite good." ,Rooms: 56,Bur Dubai,No Beach,Pool,No Spa,"Al Mankhool Road, next to Burjuman Centre", Metro: Dubai Healthcare City , Website: www.xclusivehoteldubai.com , Phone: (04) 3599925

Suha Hotel Apartments,4 Star Hotel Apartments, Dubai Marina, residential style JBR setting flats, better than average apartments on SZR and close to the palm ,Rooms: 90,Dubai Marina,No Beach,Pool,No Spa,"Jumeirah Beach Residence, behind Moevenpick Hotel", Metro: Dubai Marina , Website: www.suha-hotel-apartments-dubai.com , Phone: (04) 4291400

Corp Executive Hotel Apartments,4 Star Hotel Apartments, Al Barsha,perfect for the business exec,"walkable to the MoE, with local shops nearby." ,Rooms: 142,Al Barsha,No Beach,Pool,No Spa,Behind Mall of the Emirates, Metro: Mall of the Emirates , Website: www.corp-hotels.com , Phone: (04) 3164040

RECOMMENDED RESORTS OUTSIDE DUBAI

Banyan Tree Al Wadi,5 Star, Ras Al Khaimah,Magical tranquility in the desert,Perfect luxury as part of a two location break to the UAE ,Rooms: 101,Ras Al Khaimah,No Beach, Pool, Spa,Ras Al Khaimah, Metro: n/a,Website: www.banyantree.com/en/al_wadi/ , Phone: (07) 2067777

Kempinski Hotel Ajman,5 Star, Ajman,Beach resort away from the hubub,Expat retreat as a getaway ,Rooms: 181,Ajman,Beach, Pool, Spa,Ajman, Metro: n/a,Website: www.kempinski.com , Phone: (06) 7145555

Palm Tree Court and Spa,5 Star,Jebel Ali,Jebel Ali Golf and Resort Hotel,Beach resort to stay at on an inclusive basis but not to commute in to Dubai ,Rooms: 134,Jebel Ali,Beach, Pool, Spa,Sheikh Zayed Road, Metro: n/a,Website: www.jebelali-international.com , Phone: (04) 8145555

RECOMMENDED HOTELS IN ABU DHABI

Emirates Palace,5 Star, Abu Dhabi Island,One of the most expensive hotels in the world to build,"Palatial and fit for a king, although it may feel slightly too blong and be too expensive" ,Rooms: 394,Abu Dhabi Island,Beach, Pool, Spa,Prior to the Breakwater, Metro: n/a, Website: www.emiratespalace.com , Phone: (02) 6909000

Fairmont Bab Al Bahr,5 Star, Abu Dhabi Island,Famous for the exquiste views of the Sheikh Zayed Mosque. Stunnning,Our favourite hotel in Abu Dhabi with service excellence and superb facilities ,Rooms: 369,Abu Dhabi Island,Beach, Pool, Spa,"Near the Sheikh Zayed Mosque, between the bridges", Metro: n/a, Website: www.fairmont.com/babalbahr , Phone: (02) 6543333

Intercontinental Abu Dhabi,5 Star, Abu Dhabi Island,Beach heaven,Renovated old timer bringing a new edge ,Rooms: 390,Abu Dhabi Island,Beach, Pool, Spa,West of the Island, Metro: n/a, Website: www.ichotelsgroup.com , Phone: (02) 6666888

Yas Hotel,5 Star, Yas Island,The F1 hotel on Yas Island,The white honeycomb exterior is match by an even trendier interior and is close by to Ferrari World ,Rooms: 499,Yas Island,No Beach, Pool, Spa,F1 Circuit, Metro: n/a, Website: www.viceroyhotelsandresorts.com/abudhabi/ , Phone: (02) 6560000

Etihad Towers,5 Star, Abu Dhabi Island,"The new ""in"" hotel in Abu Dhabi",Great location and getting good reviews in Abu Dhabi ,Rooms: 382,Abu Dhabi Island,No Beach, Pool, Spa,Close to Emirates Palace, Metro: n/a, Website: www.jumeirah.com , Phone: (02) 8115555

Aloft Hotel,4 Star, Abu Dhabi Island,The trendy hotel in Abu Dhabi,Hotel close to capital gate and the convention centre ,Rooms: 408,Abu Dhabi Island,No Beach, Pool, Spa,Next to Abu Dhabi Convention Centre, Metro: n/a, Website: www.aloftabudhabi.com , Phone: (02) 6545000

St Regis Abu Dhabi,5 Star, Saadiyat Island,First mover on Saadiyat,Picture perfect paradise on a semi building site of an island ,Rooms: 377,Saadiyat Island,Beach, Pool, Spa, Near Manaarat al Saadiyat, Metro: n/a, Website: www.stregissaadiyatisland.com , Phone: (02) 4988888

PLANNING YOUR TRIP

We have managed to put together a whole amount of information during the years and reduce this down to the core points that you actually need. Times have changed but much of this information hasn't.

VISAS

Getting a visa for the UAE differs depending on your nationality, as per any other country. We refer only to tourist visas. There are three categories:

No VtSA

No Visa required for entry to Dubai, Abu Dhabi and all other Emirates in the UAE

If you are from the GCC (Saudi Arabia, Bahrain, Kuwait, Oman, Qatar), you do not require a visa to enter the UAE, whether you are entering by air, land or sea. You just require your passport.

VtSA oN ENTRY

Visa received on entry to Dubai, Abu Dhabi and all other Emirates in the UAE

This category of nationality will just receive their visa on entry to the UAE. The countries are: United States, Canada, UK (and those with the right of abode in UK), Australia, New Zealand, France, Italy, Germany, the Netherlands, Belgium, Luxembourg, Switzerland, Austria, Sweden, Norway, Denmark, Portugal, Ireland, Greece, Finland, Spain, Monaco, Vatican, Iceland, Andorra, San Marino, Liechtenstein, Japan, Brunei, Singapore, Malaysia, South Korea, holders of Hong Kong SAR passports. It's free to receive a visa and you will receive a visa allowing you to stay for 30 days. That's more than enough for most, though you may wish to renew for another 60 days, of you are scoping out the UAE for business purposes. You should speak to a specialist in this case. You'll need sponsorship and things of this nature. However, if you are coming in for a few days on business, you can just get a 30 day business visa on arrival which essentially is the same as this tourist visa

VtSA SPoNSoRSHtP

If you don't fall into the two above categories, i.e. you can't automatically receive a visa or you don't need a visa, you will require sponsorship for tourism purposes. There are two main ways to undertake this: sponsorship by a UAE resident (who could be family or even a friend), or sponsorship by the hotel where you are staying. You will need to get your sponsor to arrange all the paperwork in the UAE before your arrival – at least a few weeks to be sure. They will need all your details from when you are arriving to leaving. If you are staying in a hotel, you will need to stay with them for the duration of the trip and they will hold your passport for that time.

If you have an Israeli stamp in your passport, you may find it difficult to get into the UAE. The best way around this is to get a second passport created.

For more information, go to government.ae or contact your UAE embassy in your country. Don't overstay your visa period, as you will be charged a fee per day!

THE BEST TIME TO TRAVEL - TEMPERATURE

When your travel agent tells you that the UAE has all round heat they certainly are not lying to you. The issue is that the summer sun hits 50 degrees Celsius, so any time longer than 5 minutes in the sun and your skin will fry. The heat and humidity can become unbearable at times, especially in July and August. Rain is not usual, but on occasion, it can rain during the non-summer months. Let's put it like this: umbrellas are used more to keep off the sun than the rain.

It is no surprise that the hotel and flight prices are cheap during the Western Summer. The best time to visit the UAE is between October and April. December and January are the coolest months where it hits about 20 degrees. And then there is a steep climb to the Summer months. June, July and August can be unbearable if you are spending much time outdoors. The humidity during the hot period can make it particularly uncomfortable, but with air conditioning, in malls, offices and in the homes, some sort of normality can be attained. There are official ranges of temperature, but this is what we have experienced over the past few years, in degrees Celsius. The winter months can provide some great evenings to sit out side – and it can be argued that the Arabs go as crazy for cool weather as the British crave their two weeks of Summer.

January, 15-25

February, 15-25

March, 20-30

April, 20-36

May, 25-37

June, 28-40

July, 30-44

August, 30-44

September, 25-38

October, 20-36

November, 15-25

December, 15-25

It will never officially go above 40 degrees as this would mean that workers are not allowed to work in the sun, so you do sometimes hear of skewed temperature readings. But as we mentioned earlier, July and August can be extremely hot.

WHEN NOT TO TRAVEL

Depending on your capacity for heat, bear in mind the temperatures of Summer, the heat can be scathing on the skin. Apart from that, depending on your preference, the public holidays are not necessarily the best times to visit – but there are many who travel in to the UAE to be part of the festivities and spend time with friends and family. Equally, many residents, locals and expats use the holidays to travel out of the country. During Eid, some of the shops will be closed, though there is a festive feel in the evenings. Ramadan would require no eating or drinking in public during the day. It would be possible to eat in your room, for example, and some hotels have screened areas, but, many people prefer to avoid this time as a holiday – but the flight and hotel prices sometimes reduce during this period, so you could get a good deal. The main times that you may consider not travelling to the UAE are the summer months (July, August) as well as the numerous holidays.

The UAE has some holidays tied to the Gregorian calendar (Western calendar) and some that are tied to the Muslim Lunar calendar (Hijri Calendar). The holidays are January 1st (New Year's Day), December 2nd (National Day, 2 days). In addition there is the Prophet's birthday (Mawlid al Nabi), Ascension of the Prophet (Al Isra wa al Miraj), the last day of Ramadhan, Eid al Fitr (Feast of the Breaking of the Fast, usually at least 2 days), Eid al Adha (Feast of the Sacrifice, usually 3 days) and the Hijra New Year (the Muslim New Year). Since the dates of the Islamic holidays are based on the Hijri calendar they are subject to change every year, getting earlier by approximately 11 days every year. Islamic holidays are granted in accordance with the latest decree or ministerial decision by the Government and announcements are usually published in the press, to give exact public and private holidays.

Holidays like Miraj are unlikely to affect your holiday and, at worst you could spend that time at the beach or pool. The one other time where things shut down are during mourning periods where the country effectively shuts down for a few days and sometimes more – but one cannot plan for death!

Dates are dependent on the moon, so we suggest checking the following holidays and whether they will actually coincide with your holiday/trip.: Mawlid; Ramadan (for 30 days); Eid al Fitr; Eid al Adha; Hijra New Year. A simple Google search will give you the dates.

ARRIVING IN DUBAI

Dubai International Airport (DXB) is the main airport in Dubai, and recently opened, but very barely operational is Dubai World Central (DWC) based in Jebel Ali and on the outskirts of Dubai towards Abu Dhabi. Also known as Al Maktoum International Airport, which, when fully completed, over the next few years will be the largest airport in the world. Abu Dhabi International Airport (AUH) is the main airport in Abu Dhabi. Each of these airports is great for entry to the UAE. Abu Dhabi Airport is roughly 30 minutes from the city of Abu Dhabi and roughly an hour away from Dubai. Dubai International Airport is roughly 1 hour and a half away from Abu Dhabi but barely 30 minutes from most hotels in Dubai, so depending on the deal you receive, whether your hotel pays for your taxi or timing considerations, you could pick either of the airports. There are a total of 7 international airports with the other main airport being Sharjah International Airport (SHJ) If you are arriving in Dubai or Abu Dhabi, you can pay a couple of hundred Dirhams for someone to escort you through the arrivals gate, passport control.

If you are arriving in Dubai contact Marhaba Services marhabaservices.com

If you are arriving in Abu Dhabi contact Golden Class goldenclassservice.ae

NEED TO KNOWS

MoNEY

The Dirham is the currency used in Dubai and Abu Dhabi and the UAE. The UAE Dirham which is the official name of the currency. This is referred to as Dhs or AED. Each Dirham consists of 100 Fils. Notes are in denominations of 5 (brown), 10 (green), 20 (turquoise), 50 (dark blue), 100(red), 200 (green/brown), 500 (purple) and 1000 Dirhams (light brown). Rarely will you see a 1000 Dirham note, since they are not dispensed from many cash machines. The 200 and 20 Dirham notes are less prevalent than the others.

Coins are broken down to 5, 10, (coppers) 25, 50, Fils and 1 Dirham. Many shops will not carry the smaller Fils change and mark up or down. Often, you will be asked if you have the change to pay for something since it will clear out the till. "You have 1 Dirham, Madam?"

The Dirham is pegged to the US Dollar at a rate of 3.6724 Dirhams to the Dollar and has been since 1980. (The technical bit is that "The UAE is officially pegged to a special drawing right at the rate of SDE1=4.7619 UAE Dirhams, with a margin 7.25% on either side) And so currency fluctuations are wholly dependent on the greenback. There is talk of following the monetary union model for the Gulf, but if a currency were to be introduced it would be unlikely to come in for some time. Credit Cards (Visa, Mastercard, Amex and Diners Club) are accepted in the majority of shops, but not necessarily in the street stores. Traveller's cheques are accepted in less and less places.

There are many places to exchange your cash, including your hotel, specialist exchanges and banks. As with most countries, the rate that you will receive at your hotel will not be as good as at the exchanges. There are many exchanges on the street and in the malls, and it is perfectly safe to exchange your money there, and in most cases you do not need any ID. We would recommend having your passport for the odd instance that you do require ID.

The weird thing about Dubai is that despite the fact that there are many shops that trade in cheap goods that require significant change, there always seems to be a lack of coins or small notes available. You will always be asked if you have any change or a smaller note, but just be aware that you may have to accept additional goods instead of your small notes in some of the smaller establishments.

ATMS

ATMs can be located all over the UAE and most won't charge you commission. It will usually be your local card issuer who charges. So it's not too expensive to withdraw cash from a cash point, should you run short on your trip. They can located on most streets, including at the very many banks and bureaux de change. You will always find a hole in the wall in the malls.

ELECTRtCtTY

Electricity is stable and power cuts are less rare than in the West. As far as sockets go, the UAE uses 220-240v – 50Hz current. That's essentially the same as the UK with 3pins, and with an adapter, everything from Europe should work fine. You'll require a transformer if you are coming from the USA or Canada. Strangely, some locations have US sockets, which is unexplainable.

EMERGENCtES

For any serious emergency, the number you need is 999, and the police can determine and help with what you need. If it's a fire, then 997, ambulance then 998 but 999 is the number you need to remember, whether this is for police, hospitals or accidents.

HoMoSEXUALtTY

Although homosexuality does exist on the ground in the UAE, it is actually illegal, and so it is best not to declare that you swing that way. That said, you don't need your gaydar on to notice where the gay scene takes place. The secret is to not flaunt your sexuality and you should be fine. If you do, and you get caught, the penalty is 10 years in jail. Or reference, that's 6 years more than possession of drugs. The term used to describe this crime is consensual sodomy. Be wise to the culture, and you will not have any problems.

INTERNET

Nearly all hotels now offer Internet access at relatively fast speeds and many offer wireless access. There are many restaurants and coffee shops, for example Starbucks, across the UAE that offer wireless access, and sometimes it's free.

As far as Internet access goes, bear in mind that some websites are banned from the UAE, such as anti-UAE sites, voip sites, such as Skype, pornography etc. Flickr is the most notable ban. Some notable bloggers have been banned in the past including the notorious secretdubai blog. As with all technology, there are ways around bans, but that could get you in even more trouble!

NEWSPAPERS

Probably the most reputable broadsheet in the UAE is the Gulf News . Reportedly, it is largest read UAE daily in 'English', and favoured over most others. One of the newer newspaper and based out of Abu Dhabi is The National. It's not as thick as the other papers, but they have good quality writers. Khaleej Times, is another broadsheet, targeted at the Indian Subcontinent expats and although criticized with regards to quality, has some comprehensive local business commentary that is syndicated in numerous other publications. There have been in the past a number of newspaper that could be consider tabloid, but man have shut done for pure economic reasons.7 days is the free paper distributed all over the UAE. As with all freebies, it has a wide following and the letters section that has become more and more amusing over time. It is possible to get some international papers in the UAE, some which are locally printed, e.g. the FT and The Times of London, and some delivered at a later date. Check with your hotel. There are obviously a large selection of Arabic papers, the most popular of which are Al Ittihad, Al Bayan, and Al Khaleej.

TV

There are a number of English language free to air TV channels including Dubai One, playing American sitcom reruns, MBC2 showing movies and MBC4 showing American series, as well as channels like Star and Star world. In the hotels, you will pick up CNN and BBC.

SMoKtNG

There has been a large move to try and get the UAE to cut down on smoking, but it is prevalent across society. Blanket bans have been tried and have failed, but it appears as if is part of society, so people do smoke in the malls and sometimes in restaurants. And, of course, there are the shisha bars. You won't be able to escape the sweet smells of the hubble bubble in the evening.

TtME

The UAE's clocks don't change and are 4 hours ahead of GMT, making it perfectly placed to bridge the gap between the East and the West.

SAFETY

There is so much bad press about the Middle East and Arabs, that you would think there is a huge amount of crime going on. In actual fact, the UAE is probably one of the safest places in the world. With many people here to make more money than they can at home to give their families a better life, no-one wants to jeopardise their income generating potential. So, crime is pretty low. Obviously, things do happen, and some does get hidden and is not reported, but, as long as you play safe, you're pretty likely to be safe. People walk the streets late at night with their young kids – that's how safe it is. The one word of warning concerns driving. Dubai and Abu Dhabi are notorious for car accidents. Abu Dhabi was once listed as having the highest car accident rate in the world. That's not a record the UAE likes to have, but it is all to do with reckless driving of hugely powerful cars. The most fatal roads are the Sheikh Zayed Road, and the Emirates road in Dubai. Also, be aware that cars don't necessarily always stop at zebra crossings as you may be used to.

TELEPHoNES

The international code for the UAE is +971. The local code for Abu Dhabi is 02, Al Ain 03, Dubai 04, Sharjah 06, Amman 06, UAQ 06, RAK, 07, Fujairah 09. There are two telecoms providers, Etisalat and du. Mobile numbers are preceeded by 050 or 055. The numbers are usually 7 digits in length, and between Emirates local codes should be dialed. Within each Emirate the code should be dropped, and but calling from mobile to Dubai Land Line would require the 02 code. Calling from overseas requires the dropping of the 0. e.g. +971 (0) 4 765 4321.

Roaming can be expensive, and so it might be worth switching off data until you get to a free wireless area. It might also be useful to get a separate local SIM card for your trip, especially if you will be making many calls, local or otherwise. To get this you need to take your passport (plus a photocopy of your visa and entry stamp, and passport page, if you can do this easily) to any Etisalat telephone store. (or Du as well if you are in Dubai). You pay Dhs 75 to get the SIM card and this includes Dhs 25 worth of calls. You should get it directly from Etisalat or Du as activation will be a maximum of 1 day versus up to a week if you go to one of the smaller shops. If you are flying in to the UAE on a regular basis, it makes sense to get a local SIM, and if you know someone who can do this beforehand for you, it can make things easier for you. Phone call charges are minimal. VOIP services such as Skype are banned in the UAE although some expats figure ways to get round this.

TtPPtNG

How much are you expected to tip when in the UAE? It's always a tricky question. Tip too much, and you waste money. Tip too little and you may get a grunt of disapproval. The fact of the matter is that many of those in the service sector who you may consider tipping are paid very badly indeed, and sometimes rely on tips just to get by. In some cases you may not even think that some of the services are required, but feel compelled to tip. However, tipping practices are similar to those any where else in the world. We recommend that you do tip, but in the right way.

On occasion, restaurants, hotels and bars apply a service charge. That service charge is said to be pooled amongst the staff and split accordingly. Some believe that it is unlikely to end up with the waiter or waitress at some other places. So you don't have to give more, but if you do, give in cash. If no service charge is included at a restaurant, add 10 to 15% per cent of the total to the bill. If the service or meal was good, you should tip more.

You can tip bellboys 5 or 10 Dirhams or so, as you might do so for valet parkers or porters. Taxi drivers don't expect a tip, but perhaps you should round up to the next 5 Dirhams, especially if you take a short journey in Abu Dhabi. Tipping in bars is not usually expected but can get you speedier service. It might be worthwhile to do so if you actually have table service. The bag packers at supermarkets don't demand anything, but anything from a few coins to 5 Dirhams is worth giving. Places giving personal services such as salons or barbers do not expect a tip.

There has been some discussion regarding those who check your oil and fill your gas. It may be that they don't receive any of the tips that you give and this money goes to the gas station. If you do give anything, 5 Dirhams is acceptable.

When considering tipping, just bear in mind the personal situation of the people who are serving you. Some receive very little pay, and work very long hours. When it comes to tipping in Dubai or Abu Dhabi hotels, here is some advice:

Be careful where you tip. Some bills already contain a service charge as well as a tourist tax - and any additional amount may not go to the person that served you.

If you do want to tip, try and do it in cash, and up to 10% - more if you are generous

Tipping earlier during your stay will ensure consistent service from the concierge or bellboy for example

5 Dhs tip to a bellboy is always appreciated

If you want to tip cleaners of rooms, leave 20 or 30 Dhs in your bedroom at the end of your stay

Tipping in bars is not always expected, but if received will ensure prompt service with a smile for the next round

Be aware of the staff who are probably paid very close to nothing - and live on tips

Not all hotel staff receive the tips you give them. If you are unsure, then ask!

TotLETS

Toilets are generally very clean and accessible. You'll have no problem in the malls or hotels. Moving to some of the outskirts or further into the desert, you may encounter very dated toilets, which essentially are holes in the ground, along with douche sprays. You'll also encounter douche sprays in many modern toilets, and sometimes a few puddles! If you are in the very rural areas, you may need to carry a roll of toilet paper with you, or you'll have no friends.

WATER

The official line is that the water is fine to drink. The Emirates spend a small fortune on desalination to get the water drinkable and usable in the home. The reality is that the expatriates don't drink the tap water and instead go for bottled water. If you are at a restaurant ask for Masafi or Al Ain Water or the equivalent. Evian will be more expensive. Despite this – the UAE is not somewhere where you are going to get an upset stomach from the water, so it is completely safe to brush your teeth etc.

LANGUAGE

The official language is Arabic, with Gulf Arabic being the specific dialect. English is widely spoken and is the lingua franca between all the different nationalities in the UAE, so you'll be fine if you can speak English. English is used in most places, but less so, the further you go away from the main cities of Abu Dhabi and Dubai. However, English is used as a business language. It always helps to make an effort with the local language and you can find our basic Arabic phrases to help you gain some rapport. Having Urdu and Hindi would also be useful to have up your sleeve. Other languages spoken in the UAE include Farsi, Tagalog, Pashto and Malayalam due to the make up of the population.

ADDtTtoNAL BooKS ABoUT DUBAt

City of Gold (alt. Dubai, the story of the World's Fastest City) – Jim Krane – a fantastic, interesting and readable view of modern day Dubai – highly recommended for those who want to really understand Dubai.

Dubai – Gilded Cage – Syed Ali – another, slightly more critical view of Dubai, with more in depth understanding of Dubai, pre crash.

Dubai Complete Residents' Guide – The Dubai Explorer is the ultimate guide for expats or wannabe expats – the 'must get' book if you are moving or thinking of moving to Dubai to live, for a short period or long period. Updated almost annually.

Desperate in Dubai – Amira Al Hakawati – this is Sex and the City meets Desperate Housewives for the Dubai crew that came from a blog. Banned at launch, it is just about acceptable to the authorities – and hence a massive best seller in Dubai.

Escape from Dubai – Herve Jaubert – banned in Dubai, this book gives a personal experience of an escape amidst scandal.

Dubai: The Vulnerability of Success – Christopher M. Davidson – as controversial as it is informative, this will give you the societal and analytical view on Dubai

Dubai & Co – Aamir A. Rehman – understanding how strategy plays a role in tackling business in Dubai and the region

Dubai Map – Explorer - the best detailed map you are going to get on Dubai

USEFUL WEBStTES

Dubai FAQs, a compendium of data about Dubai dubaifaqs.com

Time Out Dubai, topical things to do timeoutdubai.com

I Love Dubai Facebook Group, a half a million strong group for lovers of Dubai facebook.com/ilovedubai.co

Definitely Dubai, official tourist board definitelydubai.com

Expat woman, has a wealth of information on anything and everything expatwoman.com

UAE Interact, Official country information uaeinteract.com

Expat Forum Dubai - a vibrant community who could probably give you the answer to anything. expatforum.com/expats/dubai-expat-forum-expats-living-dubai/

DoS AND DoN'TS

Many people worry about overstepping the mark and worry so much that they don't have a good time. Others who come to the UAE have a blatant disregard for the culture. There's also common sense about what you should do on holiday. We cover the dos and don'ts in the UAE.

Travel Insurance - Make sure you are fully covered for medical treatment. Although pharmacies provide medicines quite accessibly, treatment, hospitalisation and evacuation can add up to a large amount. Only emergency treatment is free. Make sure you are covered for unexpected losses or expenses such as cancelled flights, lost luggage, lost passport, stolen cash, or credit cards, as it can be difficult to request necessary documentation without it. Keep all your valuables in a safe place

Funds - Bring enough funds, for your stay and return. Although you can use credit cards, and withdraw from ATMs, bank transfers can take about a week. Use a proper teller to transfer your money rather than on the streets.

Drugs - Don't even think about getting involved with drugs. Penalties are severe, and with any proof in your bloodstream, even before you were in the UAE constitutes an offence of trafficking.

Respect local laws and customs. Dress in a modest way, covering at least the tops of arms and legs, and not tight clothes. Although, in practice, anything goes, it's best to respect the culture of the land that you are visiting. Don't behave in a manner that might insult Muslim customs or beliefs. Don't swear - as you can get fined and sent to jail! Public displays of affection are frowned upon.

Customs - Don't bring pornography to the UAE. Videos and books are often checked and may be retained by customs officials.

Driving - on a visit visa, you can drive on an international driving licence, but this changes is you are a resident. Don't drink and drive, ever. You'll go to jail. If you have an accident, remain with your car, in the exact place where the accident happened.

Sex on the beach is certainly not the thing to do, and you shouldn't really kiss in public, especially if you are not married. Holding hands is tolerated, but don't during Ramadan. The UAE is not the place to have a smooch in public.

Non Muslims can bring in alcohol to the UAE for their own consumption, but you should drink that alcohol within your hotel room or home. Apart from that, you can drink at licensed restaurants and bars which are usually attached to hotels. Don't be drunk in public and don't ever drink and drive.

Sex outside of marriage is illegal and so sharing a room could land you in jail. In practice this doesn't necessarily happen unless you are suspected of something else, and it will be thrown in as a charge. To get respect in public, you may want to refer to "my wife" or "my husband" – and wearing a ring would help things on

Respect local laws and customs. Dress in a modest way, covering at least the tops of arms and legs, and do not wear tight clothes. Although, in practice, anything goes, it's best to respect the culture of the land that you are visiting. Don't behave in a manner that might insult Muslim customs or beliefs.

Don't swear - as you can get fined and sent to jail!

Public displays of affection are frowned upon.

Photographs - Don't take pictures of governmental or military organisations. If you want to take pictures of the locals, make sure you ask first, especially with women.

Homosexuality – it is against the law here, so keep it undercover

Sunbathing – women should never sunbathe topless, even in private hotels – it is illegal.

Drunkenness – don't be overly drunk in public.

ID – Do carry some sort of ID with you, with a photo on it.

Overstaying - Don't overstay your visa period, as you will be charged per day.

Muslim Holidays - be aware when the Muslim holidays are. Don't eat in Public during the day during Ramadan

Make sure you do keep a copy of all your important documents in a separate place and perhaps online copies as a backup. Without the proper documentation, and in a worse case scenario of something being stolen, it will be a nightmare to dodge the red tape without proper information.

SoCtAL ETtQUETTE

Understanding social etiquette and social conduct can help significantly in a foreign country. Using them to your advantage and getting your social etiquette right can be crucial in establishing relations, whether business or personal in the UAE. Familiarise yourself with the local rules with them can go a long way, and with minimal effort. Here are a few customs that may differ from social norms in the West.

How to answer to how are you? Always answer with 'Al hamdulillah' which means "All praise is due to Allah". What this means is, essentially is that all is as it should be, since your wellbeing is governed by Allah. Even if you are very ill, you would answer with this phrase.

The sole of the foot is dirty and so when sitting cross legged, never point the sole of your foot in the direction of an Arab or expose it. The foot is considered dirty, and what this act is saying is the same as giving someone the finger - or even worse.

Crossing can be considered rude - crossing your legs in front of someone of high importance is considered disrespectful and should not be done.

Don't give someone your back. If someone is talking in your direction, you should always turn to face them. And not just in this part of the world. It's just rude otherwise.

I want to hold your hand! Shaking hand is the normal greeting with a male. But having your hand held for longer than usual is a sign of brotherly bonding, not that of homosexual tendencies.

I want to hold your hand some more! Your hand may even be held for longer than usual, while walking down the corridor, for example.

Always shake hands in formal situations. If you don't shake hands when meeting or leaving, it could be considered rude.

The right hand is clean. In most instances, the right hand is clean, and the left hand is dirty, so, when accepting food or drink, do it with your right hand. The left hand is resigned for picking your nose, we assume, unless it is held while walking down the corridor. That said, you will see people eating with both hands in public.

Shaking female hands is not necessarily the norm. Although some do in this part of the world, it should never be assumed that a female will shake your hand which could lead to an awkward moment. A better suggestion would be to wait if a hand is offered by the female. Females do shake hands with each other, and occasionally 3 kisses are shared between girlfriends.

Show respect to females always. Females demand a certain respect in the Muslim world. Always give women the option to sit down where she wishes to sit, stand when she enters the room, and let her go through the door before you. The basic rules of chivalry work well.

Culture demands the respect of elders. Always respect your elders. It's even more important in the Arab world.

Never give the finger. Never beckon anyone with one finger pointing up. If you do need to beckon, use your full hand pointing downwards

Say yes to drink, always! When offered something to drink, always say yes. (we're not talking alcohol here!) Saying no would mean rejecting someone's hospitality. Drink more than one small cup (tea, Arabic coffee) but never more than anyone else.

Never express admiration Be very careful when expressing admiration for an Arab's possession. You may find that he or she offers the object to you. (using "itfudul" - my pleasure) And then declining becomes a problem, followed by offering something back at a later date. Stating that you like your friend's Porsche Cayenne is somewhat risky therefore.

Polite chit chat can last for numerous meetings. When initiating business, it may be necessary to meet with a contact numerous times for him to scope you out, before committing to talking shop.

The office coffee shop can be a central meeting point. It is not uncommon for offices to contain a number of sofas, and for many people to come by while you are sitting in a meeting.

Your office could become a meeting point, even if you are in town for a short period of time. Bear in mind that while you may pay someone a visit, the pleasantries requirement may be sprung upon you, with numerous people popping by for a gossip.

The closest position is the most important one. When visiting others' office's you will be invited to take a seat according to your perceived level of importance. This might mean that someone gets up to make room for you. But you may have to move later if you drop down the pecking order!

Patience is a virtue Business may move at snails pace, but patience can buy you a big amount of respect.

DRUGS

Don't even think about getting involved with drugs. Penalties are severe, and with any proof in your bloodstream, even before you were in the UAE constitutes an offence of trafficking. There is zero tolerance for drugs – and before you know it you'll be in jail for 4 years.

BANNED MEDtCtNE

Not all drugs are accepted in the UAE, and some only with prescription, although some are administered in UAE hospitals. There is a comprehensive list on grapeshisha.com, but drugs that are banned include: codeine, amphetamines, methadone, robitussin, valium, xanax, Actifed compound linctus, tamiflu, reductil, Ritalin. This is obviously a very small list, and so it is worth checking with your local UAE Embassy. If you don't need it, don't bring it to the UAE, even in transit. If you have to bring it, make sure you bring a prescription and letter from your doctor. If you do get ill, you can very readily get drugs in the pharmacy. Essentially drugs that may be over the counter in your home country could be banned in the UAE. This could include many common cold and cough remedies. Various sleeping tablets, painkillers, anti-depressants and hormone replacement therapy drugs are banned in the UAE, as well as sex stimulants such as Viagra for example. Other things that are banned include poppy seeds, which you could quite easily eat on a bread roll in another country, and qat leaf, used as a stimulant for chewing, especially in Yemen.

BANNED GooDS

As with many countries, and over and above the banned drugs and medicine, there are other banned goods prohibited in the UAE. These are: pornography or any pornographic material, soft or hard core; non Islamic religious material for the purpose of distributing to others, weapons, ammunition, chemical and organic fertilizers, laser pens, radar jammers, fireworks, ivory, other unauthorized communication devices, endangered animal species, and anything else that does not "adhere to the religious and moral values of the UAE." The last part is a cover all, to prevent any object, such as a painting sculpture or any other media from being brought into the country – including pork or ham, even in a sandwich. Don't bring alcohol or pornography to the UAE. Videos and books are often checked and may be retained by customs officials.

TRAVEL INSURANCE

Make sure you are fully covered for medical treatment. Although pharmacies provide medicines quite accessibly, treatment, hospitalisation and evacuation can add up to a large amount. Only emergency treatment is free. Make sure you are covered for unexpected losses or expenses such as cancelled flights, lost luggage, lost passport, stolen cash, or credit cards, as it can be difficult to request necessary documentation without it. Keep all your valuables in a safe place

WHAT To WEAR

One of the most frequent questions we get asked is regarding clothing and what to wear. You know what the local Emirati's wear, and you're wondering how your own dress aligns. The good news is that you probably won't need to buy a new wardrobe, but you should err on the side of conservative, so aim to dress more modestly than if you were in the Mediterranean heat. In the hotel, near the resort, wear your bikini or trunks, but women shouldn't go topless. For women outside the hotel, dresses, knee length skirts and sleeveless tops are fine as long as they are not tight. You might want to avoid spaghetti vest tops. If you want to be conservative, cover up your shoulders and back, and go for a looser t-shirt than a tight fitting one. Don't go for skimpy skirts or tank tops for example. If you opt to wear sleeveless, carry a shawl with you in case you feel uncomfortable. Shawls are also useful when in an air conditioned environment such as the mall or the restaurant. However, when it comes to dressing for bars and clubs, you can almost get away with wearing what you wear back home. Most clubs actually encourage dressing up in order to gain entry, although keep cleavage viewing to a minimum. Short dresses are fine, as long as not overly short. For clubs, skinny jeans and a glitzy top are usually a safe bet for clubbing. For men, shorts and t-shirts are absolutely fine. You can wear sandals or flip flops. Abu Dhabi is slightly more conservative than Dubai – and Sharjah is very conservative in comparison. You'll get a very quick picture of what people wear by one visit to a mall or a bar. The aim is more for glam than for skimpy. You could probably push the limit of what you'd like to wear, but why the need? And why take the risk? Business dress, again, is more conservative – for women, go for longer skirts and no cleavage. For men, suits and a tie are good for a first impression, but in many offices ties are not necessarily worn and shirts and trousers are the norm. As far as walking around in a Kandoura or Abaya, we don't feel it is appropriate, although others may have other opinions. That said, they are great souvenirs to buy to take back home for your next fancy dress party!

Traditional Clothing in Dubai (as modelled by tourist tat)

WoRKtNG DAYS AND HoURS

In the West, traditionally, the Saturday and Sunday rule applies. Things are a little different here. Friday is the core holiday. Government and schools have Wednesday off, in addition. Some private institutions have Saturdays off, while some institutions align themselves to the West. It all depends. There are some who work a six day week and many, usually labourers, who work for all seven days. Official business hours operate around a split shift system from 8 until 1, and then from 4 until 7, Saturday to Thursday, although there are many institutions who are moving toward a straight shift system from 730 to 4 or similar. Banks are usually open from 8 til 3, Saturday until Wednesday and close at midday on a

Thursday. Over the coming years, Sunday to Thursday will become the norm.

OPENtNG HoURS

The weekend is Friday and Saturday. That has only formalised over the last few years, where, for some, the weekend was Friday and Saturday and other it was Thursday and Friday. For the unlucky, Friday is the only day off. With regards to shops, the malls tend to stay open from 10am to 10pm, Saturday to Thursday, and a little later on Fridays, depending on the mall, with supermarkets often opening for longer hours. Some malls will only open from midday onwards on Friday. The streets keep their own times, usually similar to the Malls, but closed between 1 and 4pm.

UAE EMBASStES (SELECTED)

USA

3522 International Court, NW, Suite #400 Washington, DC 2000

Tel +1-202-2432400, Fax: +1-202-2432432

United Kingdom

30 Princes Gate, London SW 7 1PT, UK

Tel: +44-207-5811281, Fax: +44-207-5819616

Canada

World Exchange Plaza - Suite 1800 45 O'Conner Street Ottawa, Ontario K1P 1A4

Tel: +1-613-5657272, Fax: +1-613-5658007

Australia

P.O. Box 173, Ggarran Act 2605, 36 Culgoa Circuit, O Malley Act 2606 Canberra, Australia

Telephone: +612-6-2868802, Fax: +612-6-2868804

India

EP-12, Chander Gupta Marg, Chanakyapuri, New Delhi-110021, India

Tel: +9111 26111111, Fax: +91-11-26873272

Pakistan

P.O. Box 1111, Plot No.1-22, University Road, Diplomatic Enclave Islamabad, Pakistan

Tel: +92-51-2279052, Fax: +93-51-2279063

France

3, Rue Delota 75116, Paris, France

Telephone: +33-1-44340200, Fax: +33-1-47556104

Germany

Address: Hiroshimastr. 18-20 D-10785 Berlin, Germany

Tel: +49-30-516516, Fax: +49-30-51651-900

For more information on embassies see uaeinteract.com

EMBASStES tN THE UAE (SELECTED)

Country: USA

P.O. Box: 4009

Tel: +971 2 4142200, Fax: +971 2 4142241

Country: United Kingdom

P.O.Box: 248

Tel: +971 2 6101100 ,Fax: +971 2 6101586

Country: Canada

P.O. Box: 6970

Tel +971 2 6940300, Fax: +971 2 6940399

Country: Australia

P.O. Box: 32711

Tel: +971 2 6346100, Fax: +971 2 6393225

Country: India

P.O. Box: 4090

Te: +971 2 4492700, Fax: +971 2 4444685

Country: Pakistan

P.O. Box: 846

Tel: +971 2 4447800, Fax: +971 2 4447172

Country: France

P.O. Box: 4014

Tel: +971 2 4435100, Fax: +971 2 4434158

Country: Germany

P.O. Box: 2591

Tel: +971 2 6446693, Fax: +971 2 6446942

For more information on embassies see uaeinteract.com

CoST oF GooDS

On holiday and excursion it's useful to know in advance how much things cost on the street, so that you know you are paying the right amount – and so you know that you can save by popping out to your local store opposite the hotel, rather than buying a grossly marked up product. Also, you may have to, on occasion, spend on goods and services that you didn't think you needed to. We maintain a price list of certain goods – and have included some prices below. We have provided the higher end price.

Type of Product, Brand, Size, High End Cost (Dhs)

White Bread, loaf, In store, medium sized 4.00

Baguette In storemedium sized 2.00

Naan bread In store 5, small 1.75

Butter Lurpak equivalent 227g 6.75

Margarine Flora 250g 11.75

Jam Bonne Maman Jam 370g 13.95

Mayonaise Helmans Mayonniase 500ml 10.25

Coffee, instant Nescafe Gold Coffee 100g 19.25

Tea bags, Tetley Tea 40 bags 14.75

Drinking Chocolate Cadburys 250g 9.95

Cola Coca-Cola 6 cans 5.25

Mineral Water Masafi Water 1.5l 1.50

Orange Juice Orange Juice 2L 9.00

Cordial Robinson's Orange 1litre 10.00

Chocolate Dairy Milk Bar 200g 10.25

Chocolate Lindt 70% Cocoa Chocolate 100g 10.50

Chocolate 8 X 2 stick Kitkat 168g 6.00

Muffins In store 6, medium 7.50

Gum Wrigley's Extra 1 pack 1.50

Crisps/Chips Pringles 163g 7.00

Cookies, Choc chip Chips Ahoy 300g 9.00

Cookies, Digestives McVities Digestive Biscuits 250g 7.25

Baby Food Ceralac Rice and Milk Baby Food 400g 19.00

Baby Food Gerber Pear Baby Food 80g 4.75

Baby Food Farley's rusks 18 17.00

Soap Lux Handwash 800ml 13.50

Laundry Detergent Tide 2.5kg 18.00

Fabric softener Comfort Softner 2 litres 13.75

Toilet Tissue Andrex Toilet Tissue 9 rolls 54.50

Dishwashing Liquid Lux Washing up liquid 500ml 6.50

Insect Killer Spray Pif Paf 500ml 10.25

Batteries Duracel Extra 6 6.75

Disinfectant Dettol 500ml 13.25

Razor Blades Mac 3 Razor 8 razors 17.50

Toothpaste Colgate Confidence 125g 5.75

Facial Tissue Kleenex Tissues 150sheets 18.25

Shampoo Baby Shampoo 500ml 16.20

Shampoo Herbal Essences 400ml 29.50

Lipstick Nivea 1 7.75

Feminine Hygiene Always Ultra 6 pack 6.50

Mouthwash Listerine 500ml 24.75

Body Soap Dove 1 bar 5.50

Shaving Gel Gillette Gel Can 19.25

Nappies Pampers Active Baby 70 Nappies 53.25

Condoms Durex 12 pack 41.25

Cough Linctus Actifed Cough and Cold 200ml 29.00

Pain Killer Panadol 48 tablets 7.30

Flu Remedies Lemsip 10 sachets 10.40

Cough Sweets Strepsils 24 tablets 14.00

National Newspaper Gulf News paper 3.00

Int. Daily Paper The Times Newspaper 1 day delay 7.00

Int. Daily Paper USA Today 1 day delay 12.00

Int. Financial Paper The Financial Times 1 day delay 15.00

Int. Sunday Paper The Sunday Times 1 day delay 15.00

Int. Business Magazine The Economist Magazine 3 days delay 35.00

Int. CA Magazine TIME Magazine 3 days delay 25.00

Int. Mens Magazine GQ Magazine 1 week delay 45.00

Int. Womens Magazine Marie Claire 1 week delay 60.00

Spirit 1 30-50 Bar

bottle beer 1 15-25 Bar

Bar/Club Entry 1 50-100 Bar

Shisha smoking 1 30-50

Marlborough Lights 1 6.5 Street Store

Cinema Ticket 1 30 Cinema

New DVD 1 65-85 Supermarket

Old DVD 1 50-60 Supermarket

Black Market DVD 1 10 Street

CD 1 60-120 Supermarket

Big Mac Meal regular 17 MacDonalds

Big Mac 1 9 MacDonalds

Chicken Shawarma 1 5-10 Street stall

Cappuccino tall 14 Starbucks

Cappuccino venti 16 Starbucks

Cappuccino grande 18 Starbucks

Mocca Frappuccino tall 17 Starbucks

Mocca Frappuccino venti 19 Starbucks

Mocca Frappuccino grande 21 Starbucks

Blueberry Muffin 1 10 Starbucks

Teryaki Entrée meal 1 22 Emirates Mall

Pizza Tom & Mozzarella 1 28 street restaurant

Chicken Shish Tawouk main course 1 40 street restaurant

Tuna sandwich with salad and fries 1 30 street restaurant

Drycleaning Suit 42

Drycleaning Shirt 13.25

Drycleaning Skirt 20

Drycleaning Trousers 18.5

Ironing Shirt 8.5

Gym Membership annual 5750-9000

Gym + Pool Membership annual, 5* hotels 7,888-14,500

Entrance to beach 10-300

Belly Dance Class 40

Photo Developing 6X4 1.5

Haircut Male 50

Haircut Male 35

Haircut Male 10

Shave Male 20

Cut and Blowdry Female 170-230

Blowdry Female 70-100

Styling Female 250+

Wax Full Leg 90

Wax Full Arm 75

Wax Full Body 260

Halawa Wax Leg 90

Halawa Wax Full body 200

Threading Eyebrows 35

Massage 1 hour 200

Facial 1 hour 200-370

Manicure both hands 50

Pedicure both legs 50

Moroccan Bath (hamam) 290

Basic Visit to Doctor 150

Basic checkup at Dentist 100

Hygienist clean 300-500

Filling 450

Optician Eye Test 250-350

Across town Abu Dhabi City Taxi 7-20

Across town (evening) Abu Dhabi City Taxi 15-30

Across town Dubai Taxi 15+

Across town Sharjah Taxi 10+

Abu Dhabi to Dubai Abu Dhabi to Dubai Taxi 270-400

Dubai to Abu Dhabi Dubai to Abu Dhabi Taxi 250-300

Sharjah to Dubai Sharjah to Dubai Taxi 75

Dubai to Sharjah Dubai to Sharjah Taxi 50

Shared taxi Abu Dhabi to Dubai Taxi 50

Shared taxi Dubai to Abu Dhabi Taxi 50

Airport taxi Abu Dhabi Airport to city centre Taxi 85

Local Taxi City Centre to Abu Dhabi Airport Taxi 50

Airport taxi Dubai Airport to World Trade Centre Taxi 60

Local Taxi World Trade Centre to Dubai Airport Taxi 50

Airport taxi Sharjah Airport to Sharjah Taxi 20

Airport taxi Sharjah Airport to Dubai Taxi 70

Local Taxi Dubai to Sharjah Airport Taxi 70

Local Taxi Media city to Sharjah Airport Taxi 250

Bus Abu Dhabi to dubai bus 15

Bus Dubai to Abu Dhabi bus 35

Car Rental 4X4 Nissan Pathfinder (or similar) 1 week 2800

Car Rental 4X4 Nissan Pathfinder (or similar) 1 month 6000

Car Rental Toyota Yaris (or similar) 1 week 630

Car Rental Toyota Yaris (or similar) 1 month 2,400

EVENTS tN DUBAt

Dubai is renowned for the huge number of events and exhibitions it organises throughout the year. In the past Dubai was probably most known for the Dubai Shopping Festival, but today there are so many other longstanding regular events, notably the Dubai Rugby Sevens, the Dubai Desert Classic and the world famous GITEX exhibition. It's no wonder Dubai is not just a beach holiday destination. Flights and hotels are now busy throughout the year so it's best to book your tickets and accommodation well beforehand. Whether you have a passion for food, pets, films, sports, shopping or beer, there is sure to be an event that will tickle your fancy - we guarantee it! You'll notice more events take place during October - April due to the cooler months and locals/expats usually take their vacations during hotter months. To find out what's going on check out Time Out, What's On and Concierge magazines when you get into town. As a guide, we have listed the events name, what it is, and the website where you can find out more information.

January

Dubai International Racing Carnival

Racing events will begin from November and run through till March every week. Please check website for details on races and schedule. Access is free to the beautiful Meydan Racecourse and guests will have a view of the horses in the Parade Ring before and after the event. If you want a seat, tickets are between 50 AED- 150 AED and if you want to make it an evening to remember spend 600 AED for a 3 course carvery meal overlooking the racetrack. For more info visit: dubairacingclub.com

Dubai Marathon

If you fancy taking a dive at this and perhaps getting the million dollar jackpot, there are 3 race options: the 43 km full marathon, the 10km road race, or 3km fun run all circuiting through the famous landmarks of Dubai. To register and for more info visit: dubaimarathon.org

Dubai Shopping Festival

If you happen to be visiting Dubai during mid January to mid February, you should pick up some pretty good bargains as most malls will be running promotions with some goods up to 70% off. Additionally, there will be a lively atmosphere with special events and concerts running through the month. Visit the official site for more info, although please note, it normally gets updated nearer the event: mydsf.com

February

The Dubai Desert Classic

The world's top golfers meet at the Emirates Golf Club in the European PGA Tour golf tournament to compete for a cool USD 2.5 million prize money. More info, check out: dubaidesertclassic.com

Dubai International Jazz Festival

Running since 2003, Dubai International Jazz Festival has kicked up a storm with appearances by some of the world's well known artists such as David Gray, James Morrison and John Legend. Atmosphere is perfect in the open air surroundings of Media City, perfect for mid February temperatures. More info: dubaijazzfest.com

Dubai Pet Show

Having pets in the UAE is not exactly a common thing, but for all you dog and cat lovers who crave to coo at cute puppies and kittens in clothes, the Dubai Pet Show will bring you a few hours of happiness and you may even decide you want a pet of your own. This hugely successful show runs at a new location 7he Sevens Stadium. More info: dubaipetshow.com

Dubai Tennis Championships

The Dubai Duty Free Tennis Championships have been running since 1993 and been hosts to many superstar players over the last few years. The Dubai Tennis Stadium is within The Aviation Club Tennis Centre and totally self contained with a 5000 seat centre court including a Royal enclosure. The surroundings are a great entertainment facility and include the popular Irish and Century Village with its huge selection of dining options. The championships normally run during February, for more info on match schedules go to: dubaidutyfreetennischampionships.com

Gulf Food Exhibition

If you are connected with the food industry then the annual Gulf Food Exhibition will be of interest to you, normally held mid February. Admission is strictly for those in the food business and if you register online before the event, admission is free of charge. On the day, you will have to pay a 200 AED entry. For more info visit: gulfood.com

The Terry Fox Run

The largest single day fundraiser in the world which started in Canada by Terry Fox is now in its 17th year in Dubai. Normally held mid February at the Mamzar Park, this 8.4km route is open to all ages whether you want to run, walk, cycle or sccoter. Refreshments will be held along the route and partcipants are encouraged to collect sponsorships or donate. Admission is free. For more info visit: premiermarathons.com

March

Taste of Dubai

With most UAE locals and expats eating out more then they eat in, Taste of Dubai has captured the heart of all true foodies. The exhibition normally runs between 3/4 days over a weekend in March at the Media City amphitheatre. Watch your favourite Chefs and Celebrity Chefs walk you through their popular dishes at fun cooking demos and sample hundreds of dishes at a fraction of the price. A belly filling day out for all the family! For more info: tasteofdubaifestival.com

Art Dubai

An extensive collection of worldwide as well as Middle Eastern art displayed at the Madinat Jumeirah. More then 80 galleries displayed their work last year along with daily presentations and talks on topics such as fashion. Normally held over 4- 5 days over the 3rd week in March. For more info: artdubai.ae

Bastakiya Art Fair

A smaller but intimate art fair mainly focusing on the work of local artists and middle eastern art. Held in the Bastikiya area within 16 traditional houses and the XVA Gallery and some other hotels where exhibitions, talks and movie screenings take place. Normally runs alongside Art Dubai so people can visit both shows. For more info: bastakiyaartfair.com

Dubai Polo Gold Cup

Dubai's premier polo competition of the year where teams from around the world compete to win the prestigious Gold Cup trophy. Spectate and have a fun day out with the kids and a picnic whilst watching the fierce competition. Gold competition normally held between late February and early March. For more info: dubaipologoldcup.com

Dubai Football 7s

If you love playing football and want to play at team level, the Dubai Football 7s is a great way to enter your team and compete against a host of others whilst having fun and making new friends. Last year, the Dubai Football 7s saw over 3000 entrants making it the largest football tournament in the Middle East. Any level of playing is admitted and the matches normally run over 4 consecutive weekends during late February and early March. If you love to spectate, entry is free for all during all match days. Enjoy the lively atmosphere. For more info: football7s.com

Dubai World Cup

Probably one of the most glitziest shows Dubai puts on is the annual Dubai World Cup, which is the finale to the Dubai International Racing Carnival. Supreme horse racers from around the globe partake in this world famous race by invitation only and compete with the some of the fastest horses on the planet for a whopping USD10million prize. The whole race or show is such entertainment with competitions for the 'Best Dressed Lady' and 'Best Hat' all taking place in the Bubble Lounge complete with live DJ. General Admission is free but views are limited to a certain area, otherwise if you want to be seated in style on the grandstand with unlimited beverages and canapes, ticket prices start from AED 1,200 and rise to AED 3,000 per person. For more info: dubaiworldcup.com

Emirates Literary Festival

An impressive book festival playing host to over 70 authors from around the Middle East and worldwide including names like Kate Adie and Tony Parsons all join together in a 4 day event partaking in panel discussions, workshops, listen to readings and generally promote education through reading. A great day out for both adults and kids. Held at the Intercontinental Hotel, Festival City normally for 4 days days during early March. For more info: eaifl.com

Dubai International Boat Show

If you're not short of cash, why not visit the Dubai International Boat Show and perhaps even buy a yacht! Seriously, you will be tempted. High end buyers and top of the range suppliers connect at this luxurious event where men really do enjoying window shopping! Held at the DIMC Mina Seyahi during the beginning of March. For more info: boatshowdubai.com

April

Gulf Film Festival

Concentrating on the talents of regional film makers, the Gulf Film Festival aims to provide a springboard for aspiring local film makers to showcase their work with a view to develop partnerships and make future film projects. Not as big as DIFF but a great way to enjoy arab cinema. Most films will be in arabic with english subtitles but check the schedule nearer the time. All screenings take place at the Grand Festival Cinemas, Festival City during April. More info: gulffilmfest.com

Dubai Fashion Week

Up and coming fashion designers from the Middle East and around the region showcase their collection for interested trade buyers and this trendy five day event normally held during mid April. For more info: dfw.ae

May

Dhow Racing

A very different type of boat race, traditional dhows race against one another to test out their power and robustness whilst maintaining the long standing UAE traditional culture. This event is hosted by the Dubai International Marine Club. For more info: dimc.ae

June

Dubai Summer Surprises

When the heat is on, Dubai need an excuse to organise more indoor events in the air conditioned malls, so Dubai Summer Surprises is essentially a summer sale spree with the bells and whistles of activities for the kids, competitions and entertainment. Huge bargains to be had especially as its the summer months and the emirate is quiet whilst the locals are away on holidays. Normally starts mid/end June and runs till end of August. More info: mydsf.ae

July/August

Hop Fest

For all the beer lovers, the Irish Village hosts the annual HOP FEST. Sample over 100 different beers from around the globe and mingle, sit or dance in a huge air conditioned marquee amongst some lively entertainment from live bands. This event can get loud so not really recommended to bring young kids unless going for the early afternoon part. Open all day from noon - 2am with pub grub served all day. Normally held during late July early August for 3 days. For more info: irishvillage.ae

October

GITEX

This is probably one of the largest events Dubai holds annually and is the Middle East's premier ICT exhibition. You'll find over 3,500 IT vendors all vying for your business or cash for their products. If you love gadgetry, make a stop here. Just bear in mind, all hotels get booked up pretty quickly around GITEX time so plan your holidays accordingly if you are not interested in attending GITEX! Normally held for 5 days during the beginning of October. More info and dates for this year: gitex.com

OktoberFest

Dubai's answer to the popular German based exhibition celebrating homegrown food and drink. This festival normally runs mid October for 2 days from 7pm, recently its seen so many visitors that booking is now advised. More info: irishvillage.ae

Desert Rhythm Festival

This one day festival celebrates music, entertainment, food, drink and shisha. Brinng the kids along too and they will be entertained with face painters, trampolining, magicians although better to plan the day to start early with kids rather then later as it will get loud. This event is normally held end of October at Dubai Festival City. More info on the next one: desertrhythmfestival.com

Camel Racing

November

Dubai Rugby Sevens

A hugely popular sporting event in Dubai which now sees an average of 120,000 visitors through its gates over the 3 day event. Played in its purpose built stadium the Dubai Rugby Sevens sees international players vying for maximum points score. Watching a game is a true experience and hang about afterward for the traditional Rugby Rock Concert held on the first two nights (normally a Fri and Saturday) where the whole place is turned into a loud party atmosphere. More info on dates for this year: dubairugby7s.com

Dubai World Championship

This golf championship replaces the previous Volvo Masters and has been running since November 2009. In 2010 the Dubai World Championship saw about 50,000 spectators attending free general admission although if you fancy viewing in style, premium viewing packages are available from 2,600 AED to 5,500 AED. More info: dubaiworldchampionship.com

The Big 5

For a city that prides itself on building the tallest tower in the world, what better then to be the annual host of one of the world's largest building and construction exhibitions and the largest in the MENA. The Big 5 has been in operation for the last 30 years and proved extremely successful. If you're connected with construction or building work you will find this exhibition hugely beneficial. More info: thebig5.ae

December

Dubai International Film Festival

Dubbed as the largest film festival in the Middle East, the Dubai International Film Festival brings together local talents aswell as global producers in one location to celebrate the success of new releases. General public are able to buy tickets for individual screenings of movies which will showcase throughout several locations in Dubai, take the opportunity to watch atleast one movie as chances are they may not be screened as a general release. The DIFF has become so prominent now that its regularly frequented by A-listers such as Colin Farrell and Sean Penn. The festiival is normally held early December for about a week at Dubai Media City. More ticket info will appear closer to the date of the festival: dubaifilmfest.com

UAE National Day - 2nd December

The whole country celebrates UAE's independence by taking to the streets and watching the local emiratis go by in their huge cars waving flags and honking. Park yourself at one of the many prominent streets such as Jumeirah Road and watch the fireworks displays and party atmosphere.

MODERN HISTORY & MAJOR EVENTS

For the uninitiated, this would be the point where we shared the customery beafore and after photos of Dubai. But it's more than just that. The history of the UAE is about the Bedouin tribes. Dubai's story comes from Abu Dhabi and Abu Dhabi is the story of the Bani Yas tribe. But the history actually goes back way further, and it is only in recent years that remains were found dating back several thousand years BC. Tombs continue to be found in places outside the main city of Abu Dhabi, places like Dalma Island. There is also history of other civilisations being in this part of the world before or alongside the Arabs with evidence of the Greeks being in this part of the world. There is also evidence of Christianity here before Islam arrived. On Bani Yas Island, there is one the oldest churches in Arabia.

Once Islam did arrive, the UAE, as a region, wasn't actually a stronghold as power moved steadily west to Egypt, with the Ummayyid and Abbasid dynasties leaving those to fend for themselves in the desert heat. It was only in the early 1760s when the history really did begin for the UAE and modern day Abu Dhabi. And it was all due to a gazelle. The story of the water in modern day Al Ain and the Emirate being named "Abu Dhabi", literally father of the gazelle, is instilled in the being of the local Emirati. The very existence of water drew the Bani Yas tribe to Abu Dhabi to create what we see today.

The British arrived in the 1800s to maintain stability over the gulf areas, the Bani Yas in the west and the Al Qasimi in the east. It was in the 1830s that a small group from the Bani Yas broke off to claim independence from Abu Dhabi and set up Dubai. Had that group been bigger and claimed more land, history may have been quite different to today. Dubai may have had a larger percentage of land, meaning a larger access to the oil, on which Abu Dhabi's economy is based. Dubai may not have gone the route of attracting foreign investment.

Diversions aside, oil was discovered in 1958, but the principal moment came with the agreement of union between two great men – Sheikh Rashid of Dubai and Sheikh Zayed of Abu Dhabi. This allegiance at the time of the British withdrawal from the "Trucial States" as they were known then was the founding of what we know now as the United Arab Emirates or Al Imarat Al Arabiyah al Muttahidah. The allegiance between these two powerful sub tribes became the stability of this great country and underpins how the UAE works, from foreign policy to internal government. The economic downturn of the 2008 onwards only sought to bring all the Emirates closer together, strength in power, strength in unity. That unity has continued to exist to the next generation of leaders. Sheikh Khalifa was unanimously sworn in as president on the passing of his father, Sheikh Zayed – and crucially, the friendship between the Crown Prince of Abu Dhabi, Sheikh Mohamed bin Zayed and the now Prime Minister of the UAE and Leader of Dubai, Sheikh Mohamed bin Rashid bodes well for the future.

The history of the UAE is an interesting one and the times before the union could be turned into a Hollywood epic. But this is no history lesson, nor is this a movie! Below are the main points that you need to know, including some of the newsworthy moments of the last 10 years.

1820 – The Sheikhs of the relevant sheikhdoms sign an agreement with Great Britain for protection.

1892 - The sheikhdoms become known as the Trucial States.

1930 – Pearl trade starts to wane

1954 – Oil is discovered in Abu Dhabi

1971 – UAE Formed as an independent state of 6 states (Emirates), with Sheikh Zayed appointed as the First President of the United Arab Emirates.

1972 – Ras Al Khaimah joins the UAE as the 7th Emirate.

1985 – Emirates Airline launched

1990 – Death of Sheikh Rashid – succeeded by Sheikh Maktoum as Ruler of Dubai

1996 – Dubai World Cup launched

1996 – Dubai Shopping Festival Launched

1998 – Burj Al Arab opens

1999 – Dubai Internet City (Freezone) opens

2001 – Reclaiming of Palm Jumeirah begins

2003 – Freehold property law agreed allowing expatriates to buy property in Dubai

2004 – Death of Sheikh Zayed – succeeded by Sheikh Khalifa as Ruler of Abu Dhabi and President

2004 – Saadiyat Island announced to be the cultural centrepiece of Abu Dhabi with museums from the Louvre and Guggenheim amongst others.

2005 – DIC buys the Tussauds Group

2005 – Ski Dubai, the largest indoor ski slope in the Middle East opens

2005 – Emirates Palace, Abu Dhabi's landmark hotel, which cost $2bn to construct, is opened

2006 – Dubai Ports World buys P&O, leading to a furore within the US regarding security

2006 – Death of Sheikh Maktoum – succeeded by Sheikh Mohammed, his brother – as ruler of Dubai, vice President and Prime Minister

2007 – Dubai World invest in Las Vegas casinos

2008 – Atlantis Hotel opens on the Palm

2008 – Grooverider, a famous British DJ jailed in Dubai on drug possession

2008 – Pakistani cricketer Mohammad Asif detained in Dubai on drug possession

2008 – Abu Dhabi buys Manchester City Football Club

2008 – British couple Vince Accors and Michelle Palmer sentenced, jailed then suspended for having "sex on the beach"

2009 – Dubai denies a visa to Israeli tennis player Shahar Peer provoking an international storm of outrage. Andy Ram, another Israeli, is granted a visa and becomes the first Israeli to play a professional tennis match in the UAE

2009 – Dubai Metro opens

2009 – Dubai bans author Geraldine Bedell from attending the Emirates International Festival of Literature over references to a gay Sheikh in her novel, The Gulf Between Us.

2009 – Dubai World, the emirate's main holding company asks for a 6 month delay to repay its debt, sending world markets into turmoil.

2009 – Maiden Formula 1 Abu Dhabi Grand Prix takes place in Yas Marina Circuit

2009 – Abu Dhabi bails Dubai's out to the tune of $10bn

2010 – Burj Khalifa, the tallest building in the world, opens

2010 – A senior Hamas official, Mahmoud al Mahbhouh is assassinated in the Al Bustan Rotana in Dubai. The hit team had forged European passports and were allegedly from Mossad

2010 – The UAE jails two Brits Ayman Najafi and Charlotte Lewis for kissing in public

2010 – The UAE's telecom's authority threaten to block Blackberry services over privacy issues but later comes to an agreement with its owner RIM

2011 – The UAE manages to avoid any major uprisings from The Arab Spring, but had to quash a small number calling for political reform

2013 – Dubai announced as the host of the 2020 Expo (and the building starts again!)

2014 – Dubai Airport becomes the busiest airport in the world.

THE UAE FACTFILE

The Country

Formal Name (Arabic): Al Imarat Al Arabiyah al Muttahidah (or Al Imarat) and formerly called the Trucial States prior to independence. The referred name is United Arab Emirates (or UAE) (n.b. Although the United Arab Emirates (UAE) is generalized as being a country, strictly it is a federation consisting of seven Emirates)

Emirates: Abu Dhabi, Dubai, Sharjah, Umm al Qawayn, Amman, Fujairah, and Ras al Khaimah

Cities

Abu Dhabi is the capital of the UAE, and Abu Dhabi the Emirate holds the seat of government and has done since the UAE was formed in 1971. Dubai as a city and an Emirate are essentially used interchangeably these days with construction edging further and further outwards. Abu Dhabi City, is basically an island just off the coast of the Emirate and linked to the land by two bridges. Dubai as a city is the most populated but as an Emirate, Abu Dhabi is the most populous, with cities such as Al Ain and Madinat Zayed in the East. Other key cities include Sharjah and Khorfakkan, both in Sharjah.

Location

Location wise, the UAE is located in the "Middle East" between the Arabian Gulf and the Gulf of Oman with borders in the North with Saudi Arabia and in the North West with Oman. The geographic coordinates are 24 00N, 54 00 E. In square kilometers, the UAE is 83,600 square kilometres which is about 30,000 square miles. Abu Dhabi, the Emirate, by far the largest of the seven, is 67,350 square kilometres.

People

The people of the country are referred to as Emirati although the term UAE National is used more and more often. On occasion where comparisons are made between UAE Nationals and Expatriates, the terms local and expat are used. The population was estimated to be 4.7 million in 2010, with the percentage of UAE Nationals between 15 and 20%, depending on which figures that you look at. In Dubai, that percentage would be close to 10%. As far as the large number of expatriates that live and work in the country, the majority are Indian, Pakistani, Bangladeshi, Egyptian, Jordanian, Iranian, Filipino. From the West, there are increasing numbers of British, French, other Western Europeans as well as Americans, Canadians, South Africans and Australians, with almost every nationality represented. To understand the make up, at least half of the population are from the Indian subcontinent, and certain areas resemble the streets of India rather than Arabia.

Religion

The UAE Nationals are majority Sunni Muslim, with about 15% of Muslims in the UAE of the Shia minority. Many of the expats who come here are also Muslim, especially since some come from the Gulf states. Other religions that are represented include Christianity and Hinduism. It is not illegal to practice another religion here, as opposed to some other countries, but it is illegal to essentially preach with the intention of conversion. There are churches in allocated areas, as well as temples, but of course, you see Mosques at every corner, and Islam is the most practiced religion.

Geography

The land is flat by the coast of the Arabian Gulf, with deserts in the central undeveloped part of the country. There are also some mountains towards the coast of Oman. Much of the land is desert area with some small agricultural regions. Sometimes you will be astounded with all the greenery that you actually see in the desert!

Political Parties

There are no political parties. The government type is a federal system with a Federal Supreme Council consisting of the rulers of the 7 Emirates, a ministerial council and a federal national council (20 of the 40 members are elected by local Emiratis)

President and Ruler of Abu Dhabi: Sheikh Khalifa Bin Zayed Al Nahyan

Prime Minister and Ruler of Dubai: Sheikh Mohamed bin Rashid al Maktoum

Crown Prince of Abu Dhabi: Sheikh Mohamed Bin Zayed Al Nahyan

Crown Prince of Dubai: Sheikh Hamdan bin Mohamed al Maktoum

International Groups: GCC, Arab League, OIC, UN

Flag

The UAE flag has three horizontal bands of green, white, and black (top to bottom), with a wider vertical red band on the side. The colours are the pan-Arab colours and have been historically linked to the Arab people and Islamic faith and signify Arab unity and independence. Other flags in the region use similar colours in the their flags. Supposedly, red means blood, white is peace, green is Islam and black is oil.

Financials

GDP: $230bn (2009)

GDP/capital: $38.9k

Annual Growth: 3%

Inflation 3%

Major industries: Oil, Gas

DUBAI AND THE FINANCIAL CRISIS

For the greater part of the first decade of the 21st century, Dubai prospered from an economy driven excessively higher by property speculation. Take a step back and this was a result of Dubai redefining itself as a tourist hub, and creating a lure for the place, making it stable for business and for expatriates to come and help build Dubai into a 21st century phenomenon. Dubai had very little oil – most of the reserves were within Abu Dhabi's boundaries – and so this redefinition to trade, tourism, finance and business was a necessary one. But what happened? It grew too fast too quickly, leveraged too quickly and the one thing that injected an unknown factor to the problem – opening up property to foreign investors. It was an ingenious move, because it encouraged an influx of multiple investors, but on the downside, many flipped their properties off plan making a tidy fortune. Unfortunately, that quick growth led to a bubble effect - whose peak coincided with global meltdown.

Problems started after Lehman Brothers folded which lead to the beginning of the property crash in Dubai. The real estate, fuelled with liquidity, had the rug taken out from under it and property prices tumbled, in some cases more than 60% within 12 months. And almost exactly a year after Lehman fell came the very public announcement that the government of Dubai asked the creditors of Dubai World and Nakheel, the companies responsible for Burj Khalifa and the Palm Island, amongst others, to freeze debt repayments. Part of the problem was that this announcement wasn't planned in advance and that it came as a big shock. There was no shock that Dubai had debt, but its inability to pay sent shock waves around the world. The actual debt was thought to be $80bn, but it was also Islamic bonds that were due to be paid that caused problems. With many of the properties pre sold before being built – many sole investors also lost money causing frustration and unrest.

Dubai Marina and Jumeirah Beach Residence

Has Dubai recovered? It continues to hold debt, but unity with Abu Dhabi, who helped bail out some of the debt has added stability to the Emirates. Even with all its money, Abu Dhabi has also come a little unstuck on its own property developments in recent years, slowing some of its key projects. Will Dubai survive? Well, Dubai's reputation has been dented in a big way, but there is much to be done to clear the debt. But the fact remains. After all is done, Dubai has emerged as a top destination for tourism, and will continue to grow in reputation for business.

THE OTHER EMIRATES

Dubai is the most famous of all of the Emirates and takes up the bulk of the media and tourism interest. However, there are, in total, seven Emirates. We have provided you with some information should you decide to visit Abu Dhabi or any of the other Emirates as part of your trip to Dubai.

Location of the Abu Dhabi Grand Prix

ABU DHABI – THE EVOLVING CAPITAL

Abu Dhabi is a city morphing into a global destination competing with some of the elite centres of culture and tourism to become a modern city state, inviting the world to sit up and take notice. Yes, Abu Dhabi, the capital of the UAE, is slowly shrugging off its capital city shackles and becoming a real destination that prides itself on being truly Arabian for a modern era. One need only to look back fifty years to see the transformation from coastal village to skyscraper metropolis – and now a new era is emerging, one that will draw a new crowd, and new fans to its futuristic view of the world tomorrow. Abu Dhabi is on round three of a city rejuvenation that has catapulted it onto the world tourist stage. Having previously been a consortium of Bedouin sand huts, Abu Dhabi emerged from the desert as a Middle East skyscraper haven for Oil execs. Now, Abu Dhabi is on a transformation that has started to cement itself onto the global stage.

Think back twenty years ago and many had never heard of Abu Dhabi. Even ten years ago, Abu Dhabi was piggybacking on Dubai's fame. But while the world marvelled in the rise of Dubai, the oil money was doing all the talking in the background. With roughly 9% of the world's oil reserves Abu Dhabi has amassed one of the largest sovereign wealth funds in the world. And, it has done this almost in stealth mode, investing in some of the most lucrative companies around the globe – without the need to scream and shout.

And now, the plans are coming to fruition.

The ideology for modern day Abu Dhabi had been a long time coming and when they arrived they certainly put Abu Dhabi on the map. Buying Manchester City Football Club and launching the Formula 1 Abu Dhabi Grand Prix were great marketing for a city starting to redefine itself for a new era. But with Dubai so close by, there was great need to place a flag in the Abu Dhabi sand. "Abu Dhabi has arrived – and we are different."

And while Dubai has created its own modern city in the sand, Abu Dhabi hasn't sat on its laurels. There have been plans to redefine green energy with ground breaking initatives such as Masdar, the world's first carbon neutral city. Whole islands have been transformed from desert nothingness to infrastructural marvels. Yas Island proudly boasts possibly the best ever Formula 1 track ever created along with amazing marinas and golf courses to compare with a playboy's paradise. And with another fell swoop Saadiyat Island is being transformed to a cultural island like no other – there will be local versions of the Guggenheim as well as the world's first

Louvre outside Paris – along with wetland reserves and uber exclusive beach resorts. And that is just a snapshot.

The grand master plan of transformation has only just begun. However, ask a layman about Abu Dhabi and you will receive a peppering of responses from the mundane to the ignorant. Here are a selection:

1.   The place where Garfield sent Nermal

2.   "That place close to Dubai"

3.   The owner of Manchester City Football Club

4.   Where the Emirates Palace, the most expensive hotel in the world is

5.   Where the final F1 Grand Prix of the season is held

6.   The instigators of the world submission wrestling championships

7.   Those who bailed out Dubai

8.   Oil Money

9.   Desert, sand, and Bedouin

10.   Where Sex and the City 2 was based but not filmed.

Aside from any xenophobic reaction, the perception of Abu Dhabi essentially revolves around the unknown and the glamour. And while Abu Dhabi has about a hundred years until the oil runs out, expect big things over the coming ten. Many people are unsure just what Abu Dhabi will offer. Well, the offer is this – a city rich in Arabic heritage, in Bedouin hospitality and modern day marvels. Abu Dhabi is a city that welcomes visitors and its people, both the UAE Nationals and the transitioning expatriates to watch the steady growth of a brand new world.

There are hundreds of things to do in Abu Dhabi and it is difficult to single out what specifically one could do, but here are our favourites:

Visit the Sheikh Zayed Mosque, which for us is the best tourist spot in the whole of the UAE. Both amazing and beautiful, it also gives you an opportunity to understand the culture.

Indulge in a bit of shopping both at the Central Souk Abu Dhabi, but also at Marina Mall

Nearby to the mall is the Abu Dhabi Heritage Village where you can understand the past of the UAE, and attempt to hump a camel's hump

Take tea at the Emirates Palace where there you can indulge in some gold cake and marvel at one of the most expensive and extravagant hotels in the world.

Get your adrenaline pumping at Ferrari World Abu Dhabi, followed by a drive around the Yas Formula 1 Race Track at the Yas Hotel

Visit Yas Water World – although not as amazing as Atlantis in Dubai, it's great for families

Visit Manarat al Sadiyat and see the becoming of a new cultural zone – and visit Masdar, the future city, built for a new age.

Hotels are coming to market almost every month in Abu Dhabi and there really are some great hotels. Aside from the Emirates Palace which may be too extravagant for some, we would recommend the Fairmont and the Shangri La as well as Intercontinental or Beach Rotana if you want to be closer to town. The food scene is to die for – and you can spend a lot of money on some amazing food, as well as not very much money on some great street grub. If you want to go all out, try Hakkasan, Hoi An Cipriani or Chamas. Our favourite street food is the shawarma from Lebanese Flower – probably the best in the UAE. But you'll be spoilt for choice in Abu Dhabi.

A TRYST WITH CULTURE IN SHARJAH

The city of Sharjah is the third largest city in the United Arab Emirates and is unique for its being one of the more traditional Emirates. Having been under the reign of the Al Qasimi dynasty since 1972, it is known as the most cultural Emirate in the UAE and thus one of the more popular places to visit for tourists coming to the UAE.

Sharjah is located on the southern coast of the Arabian Gulf is flanked by the cities of Dubai and Ajman on its borders while Abu Dhabi is about 180 kilometres away. The geographical significance of Sharjah is emphasized by the fact that it overlooks the 16-kilometre long Arabian Gulf coastline and touches the Gulf of Oman coast on its eastern side wherein the terrain transforms into a rugged shore backed by high mountains. It is a fantastic coastline – and one to be seen.

As a city, Sharjah does not have any real public transportation system That is no real problem as one can either hire a car, take a taxi or just visit Sharjah through one of the many tours that are definitely worth considering. Taxis in Sharjah are plentiful. Many people working in Dubai live in Sharjah, due to the cheaper rents which accounts for the heavy rush of road traffic between the two cities during rush hour. There is a Government-operated inter-emirate bus service as well, located next to the Sharjah fish market and the Sharjah Fruit and Vegetable market. If visiting Sharjah as a tourist, try to avoid the rush hour.

Tourists who want to come directly to Sharjah could use the low cost airline Air Arabia flights as well which flies to Sharjah International Airport and are well connected to most of the Middle-East and Indian Sub continental cities. A better option, in our opinion, is to fly to Dubai and get to Sharjah take a taxi from there.

A trip to Sharjah is a must not just due to the endless shopping opportunities which it offers but also because it reflects its rich cultural heritage and traditions in every possible aspect of life. Sharjah really is the traditional cultural heartbeat of the UAE – and while Dubai and Abu Dhabi look to create their own cultural niches, no one will dispute that Sharjah, as a place holds truer to being intriguing from an Arabian standpoint.

As we have mentioned, the cost of living in Sharjah is lower compared to Dubai and many of the expats living in Sharjah have made it their home due its cultural focus, its slightly more conservative concentration on life and although the higher paying jobs are actually located in Dubai, Sharjah has more of a reality to those attracted by the buzz and glam of its neighbour

It would be natural for any foreigner to be enamoured with the city of Sharjah as it is an ideal showcase of rich Islamic heritage. From the museums, the traditional houses and the forts on to the artistically designed souks, a tourist could expect to be treated to a healthy dosage of history, tradition and art.

Things to do in Sharjah

As part of one's itinerary, the following are some of top spots and some of the top things to do in Sharjah:

Al Hisn Fort which occupies a majority portion of the heritage area features many exhibits and displays in addition to the Sharjah Fort Museum which provided a deep insight on the social history of the area.

Tourists interested in history must visit the museums, especially the Sharjah Museum of Economic Civilization, the Sharjah Heritage Museum, Sharjah Art Museum and the Museum of Arabic Calligraphy.

Souks form an important part of tourism in Sharjah and while the Souk al-Arsah must be included because it is the oldest souk in the country, the Blue Souk deserves a visit for its eclectic shopping experience. In actual fact, the Blue Souk is one of the must do things to do in the UAE and probably the top thing to do in Sharjah.

The Sharjah Desert Park is an attraction in itself as it offers something for every age group. So when the adults are busy exploring the thought provoking exhibits in the Natural History Museum, the kids can entertain themselves at the Arabian Wildlife Centre and the Children's Farm.

The Al Qasba Ferry provides tourists with a unique view of the city in the form of a boat tour.

Sharjah could be an international tourist destination in its own right proven by the fact that it has something in store for all types of budget. Hence, while tourists who are willing to splurge can opt for the Holiday Inn Sharjah or the Holiday International Hotel, the ones thosewith a tighter budget could settle for Crystal Plaza Hotel, The Suites Hotel Apartments, Millennium Hotel, Radission SAS Resort, Grand Hotel or the Al Sharq Hotel.

You could spend anything from a few hours to a week to get the full flavour of Sharjah. However long you decide to spend in Sharjah, it will be definitely be fun filled and enriching. Just be aware that this fun will be booze free, because, for some, Sharjah's downside is that it is dry. For others, that's another of the big pulls.

THE BASE OF FUJAIRAH

Fujairah is one of the seven Emirates which make up the UAE and is exceptional in the sense that it is the only one which lies on the coast of Gulf of Oman unlike the other six which flank the Arabian Gulf. Having gained independence from Sharjah in 1952, over the years the region has emerged as a prominent commercial destination due to rapid economic growth and social evolution not to mention its flourishing tourism industry.

While the Fujairah International Airport facilitates connections with most of the well traveled flight routes, it takes two hours by car to reach here from Dubai and likewise a short time from Oman as well since it lies close by. There are regular bus services connecting Fujairah with Dubai, Sharjah and the other Emirates wherein the buses are affordable as well as comfortable.

Fujairah is an exception amongst the other Emirates in more ways than one. Apart from being located on the west coast, it is totally mountainous unlike the arid deserts of Dubai and Abu Dhabi. The area also experiences a significantly larger proportion of annual rainfall compared to the rest of the UAE.

There was a time when Fujairah's economy was dependent on cement, stone crushing and mining activities but commercialization soon became the order of the day through establishment of free trade zones and encouraging construction activity in the area. Shopping in Fujairah is not tourist oriented and apart from a couple of shops which offer souvenirs most of the others sell grocery type items. There are a few restaurants as well which are economically priced and offer delectable Arabian cuisine.

Things to do

Fujairah is not exactly a tourist destination but can be selected as the base city from where excursions to nearby areas could be planned. Some of the common points of attraction are the Fujairah Fort located on the fringes of the city, beautiful beaches in the city of Diba located 30 kilometres away, driving through the Hajar Mountains, a trip to Khor Fakkan and a boat ride in the Gulf of Oman as a method of exploring the islands.

Marine activities like fishing and diving are popular amongst people while desert driving and power boat racing are meant for the adventurous.

Accommodation is plenty in Fujairah and while there are as many as six luxurious five-star hotels, it is possible to find budget accommodation comprising of clean and comfortable rooms.

RAS AL KHAIMAH

Ras Al Khaimah, meaning the 'Top of the Tent', is located in the northern region of UAE and lies sandwiched between the Arabian Gulf and the Hajar Mountains. Featuring a capital city of the same name, its coastline stretches for 27 miles and is inclusive of numerous lagoons and beaches while the border with Oman consists of an unbroken chain of mountains. Ras Al Khaimah is how you would expect an Arabian costal village to be. Its charm is its simplicity and is almost the antithesis of Dubai.

Foreigners holidaying or visiting with investment intentions describe the emirate as peaceful, relaxed and unspoilt. RAK's natural beauty of the Hajjar mountains and short distance to Oman make it an attractive alternative to those tired of Dubai.

RAK initially concentrated on developing its industrial sector and has now become the world's largest producer of ceramics under the brand name RAK Ceramics. It also created the Gulf's leading pharmaceuticals company Julphar. It is only within the last 3 years that RAK has put more energy into the real estate sector. Diversifying into this area made sound economic sense as RAK does not have the natural abundance of oil unlike its fellow emirate Abu Dhabi. Watching the success of the Dubai property boom, RAK felt they could regenerate and develop the emirate too and with RAK's beautiful scenery, who wouldn't be tempted?

Ras Al Khaimah enjoyed a prestigious status of being an important trade centre during the yesteryears and a glimpse of this glorious epoch is still visible in the rich and varied heritage of the city. Overall, Ras Al Khaimah has something to offer everyone with its tranquil beaches, majestic mountains, dramatic sand dunes, wildlife sanctuaries and emerald green golf courses. But for many, the three letters of RAK are those found on some of the best ceramic in the world. Yes, Ras al Khaimah is known for its ceramics industry, globally.

Once upon a time, the harbour settlement of Ras Al Khaimah was known as Julfar and early Julfar was located in the Shamal area inhabited by a tribe named Azd. Archeological excavations in the area revealed that residential quarters during that period were built of wood and over a period of time the port shifted location due to the silting in the channels. Owing to its strategic location, the town was the scene of many conquests involving the British and gradually usurped its independence not only from foreign powers but indigenous emirates as well to eventually become a part of UAE in 1972.

Many foreign investors are homing in on the quick investment opportunities to be had in RAK. There are now many designated areas that are available as freehold and when buying a property, you will usually be given a resident's visa for yourself and the your family. Many existing UAE expats are interested in purchasing second homes in RAK for investment as the price of property varies enormously between RAK and say Dubai or Abu Dhabi. Some quote prices as being a third of what you'd pay in the popular Emirate states.

One of RAK's biggest advantages will be its close proximity to Dubai. The Emirates Road, which is the main highway connecting Dubai, Sharjah and Ajman is extending to RAK and it is expected journey times form Dubai to RAK will be less than an hour. It will therefore make sense for expats to consider renting in the nearby emirates rather than pay extortionate rentals in Dubai.

Tourists who visit the area in December and January get an opportunity to witness the Awafi festival which is a three-week event filled with cultural enjoyment. This festival is held in Al Awafi, a traditional heritage village and while the food lovers are busy sampling the ethnic cuisine, the adventurous try their hand at the dramatic sand dunes drive and the rest of the family spends time shopping for souvenirs.

People living in the area lead a life of good quality as there are plenty of schools, healthcare facilities, shopping malls and a park for recreation. The majority of the country's income comes from industries and it is courtesy of this that the region is at present the country's largest producer of cement and the world's largest producer of ceramics. Had it not been for severe power cuts, this area would have long since emerged as one of the most investment friendly regions of the world.

Things to do in Ras Al Khaimah

This place is all about the outside – the beaches and the lagoons are there to be enjoyed - get involved in the water activities.

A must-see is the National Museum of Ras Al Khaimah which is housed in a former royal palace and provides a deep insight on the history and tradition of the region.

Jazirat Al Hamra is fabled as being an abandoned ghost town – are you man enough to go and check it out?

Shamal and Sheeba's Palace could be visited to appreciate the ruins and the tombs.

Dhayah Fort is the only surviving hilltop fort in the country and should be explored for its uniqueness.

Hiking in the mountains which would last for a couple of days and visiting the camel races along with the local people.

Some of the famous hotels in the area are the Hayat Plaza Hotel, Creek Plaza Hotel and Banyan Tree Al Wadi, which happens to be the first desert resort of its kind in the UAE. Our choice is the Al Hamra fort hotel and beach resort – which has been constructed as a fort with the traditional wind towers. Ras Al Khaimah is an ideal destination to relax for a couple of days nestled amidst ethnic surroundings.

UMM AL QUWAIN

Umm al Quwain is the second smallest of the seven Emirates and probably one of the most chilled out of them all. We're not saying that this place is hippyland, but it's quite easy to soak in the atmosphere and greenery and not really feel too rushed to do anything at all.

Despite UAQ having some energy deposits, the economy hasn't really kick-started here and it's probably safe to say that this is one of the poorer Emirates. That said, they are always looking for ways to attract investment. The sleepy village type feel is synonymous throughout the whole of the Emirate, but essentially the most interesting part is around the lagoon where you will find the dhow yard and the food markets.

Things to do in Umm al Quwain

Although there isn't that much to do in Umm al Quwain, there is one place which is almost as if it was from the Wild West – Lazimah – which is like a ghost town with old houses which is great because they haven't been bulldozed down and replaced by skyscrapers. It makes a nice change.

The other place you are likely to find interesting if you haven't been to one before is the Dhow yard where you can watch the boats being created.

You are unlikely to find yourself in UAQ, and if you do you will likely stay somewhere else. There aren't many high end hotels, but most of them including the Flamingo and the UAQ Beaach resort are reputable. Dubaians know UAQ as the location of Baaracuda. This is the massive off licence and the place to stock up on booze that warrants the drive for many expats to make on a quarterly basis, especially during the summer months.

AJMAN

Ajman, meaning small city in Arabic, is the smallest of the seven emirates and while its west flank touches the Arabian Gulf, the rest of the Emirate is engulfed by Sharjah. Ajman is a city that benefited from the influx of people from the bigger cities of Dubai and Sharjah and thus embarked on its own development drive, the resonance of which is still reverberating in the region. At present, the city of Ajman is regarded as being one of the most lucrative investment regions in the world with a number of ambitious projects waiting to take off. To Dubaians, it's the place that wants to be a mini Dubai near Dubai. It is mini – that's correct. It's the smallest Emirate.

Ajman's location could be best described as being centralized in the UAE thus implying that it is not far from any of the major cities. With Sharjah on one side, Dubai being only 10 kilometres away towards the south and Umm Al Quwain being the third city in close vicinity, most of the roads connecting these cities pass through Ajman. It's not difficult to get to.

The 16-kilometre long beach and the natural port courtesy of the Arabian Gulf have provided this city with an influx of tourists looking for more secluded relaxation.

Things to do in Ajman

While in the area, a visit to the Ajman Museum is a must. The building itself dates back to the eighteenth century and is actually a fort which served as the Royal Palace, then was converted into a Police Station and in 1981 was opened as a museum showcasing a variety of traditional artefacts.

Dhow Yard is a boat building Yard occupying the northern portion of the creek and since it is just a short distance from the city's centre is worth a peak.

Mowaihat is an archaeological site on the outskirts of the city which came into prominence in 1986 when an accidental discovery of a 2000 B.C. tomb by some workers brought it into the limelight as a historically significant area. Since then the site has been witness to constant excavation and many of the unearthed objects find their way to the showcase of the Ajman Museum.

Ajman is also the proud owner of two inland enclaves namely Masfout and Manama. Located at a distance of 110 kilometres from the city on its south eastern fringe, it is close to Hatta and is home to the 'farfar' trees which bear beautiful yellow flowers. Manama lies in the east, approximately 60 kilometres away.

There are plenty of eating joints in the city and it is possible to sample everything from cheap vegetarian meals, global food chains and ethnic Arabian cuisine. If you are visiting Ajman, stay at the Ajman Kempinski, or go for the Ajman Beach Hotel if your budget doesn't quite get you to luxury. That said, the beach at the latter is pretty damn good – and clean!

OTHER EXCURSIONS

For the long termer in the UAE, there are a great number of places to go and see. From the wider Abu Dhabi Emirate, Al Ain and the islands to Oman and its intrigue, we provide you with a list of our favourites.

GREENERY IN THE GARDEN CITY OF AL AIN

The garden city of Al Ain is one of the three cities which form the geographical triangle in the centre of the United Arab Emirates, the other two being Abu Dhabi and Dubai. As each of the three cities is located at a distance of 130 kilometers from the other two, it is an equilateral triangle which is formed with Al Ain lying to the south of Dubai and being east of Abu Dhabi.

Although this city is the second largest in the Abu Dhabi Emirate and is home to the large number of Emiratis, it offers a welcome change from its vibrant counterparts, Dubai and Abu Dhabi. For the fact that that it has been inhabited for the last 4000 years and that it is the birthplace of the first president of UAE, Al Ain has been a symbol of cultural heritage attributed to have sprung from the numerous underground water springs responsible for its unique identity. But while Al Ain is known for its greenery, it also is a city, which is distinct – almost a contemporary avatar of the city. Some say that Al Ain is a green version of Abu Dhabi 20 years ago.

While bus services are provided to travel to and from Abu Dhabi, transportation from Dubai is a little more difficult in the absence of a regular bus service and the mini bus service being only one way from Dubai to Al Ain. And because, Al Ain is so close to Buraimi, short trips to Oman by car without the need to get a visa are possible. If you are hiring a car, make sure you are covered for this. Although you can fly directly to Al Ain, we would recommend flying to Abu Dhabi, and either taking a bus or taxi to Al Ain – or hiring your own car. There are heaps of cheap taxis in Al Ain.

While Dubai and Abu Dhabi have always been well known as international tourist destinations, Al Ain in contrast has always been the favourite haunt of the Sheikhs probably due to its surrounding red sand dunes and indomitable mountain ranges. An oasis in the midst of the arid surroundings, the beautiful garden city is replete with forts and settlements not to mention the recent additions of theme parks and shopping plazas. Al Ain has managed to maintain its charm and grow with the modern age.

As a visitor, this is an once-in-a-lifetime opportunity to embark on a desert safari, 4WD expeditions as well as camel trips. In fact, many of the desert safari's booked in Dubai and Abu Dhabi come in the direction of Al Ain, as the dunes are better! Al Ain is also a shopper's paradise since everything is cheaper here but also has some specialized stores. The city sports a soothing aura of relaxation and easy-going lifestyle as circling the gardens, fountains, sculptures and statues imparts a feeling of well being and calmness. It's also a breath of fresh air with the balance of desert heat. You don't get this in the main cities in the UAE.

One thing to watch out for is a remnant of past heritage in Al Ain. Although this exists elsewhere in Arabia, you must see the Falaj, the traditional irrigation system dating back to 1000 B.C. that surrounds the farms and date groves even today.

Things to do in Al Ain

A must-visit is the famous landmark of Jebel Hafeet, the second tallest mountain in the UAE standing high up at 1350 metres. While the summit of this limestone monolith has been made accessible by a three-lane highway which snakes all the way to the top with three resting points for viewing, the face of the mountain is honeycombed with coves and thus ideal for pot holers. The zenith provides a panoramic view extending all the way beyond the borders to Oman

The Al Ain Museum and Fort had been constructed to serve as a safety haven from raiders and served as headquarters of the erstwhile ruler of Abu Dhabi as well. Exhibits at the museum showcase the way people lived prior to the formation of the UAE.

Something which must never be passed over during a trip to the region is the Al Ain Oasis, its rustic atmosphere and the shade of the date palm trees.

Located close to the Oman border is the Camel Souk in which hundreds of camels are traded everyday and some could even be used for providing children with rides in return for a small fee.

The three five-star hotels in the city are The Hilton, The Rotana and the Intercontinental with innumerable options for budget travelers looking for a roof over their heads. If you are staing at Jebel Hafeet, you should stay at the Mercure Grand Hotel.

Normally a day or two would be enough for the city, but added attractions like a hassle-free trip to Oman and a healthy dose of relaxation may tempt one to stay longer than usual. After having covered all the tourist spots, sampling the ethnic Arabic cuisine is an ideal way to end the day. Al Ain is a great visit away from the fast life of the city – and while many Emirati live there, many locals from Abu Dhabi have their country home there – it's an Arabian equivalent of a place in the Hamptons.

AL GHARBIA, THE REGION – ECLECTIC AS CAN BE
Overview

Spread over an area of 60,000 square kilometres, the Al Gharbia region in the Emirate of Abu Dhabi accounts for more than 70% of the total land mass of UAE in which are located its seven main cities. Although politically belonging to the UAE, this region is in close proximity with the borders of neighbouring Saudi Arabia and Qatar and its administrative capital is located at a place called Madinat Zayed. In spite of the large area, not many live here and thus it has retained its historic beauty.

Al Gharbia, up to very recently, hasn't had any real prominence – and the fact the Al Gharbia is being talked about as an area is due to the huge amount of marketing it is getting from the Abu Dhabi government. Actually, if you look to the future, 50 years from now, Al Gharbia could continue down the route of Arabian haven. But now that the tourist board have grasped this area, expect great things from the region. As a result, a sustainable plan of development was chalked out which pivoted on infrastructure and was an encouragement for the tourism industry in the region.

Colloquially termed as the region which is the meeting point of the land and the sea, Al Gharbia is a perfect blend of rich cultural heritage and economic growth. The area offers attractive and lucrative investment opportunities while retaining its old world charm so that people can cherish their traditional lifestyle while enjoying the benefits of increased spending power.

Things to do in al Gharbia

One of the best ways to experience the essence of Al Gharbia is to get involved with some of the famous festivals and if possible also rejoice with the locals. These festivals aptly showcase the diverse traditions of the region and provide plenty of adventure as well for the strong hearted. Some of the renowned festivals celebrated in the region are discussed as follows:

Bike enthusiasts can derive their share of excitement at the Abu Dhabi Motors Club festival termed as the 'Desert Challenge'. This festival attracted bike lovers from all over the world due to its novel location and the crazy roads!

The Liwa Date Festival has evolved into an epitome of folklore not only due to its unique logo but also its style, pattern and inspirational message which it claims to have received from nature. If you want cultural heritage, a festival celebrating dates is as good as you can get – after all, the people survived with just the date palm tree back in the day.

The Al Dhafra Festival which is held in Madinat Zayed in December is one of the most popular events in the region, a fact which is proved by the mass participation in all its contests. This festival is all about preserving culture, so anything and everything associated with the roots of the Emirati people is covered. The most amazing one of these is the camel festival. You will never see this in the West, so a camel festival as part of this is probably one of the most unique things you could possibly do in the world! Firstly there are camel markets where camels are traded – but then there are "contests" – where prizes are awarded for best bred and most beautiful. Yes – you can come and visit the Camel Beauty Contest! Late January is the time to come for this. If you have a camel to enter, you may win a luxury car, but top prize is nearly $10m. Are you in the wrong business.

Water sports enthusiasts can have their share of fun at the Al Gharbia Water Sports Festival which is held in April and is a nine-day extravaganza. Described as being the wettest and wildest event in UAE, the highpoints of this festival are the various water sports and participation from world renowned athletes. Essentially, a competition for surfers, kite surfers – this new festival will continue to grow as Al Gharbia becomes more prominent. Expect more and more water junkies, year on year.

NATURE AT ITS BEST ON THE BANI YAS ISLANDS
Overview

Located 250 kilometres southwest of Abu Dhabi, Sir Bani Yas is the largest natural island which serves as home to the largest wildlife reserve in Arabia. Established in 1971 by the late ruler and founder of UAE, this ecological investment spans out over an area of 87 square kilometres measuring 17.5 kilometres from north to south and 9 kilometres from east to west.

For anyone who wishes to take a break from the skyscrapers and bustle of Dubai and Abu Dhabi, Bani Yas is an ideal retreat and is accessible through ferry service which plies between the island and the two cities. If you take the E11 from Dubai and cruise past the cities of Abu Dhabi, Mirfa and Tarif in the direction of Liwa Oasis, then taking a turn off the road at Jebel Dhanna after four hours would lead to the jetty from where ferries go to Bani Yas and the other desert islands. From Abu Dhabi, the jetty is two hours away.

Not to be confused with Yas Island which holds the grand prix, a trip to Bani Yas is a unique experience, and one that has been kept secret amongst the local Emiratis up until now.   It is an opportunity to sample Arabian wildlife at its best not to mention a horde of nature related activities which can be undertaken. The island gets its name from the Bani Yas tribe which inhabited the area many years ago and archaeological sites discovered on the island reflect humans of different descents through the years.

The green haven of Bani Yas Island is all about responsible tourism as it serves as a safety zone for a number of endangered species of animals like the Arabian Oryx, a species of antelope which is now extinct in the wild. This island is probably the only place where as many as 400 Oryx roam around freely along with gazelle, deer and giraffes. While dolphins and sea turtles account for the marine life the circle of life on land is completed by the presence of many grassland animals like emu, Eland, Gemsbok and the Urial sheep along with predators like hyena and cheetah.

As the hunters and the hunted thrive within the confines of the wildlife reserve the Bani Yas Island makes its bid towards eco tourism by deriving its electricity from wind turbines, the first of which was set up in 2004.

Things to do

Bani Yas Island is a dream-come-true for sea-loving and adventurous individuals and after having appreciated and cherished nature to the fullest some of the other activities which can be indulged into are:

Snorkelling in the neighbouring reefs

Kayaking in the bay and the sea

Both beginners and experts can try their hand at archery.

Mountain biking on the rugged terrain

Exploring the historical aspect of the island through a number of Stone Age and Islamic structures and also the remnants of the 7th century Christian Church which also happens to be the only pre-Islamic Christian site in the UAE.

Accommodation on the island is looked after by the Desert resort and Spa managed by Anantara. With 64 rooms, 6 private lodges by the beach, three restaurants, a spa, a health club, a kid's club, swimming pool and business facilities, the resort is luxury personified and an ideal holiday retreat. It's also ideal as an nouveau honeymoon destination. Bani Yas is a secret to some – just don't tell them that we told you about it!

THE OASIS TOWN OF BURAIMI

The oasis town of Buraimi in Oman shares a border with its counterpart Al Ain in the UAE as both belong to the desert oasis complex which is supported by a number of water wells in the area. Although Oman as a country is not as prosperous as UAE, the difference is hardly visible in case of Buraimi and Al Ain and people travel to and fro between the two cities without having to face any diplomatic hurdles.

Legend has it that when borders were being drawn to demarcate Oman from UAE, inhabitants residing in the area were given a choice to choose their Emir as a deciding factor as to which side of the border they would like to be in. Hence, the two towns on either side of the border were created and even though they politically belong to different nations, the people still mingle with each other like before. Tourists follow the same split but for different reasons- they arrange their hotel in Buraimi since the hotels are cheaper.

The best way to get to Buraimi is to drive from Al Ain and it is at a destination named Hilli, 8 kilometres away from the traditional border, where you can get your visa. Within Buraimi, it is the local orange and white Omani taxis which are the best option for getting around the town and accept Omani Riyals or UAE Dirhams as payment.

Al Buraimi, meaning palm groves, has been an oasis in an otherwise arid desert since time immemorial and it was only as recent as 1972 that a political border was drawn thus dividing the oasis into two distinct identities, Buraimi and Al Ain. Since the town has been under the reign of different monarchs before it officially became the capital of the Al Buraymi governate.

The overall impression of the town is that of being less affluent as compared to its UAE counterpart and infrastructure is characterized by unnamed streets and absence of footpaths. However, it is still considered as a shopping destination since most of the shops here accept UAE currency.

Things to do in Buraimi

One of the main tourist attractions is the Wilayat Al Buraimi, which is a conglomerate of three main buildings forming the Governorate of Al Buraimi. The entire cluster occupies the north-west corner of the Sultanate of Oman and comprises of wilayats of other provinces as well.

Within the Wilayat of Al Buraimi, there are innumerable forts and houses both being historically significant. The visit is made worthy by the Al Khandaq fort, the emblem of the province.

Another major attraction is the Al Hillah fort which has been recently restored and refurbished. The list of forts goes on to include Al Fayyadh, Hafeet and Wadi al Jizzi.

Among the must-see spots is also included the historic house named Bait Bahr which provides a deep insight into the history and cultural heritage of the area.

If you are going to Al Ain, it is worth stopping by in Buraimi, and at a minimum to check out the oasis.

TAKING A BREAK IN DELMA ISLANDS

In the extreme west of the UAE at a distance of 30 kilometres offshore lies the volcanic Delma Island which is home to approximately 6000 people and has been inhabited for thousands of years. Although the island measures 10 kilometres from north to south and 5 kilometres from east to west, it has been blessed with the presence of numerous natural water wells and springs to enable the inhabitants to lead a stable life.

There was a time when fishing and pearl diving were the only professions practised by the residents of the island but courtesy of the tree plantations and afforestation projects which have sprung up during the recent years the horizon is now a picture of greenery. Apart from being one of the flourishing pearl production centres in the past, this island is important as an archeological site as well since it served as a cradle of civilization as long back as seven thousand years ago.

Its growth as a prominent tourist attraction was spurred by the commencement of the two new ferry services traveling between the island and Abu Dhabi. A recent addition has been the introduction of bus services operating in tandem with the ferry timings. The intention behind this is to integrate the land and water transport so as to bring about economic growth in the region by encouraging investment.

At one point of time, Delma Islands were inhabited only by Arab nomads who indulged in pearl trading and animal breeding to earn their livelihood - and used to travel to and fro between Delma and Liwa. They used to meet in the mosque to pray and congregate

Things to do on Delma Island

While spending time in the vegetable fields and fruit orchards, archeological excavations also serve as a local attraction as it provides an insight into the life of people and the gradual evolution of the island.

There are three mosques in Delma namely Muraykhi, Al Dawsari, Al Muhannadi and although they are similar to each other in terms of layout, design and decorations, they could be included in the travel plans.

Another noteworthy inclusion in the itinerary should be the Al Muraykhi House Museum, which was formerly the residence of a prominent pearl merchant and was established in 1931. It now serves as a museum and features interesting exhibits pertaining to the island.

A visit to Delma Islands would be a welcome respite from the hustle and bustle of Abu Dhabi – worth a trip if you are staying in Abu Dhabi on an extended stay.

JOZOR AL SAHRA'A - THE DESERT ISLANDS OF ABU DHABI

The desert islands of Abu Dhabi, known as Jozor Al Sahra'a in Arabic, are an archipelago of eight islands which were envisioned by Sheikh Zayed, the founding father of UAE and were converted into reality thanks to his efforts. Comprising of Sir Bani Yas Island, Dalma Island and six discovery islands, they serve as home to some of the most cherished natural treasures of Arabia with landscapes sculpted by nature, indigenous animal species and mangroves.

These islands are well connected with Abu Dhabi and it takes two and half hours from the capital city to reach Sir Bani Yas Island jetty having driven on the E11 highway and crossed the town of Ruwais en route. On arriving at the terminal in Jebel Dhanna a ferry takes people across to the Sir Bani Yas Island after a ride on the water lasting about 20 minutes and having reached the island the tour buses and chauffeur driven cars are responsible for the mobility.

Another quicker, easier and cheaper alternative would be to fly to the desert islands from Abu Dhabi in one of the many scheduled flights which depart from the Abu Dhabi International Airport and land at the airport on Sir Bani Yas Island.

The Desert Islands Abu Dhabi are another of the areas that are being marketed heavily as a natural, tourist destination as Abu Dhabi evolves to a life after oil and alongside Al Gharbia, the Desert Islands feature prominently in the future focus. One only need to touch down at Abu Dhabi airport to see such marketing. In fact, no tourist would have even considered these islands as spots to visit.

The desert islands are meant serve as a haven for natural wonders and provide plenty of opportunities for water sports and adventure activities. When these islands were conceived, the intention of the creator was not only to conserve nature at its optimum but also to encourage its propagation so that it can be cherishes, valued and enjoyed by the forthcoming generations as well. Who would have thought that so close to the desert lands were such beautiful natural islands?

It is at these desert islands that intensive research work is evident aimed towards maintaining the delicate balance of the ecosystem. Some of the high points of the programmes include relocation of non-indigenous animals, monitoring of breeding programmes, removal of human interface from within the park, saving water and preventing its wastage and monitoring visitors throughout their activities on the islands.

Wildlife forms an important aspect of these islands and while Oryx, gazelle, deer, giraffe, sheep and cheetah constitute the land animals, dolphins, sea turtles and a variety of aquatic species reside in the waters and more than a hundred individual species of birds rule the roost. All these signs of life are supported by the tenacious flora which comprises of a number of different desert tolerant plants as well as mangrove forests.

Things to do on the Desert Islands

Good facilities and infrastructure for activities ensures that a visitor to the island would remain occupied for days on end and may never want to leave. Some of the most popular activities include:

Going on a nature and wildlife drive in a group which lasts for approximately two and half hours to see the indigenous plants and animals, archaeological sites and geological formations. An alternative to this is the one-and-half-hour long nature and wildlife walk within the animal enclosure.

Mountain biking tours last for about one to two hours and follow two routes. The first is a basic route replete with scenic beauty while the second is advanced and hence more strenuous.

Water activities like kayaking and snorkeling these are dependent on tide levels and weather conditions. A guided snorkeling expedition is a wonderful way to relax with the whole family while kayaking at leisure could possibly be the best way to see the sunrise.

Provision of bows and arrows makes it possible for a visitor to try the Arabic tradition of archery.

Then there are scenic seaplane flights and sunset cruises both of which are dependent on weather conditions and provide fantastic panoramic views.

Accommodation is provided by the Desert Islands Resort and Spa by Anantara which is a part of the Luxury Hotels of the World Property and hence well equipped with all the modern amenities.

SPENDING A LIVELY DAY IN DIBBA

The coastal strip of Dibba occupying the north eastern stretch of Gulf of Oman is politically split into three parts namely Dibba Al-Fujairah, Dibba Al-Hisn and Dibba Al-Baya. While the first two regions are governed by the Emirates of Fujairah and Sharjah, UAE, respectively, the third region comes under Oman.

Described as being an Omani territory surrounded by the UAE on all sides, its location on the southern end of the Musandam peninsula makes access a little difficult. As a result, while it is well connected by air with Dubai and Abu Dhabi, the same cannot be claimed about flight connections with Muscat which are not only infrequent but undependable as well. Another alternative is to travel by road as it is connected with UAE via a single road and with Musandam, Oman, via two roads but the journey is believed as being arduous and tiring.

Dibba's existence is an essential aspect in the history of the region as during the ancient years it was an extensive settlement on the coast of Oman. Its high point was an international trade market in which Indian and Chinese merchants plied their wares while crossing the Arabian Sea. Many of the archaeological expeditions in the area have been attributed to this historical role as a natural harbour which was witness to varied cultures and ethnicities.

Being one of the rare regions in the world which feature an active fault, Dibba is of considerable interest to geologists. The fault is a geological consequence of recent seismic activity and while its point of origin lies in the UAE, it runs into Oman from the north and continues southwards to taper out around the middle of the Arabian Peninsula. As per the geologist's jargon, it is the Dibba fault which separates the ophiolites of the Oman Mountains from the Mesozoic carbonates characterizing the Musandam Peninsula.

Each of the three segments of the town enjoys its own distinct identity and culture, the difference arising due to the varied governing bodies. All three segments, however, make worthy tourist attractions as well with Dibba Al-Fujairah on the east being well known for beautiful beaches and water sports, the smallest Dibba Al-Hisn featuring a Portuguese fort and the northern Dibba Al-Baya serving as the gateway to the Musandam Peninsula.

While campers and adventure lovers prefer Dibba Al-Fujairah during winters, the heavily populated section of Dibba Al-Hisn is noteworthy for its fish market.

Things to do

Many people come to Dibba to visit the Al Bidyah Misque which is one of the oldest in Arabia. It has 4 small domes – with architecture unknown for the region. Definitely something to check out.

A trip under the surface of water to view the diverse marine life is a must in Dibba and the onus is on the visitor to make the most of the numerous diving sites as well as those close to Fujairah and Musandam. It is not just the aquatic habitat which is mesmerizing but an opportunity to explore the wreckage on one of the wreck dives is indeed a memorable experience.

On undertaking a dhow cruise on one of the traditional Arabian dhows, one can get up close to the fjords and appreciate their barren surface which tends to make them appear unearth-like.

The highlight of the town is Dibba castle and the Portuguese fort, both of which are cherished historical landmarks in the area.

Enthusiasts can opt for the Khasab Wheel Drive tours and embark on a mountain safari which is a journey through the barren mountains.

Other local attractions in the area include hanging around the beaches, swimming and snorkelling, greeting the fishermen or alternatively admiring the rugged beauty of the Hajjar Mountains.

Being out of the way, this spot does not feature among the usual tourist itineraries but if you can get a trip there, and you like diving and empty beaches then Dibba is for you.

A BEACH HOLIDAY AT KHOR FAKKAN

Khor Fakkan, meaning "creek of two jaws", gets its name from the bay in Gulf of Oman on which it is located. Occupying a small portion of the east coast of the UAE, this city officially belongs to the Emirate of Sharjah although on three sides it is surrounded by the Emirate of Fujairah, the fourth side being water which is responsible for the town's importance in being a major container terminal.

It takes two hours to cover a distance of 137 kilometres from Sharjah and arrive at Khor Fakkan and the first sight which greets the eye is the splendid bay of sparkling blue water which stretches out till the horizon. Some of the high points of the town are Shark Island is the midst of the sea, Port Khor Fakkan, The Oceanic Hotel distinct because of its porthole style windows as well as the magnificent palace of the Ruler of Sharjah perched on the hilltop.

By the side of the port lies the rocky mountainous terrain wherein the inhabitants have carved terraces on the slopes for to grow date palms, vegetables and mangoes. Even though there is water everywhere, flooding is least among the concerns courtesy of the man-made dam which also acts as a reservoir for the town.

Khor Fakkan is an important archaeological site due to the traces of ancient human settlements unearthed in the area. Further interest was generated when an excavation team identified 34 graves along with remnants of settlement believed to have existed early-mid 2nd millennium B.C. on a rock outcrop facing the harbour.

Things to do in Khor Fakkan

The natural backdrop of the bay lends Khor Fakkan a unique beauty and also makes it a thriving tourism spot which has a lot to offer. There is plenty to do at Khor Fakkan:

This is an ideal place for beach lovers as the gorgeous beaches are not only meant for lazing around but also for diving, snorkeling and various other sports like water skiing and wind-surfing. There are a number of popular diving locations where you can see kingfish, tuna, barracuda and sometimes even sharks! You can also go night diving on request.

A drive through the rugged mountains is recommended and on the way after having crossed the town is the Rifaisa Dam followed by a number of stone houses.

Khor Fakkan has something for everyone and the historically oriented can spend a day exploring the hundred of year old fort and a four-domed mosque which had been long since destroyed by the Portuguese.

One of the most popular tourist destinations is the Al Wurrayah Falls located at a distance of 4.5 kilometres to the north of Oceanic Hotel.

Along the Corniche Road lies the Corniche Park, Ladies Park, Al Marjan Diving centre and the Central Souq and at the southern end of the Corniche Road lies a fish, fruit and vegetable souq which could be visited for sampling the local fresh produce.

Stay at the Oceanic Hotel next to the Hajjar Mountains. This is where the locals love to holiday. It's a fantastic spot!

EXPERIENCE THE QUAINT AND RUSTIC MASAFI

Masafi in the United Arab Emirates is located at the edge of the Hajar Mountains which also happens to be the cross-point of three roads leading to the important settlements of Dibba, Dhaid and Fujairah. A small village which started out as a fuelling stop for people driving to and fro between Ras Al Khaimah and Fujairah soon evolved into an important oasis town fortified with a trading post and laced with modern highways.

Masafi in Arabic means pure water and it is no surprise that this is home to the largest manufacturer of bottled water in the area. Named after the town which is well known for its fresh water springs, the company was established in the village itself in 1976 and draws its bottled water from wells some of which are as deep as 300 metres. It has risen to a position that the name 'Masafi' is more synonymous with bottled water in UAE than the place.

On the whole, Masafi is divided between the two Emirates of Fujairah and Ras Al Khaimah. The border is symbolized by an unfinished building which was the scene of violence during the dispute and still exists in the same incomplete state. The nearest airport is that of Ras Al Khaimah and following the motorway by car would lead to the Masafi Friday market and the town.

Although located next to the motorway, you'll be surprised by the calm and peaceful ambience of the town which features imposing contemporary residential houses standing next to ancient shabby dwellings

Things to do in Masafi

It is the Masafi Friday market, locally known as the Souq al Juma, which attracts visitors to this town. Operational seven days a week, it lives up to its reputation of being one of the most eclectic markets in the country and a visitor would find everything from rugs, antiques and souvenirs to fresh fruits and vegetables.

Initially started by Emirati local farmers who stood by the roadside after the Friday prayers to sell their wares its popularity soon acquired phenomenal proportions and success led to the original sellers hiring other nationals to do the selling while they looked after the management. As a result, in the present day version of the market, while Afghanis and Pakistanis sell carpets, mats and shrubs, the Bangladeshis ensure the supply of fruits, vegetables and garden plants. ornate Pottery with local designs is also sold

Reputed as being one of the greenest towns in UAE, Masafi may not feature prominently in a travel itinerary but when some prefer brunches in the plush hotels, others may want to check out the market if not for shopping then just for the sake of experiencing its unique atmosphere. Get down to the masafi market – you wont regret it

MUSANDAM PENINSULA – BEAUTY IN ISOLATION

The isolated enclave of Musandam is the northern most region of Oman and could be described as the extension of the eastern coastline of UAE. Being the smallest area with an expanse of just a little over 3000 square kilometres, it juts out into the Strait of Hormuz like a rocky headland and hence is regarded as being one of the most strategic points in relation to the existent sea route.

There are regular flight services going between Musandam and Muscat and the location of the area is such that the only other alternative is to make an entry by road from the neighbouring UAE. While one road originates from the eastern side of Oman and enters Musandam after passing through Dibba in UAE, the other road starts from Dubai and snakes along the coast passing through cities like Sharjah, Ajman and Ras Al Khaimah to eventually end in Musandam. It's a great coastal drive

You need an entry visa to visit Musandam and is now becoming the preferred holiday destination for many UAE expats who wish to take a weekend break away from it all.

While perched on the towering rocks of Musandam which form the elbow of the Gulf, the horizon dotted with ships and tankers carrying goods and oil to and from the ports in the Arabian Gulf and closer to land you can spot numerous fishing dhows and speedboats carrying a variety of goods on board ranging from seafood and goats to contrabands.

Prior to the 1980s' Musandam did not even have roads and the only landmark which was visible from miles around was the Hajar mountain range extending unbroken for 640 kilometres between Ras Al-Hadd in the south and plunging dramatically into the sea at Ru'us Al-Jebal. Hence, most of the terrain here is mountainous comprising of gorges, hairpin bends and wadi beds while the sea has variety of marine life. Likewise, the lives of people is all about fishing and traditional handicrafts, the most prominent being manufacture of Musandam axe or Jirz. Commercialization is limited to the town of Khasab which serves as an administrative centre and is inhabited by a population of around 30,000.

In recent years, Musandam has acquired popularity due to its focus on eco tourism which is actively pursued byOman in this isolated area. As a result, it is one of the best examples of environment conservation featuring among other species 130 varieties of birds and supporting another 372 which migrate annually.

Things to do in Musandam

Musandam is famous for adventure sports related to the mountains and the sea and most of the tourist spots are also concentrated in these areas.

The highest peak in Musandam is Jabal Harim but due to military reasons, tourists are not allowed to climb to the summit but you can go close by and stop short at a close distance. This place could be any rock climber's paradise as there are more than 160 climbs for all levels with some of the spots being well known and the other limestone peaks waiting to be scaled. Some of the common trails undertaken by mountain lovers are the steep cliffs bordering the peninsula and the highest cliff in Arabia – Wadi Dhum in Nizwa.

The sea has its own charm in terms of fjords which offer a unique canoeing experience and which have earned this place the nickname of 'Norway of the east'. Some of the popular sea related activities are scuba diving snorkelling and taking Dhow cruises out into the Strait of Hormuz wherein a spot of luck would lead one to dolphins as well.

While in Musandam, you might as well forget about the shopping and sky scrapers prepare for a close tryst with nature. Accommodation on this island is provided six senses Zighy Bay and a number of budget resorts all of which boast of friendly and warm hearted staff.

You could wile away many days here without even realising it. Not only does it offer a welcome break from the hustle and bustle of city life but also completely redefines the Gulf experience.

THE CHARMING CITY OF MUSCAT

The official capital city of Oman, Muscat, is in fact a combination of three small towns namely Muscat, Matrah and Ruwi because of which it is the largest in the Sultanate. Lying alongside the coast of Gulf of Oman, this city is a part of a long conglomerate of numerous cities and towns which stretch for over 40 kilometres sandwiched between the sea in the north and the barren mountains in the south like an unbroken string of pearls.

In olden times, the city served as an important port in the Arabian Peninsula which accounted for its rapid commercial growth and its ascension to the status being declared as the capital city. However, the medieval appearance is still retained in form of the two Portuguese forts of Jelali and Merani which exist alongside the modern and contemporary buildings. This all makes Muscat an intriguing place to visit.

On an international scale Muscat is well connected by air to most of the prominent cities around the world and its international airport is served by many well known airlines with Oman Air representing the country. There are also domestic flights between Muscat and Salalah a couple of times during the week. Road transport features daily bus services between Muscat and Dubai, taking 6 hours, as it also services to Abu Dhabi, Buraimi, Nizwa, Salalah and few of the other cities in close proximity. Traveling by car is probably one of the best ways of travel between Muscat and the UAE with Hatta and Al Ain being the border areas. It's not difficult to do – and something you really should consider to split a holiday between Dubai and Muscat.

It is not only Muscat which should be concentrated upon during a visit and traveling to the neighbouring cities and towns flanking the main highway of Sultan Qaboos could be an equally rewarding experience. While Muscat is a walled city and is home to royal palaces, a visit to Matrah would reveal the presence of a charming fishing village by the bay and a maze like formation popularly known as the Matrah Souk. The town of Ruwi was traditionally the commercial centre and has continued to live up its reputation to this day looking after diplomatic aspects as well.

On driving down the Sultan Qaboos highway, something that would be hard to miss is the 50-kilometre long beach extending from Qurum up to Seeb. This beach is symbolic of social contradictions because while on one hand it is dotted with world renowned hotel chains, it also provides one with the opportunity to mingle with the fishermen handling their drag nets. With hot summers, warm winters and scarce rainfall, Muscat as a city depends predominantly on trade for its economy with dates, pearls and fish.

Things to do in Muscat

The Sultan Qaboos Grand Mosque, which is the third or fourth largest mosque in the world deserves a visit courtesy of the sparkling Swarovski crystal chandelier, hand woven ethnic carpet and marble panelling. It is one of the few mosques which are open to non-Muslim visitors, similar to the Sheikh Zayed Mosque in Abu Dhabi - and one should dress conservatively.

Amongst the number of big and small parks, the Qurum National Park with its rose gardens, waterfalls, lake and amusement park is the largest. Another prominent park is the Riyam Park which features an Arabian watch tower in addition to a number of rides.

Wadi Shab, located 100 kilometre south-east of Muscat, offers one of the mostspectacular sights with its emerald green pools, enigmatic caves and dramatically steep sides.

The city is home to a number of museums, each specializing in a particular theme so that there is something of interest for all age groups and professions.

There are a number of activities which would capture the imagination of tourists here, the foremost being a walk in the Corniche area and other equally interesting alternatives being scuba diving, night safari, trekking, rock climbing and watching aquatic animals in their natural habitat.

Muscat is a gourmet king's paradise as is evident from a wide range of eating joints serving a variety of cuisines and catering to a variety of budgets. However, you should keep to your bottled water if he wishes to remain on his feet throughout the trip. Likewise, one is spoiled for choice when it comes to accommodation as well and while the Grand Hyatt feels like an Arabian palace Arabian palace there are a number of conveniently located mid-range and budget hotels as well. Our favourite is the Shangri-la Muscat, perfect for a family getaway.

TRAVELLING DOWN THE HISTORICAL LANE IN OMAN

Overview

Occupying the south-eastern tip of the Arabian Peninsula, the Sultanate of Oman, which is its official name lies between the Arabian Sea on one side and the Gulf of Oman on the other. Being surrounded by Saudi Arabia, Yemen and the United Arab Emirates, Oman is probably one of the hidden gems for a tourist – it's perfect for those looking for a relaxing holiday mixed with culture, Oman is the place. It's great to combine with either Dubai or Abu Dhabi for a holiday –because they are all so different.

You can easily drive down to the UAE, assuming you have a visa which is issued on entry by the Royal Oman Police. Getting there is simple and you can go via a host of cities including Buraimi which is in Al Ain, Bukha, Waddi Hatta and Khamat Mulahah For the seasoned traveler one can get to Oman via Saudi Arabia crossing the desert of Al Mashash. Again, from Yemen, there is a choice of two roads namely the Route 47 and the road from Thumrait to Al Mazyonah on the border.

However, most people fly in to to the Muscat International Airport, Salalah Airport or Khasab airport all of which are well connected with most of the major airports with many of the prominent airlines. Our advice would be to fly in or fly out and combine a drive to or from the UAE, depending on where you intend to stay. Once you are there, taxis and buses are easy to get.

Oman is believed to be the cradle of civilization making this is a must-visit destination for travelers who are inquisitive about their pre-historic origins. Some say that Oman is the Arabian antithesis of Dubai. While Dubai is the gogetting future city, Oman is the historical, cultural hub of Arabia. While on a trip here, you can see a number of successive phases of history beginning from the Stone Age and continuing along to include the arrival of Islam, European colonization, sovereignty and relations with Africa. It really is all around.

Characterized by a hot climate with very little rainfall, there is no particular tourist season for planning a trip here although, as with the UAE, you should try and avoid the summer months between May and September. Having landed, there is a lot to see unlike the usual reputation of Gulf countries being associated with shopping, Oman offers a rare glimpse into its traditional villages as well. The people are friendly and helpful – and have a contentment with life that befits to relaxing nature of the place.

The culture here is not just limited to the big cities with sky scrapers but can be found reflected as much in archeological sites, religious places, ancient forts and of all things the Frankincense Tree. Unique as it is, Frankincense has been associated with human civilization since time immemorial and it is courtesy of this age-old relationship that the Dhofari people regard this tree as an embodiment of life, culture, history and traditions.

Things to do in Oman

All the eclectic things to do in Oman fall broadly under the categories of nature, festivals, activities and shopping. If that's your idea of holiday heaven, Oman is the place to be.

Nature lovers can look forward to a wonderful time here as they would get the unique opportunity of appreciating the diverse flora and fauna in the various natural reserves, lagoons, botanical gardens and protected areas. Some of the other natural landmarks which are worth a visit are the Strait of Hormuz, Al Hajar Mountains, archeological caves and natural water springs believed to possess curative and therapeutic powers.

There are three most important festivals in Oman namely the Cultural Theatre Program, the Muscat festival which is all encompassing and the Salalah Tourism festival which is celebrated in the Dhofar province to mark the advent of autumn.

There comes a time when you need to get your adrenaline going and this can be achieved in Oman through numerous activities ranging from water sports like scuba diving and boating to land activities like camping, caving and trekking. Watching whales, birds, turtles and dolphins in their natural habitat is also a popular way of spending time while the true thrill can be derived from indulging in camel racing, horse racing and four-wheel driving.

Oman has its share of souks like its neighbours, the wealthy Emirates, but it has old markets as well where one is likely to come across traditional industries like dagger-making and handicrafts.

It would be impossible to capture the beauty of this country in a few hours or even a few days and the only way to do full justice would be to plan a full fledged vacation lasting over at least a fortnight. Many people return year on year to get away from it all. Accommodation is not a problem as there are innumerable hotels here to suit every kind of budget and while 5-star hotels offer their own luxurious charm, the budget hotels, resorts, hotel apartments and guest houses represent an insight into the rustic local life.

Printed in Dunstable, United Kingdom